CHIVALRIC ROMANCES

CHIVALRIC ROMANCES

Popular Literature in Medieval England

Lee C. Ramsey

Indiana University Press BLOOMINGTON

Manufactured in the United States of America

Library of Congress Cataloging in Publication Data

Ramsey, Lee C., 1935–
  Chivalric romances.

  Includes index.
  1. Romances, English—History and criticism.
2. English poetry—Middle English, 1100–1500—History
and criticism.   3. Chivalry in literature.   4. Popular
literature—England—History and criticism.   I. Title.
PR321.R35   1983   821'.1'09   83-47659
ISBN 0-253-31360-0
1 2 3 4 5 87 86 85 84 83

For Lawren and Todd

CONTENTS

CHIVALRIC
ROMANCES

1 The French Book

Today few people read medieval romances, and even fewer enjoy them. Yet most of us know something about them, and it is probably the romance more than anything else that has supplied the modern world with its idea of what the Middle Ages were like: knights jousting on horseback, fire-breathing dragons, and chapels in the forest. Unknown or forgotten are the more accurate pictures of the quiet, regulated life of the monasteries, the bustling trade of the cities, the rural villages dominated by their cathedrals, the splendid courts, and the harsh agrarian life of the peasantry. Fiction has replaced fact, as it will in the popular mind, which loves a good story and is impatient with history and scholarship. But some of the blame for this state of affairs also lies with medieval writers and illustrators, who, anticipating their later counterparts, liked to represent their world in terms of conventions of the romance genre.

Romances never pretended to give an accurate picture of life in their times, and they were not even the dominant form of medieval literature. To judge by the numbers of surviving manuscripts and the lists of library holdings during the Middle Ages, serious works in Latin and devotional works in the vernacular languages were more widely read, and both were certainly more esteemed, even among that part of the population which made up the principal audience for the romance. But in the eighteenth and nineteenth centuries, when writers and editors such as Walter Scott, George Ellis, and Thomas Percy revived interest in the Middle Ages, they turned their attention first to the romances and to the fictional world of the romance. The resulting stereotypes, as perpetuated by Tennyson, Mark Twain, and T. H. White, have given most of us our first and, in some cases, our only idea about the realities of life 700 years ago. In effect, the medieval world became transformed into the fiction created by one limited part of that world. It was neither the first nor the last age to have become so transformed.

1

   The romances have much to tell us about the age in which they were written. They were, if not the literature of most people in the Middle Ages, at least the literature of the most important and influential people, the nobility and prosperous middle classes. If the men and women of those times did not read romances as a steady fare or treat them as seriously as they treated other kinds of writing, they did turn to them for pleasure, they did learn from them (or say that they learned from them), and they did find expressed in them some of their most intimately held ideals. The romance could reflect some of the deeper anxieties and desires of its medieval audience, and, strange as it may seem to modern readers of these works, it had the power to delight and to move—witness the sermon writer who spoke of those who were stirred to tears when *Guy of Warwick* was read aloud to them.[1]

   The romance heroes, although few of them are well known today, had names that created excitement just in the mentioning, and writers loved to recite these names. The author of the *Laud Troy Book*, for example, begins his poem by remembering the names of "men who were once doughty in deed while God gave them life but are now dead and gone: of Bevis, Guy, and of Gawain, of King Richard, and of Yvain, of Tristran, and of Perceval, of Roland Ris and Aglavale, of Archeroun, and of Octavian, of Charles, and of Cassibaldan, of Havelok, Horn, and of Wade." The romance of *Richard Coer de Lyon* slips in the names (in a manner that Chaucer parodied in *Sir Thopas*): "I intend to tell no romance of Partonope, nor of Ipomedon, of Alexander, nor of Charlemagne, of Arthur, nor of Sir Gawain, nor of Lancelot de Lake, of Bevis, nor Guy, nor Sir Urrake, nor of Ury, nor of Octavian. . . ."

   Medieval romance was the creation of French writers during the latter half of the twelfth century. An astonishingly original and vigorous type of literature, it grew, flourished, and went into decline in France—all within a period of little more than a century. Before the decline set in, however, the romance had spread to other parts of Europe, most notably to Germany and England, where native traditions, quite different in some respects from the original one, sprang up. It is usual to equate romances in England with romances in English, but if we recognize that the English tradition began with works written in French for the French-speaking court of England, we see that the romance came to England quite early, almost simultaneously with the origins of the form itself. Later developments took the French and English traditions in two different directions. While verse was giving way to prose in France during the thirteenth and fourteenth centuries, verse romance continued to be in vogue in England, at first in the form of translations but later as original compositions, influenced only in a general way by their continental forbears. Even from the beginning, however, the romances of England were distinct in subject and style.

This new form of literature, the romance, was a modification of the *chanson de geste*, which in turn seems to have derived from the ancient Germanic epic, of which *Beowulf* and the *Hildebrandslied* are examples. The *chansons de geste* are lengthy narrative poems depicting and apparently written for a warrior society. Their central subject matter is the establishment and defense of nations, Christian nations in particular. These works, of which the *Chanson de Roland* is the best known example, place great emphasis on fighting and military virtues such as courage. They show Christian heroes struggling against foreign or pagan ("Saracen") foes, but they exhibit no special interest in Christian virtues or in Christian doctrine.

In form, length, and even in subject matter, the romances are similar to the *chansons de geste*, but their attention shifts away from the military society and military virtues, their battles tending to be stylized into the form of jousts and single combats. Instead of the defense of Christendom, their subject is the search for individual identity within an already established society. When the romance's hero is a king, his usual task is to restore just rule to a nation that has lost it as a result of assaults either from within or without; other heroes of the romance are engaged in making places for themselves within their society, in finding lords or families, in giving purpose to their lives, in getting married. The love quest is particularly characteristic of the romance, although it does not occur in all of them; the *chanson de geste*, on the other hand, seldom portrays its heroes as lovers. Its world is, first and foremost, the battlefield; the world of the romance is the court.

The traditional way of defining these differences is to associate the *chanson de geste* with the "heroic age" and the romance with the "age of chivalry."[2] Chivalry is, certainly, the central theme of the medieval romance, but it is not an easy concept to define. It is, above all, the mode of behavior appropriate to the knight, the warrior on horseback, as opposed to the ordinary foot soldier.

Chivalry includes within it the knight's duty to fight for those who
are below him, especially the poor and the weak, but the behavior
that it prescribes is primarily social rather than military. Chivalric
virtues are those that ensure just and stable rule, defense of the
existing order, and observance of social form and rank—the virtues
of civilization. Chivalry involves an inherent contradiction between
the hero's role as warrior and as courtier, between the hard life and
the soft life. This contradiction has its classic expression in
Chrétien de Troyes's romance *Erec and Enide* when Erec, fresh from
winning his lady and enjoying the benefits of his victory in the
bedchamber, must be reminded by her of his obligations as a war-
rior.

The differences between *chansons de geste* and romances may well
indicate that they addressed different segments of the society but,
more than that, seem to point to historical changes in the nature of
the society. After all, the most important characters in both genres
are those who comprise the warrior class. The *chanson de geste* would
appeal to those who are actually concerned about proving them-
selves through combat and who are anxious to identify themselves
with a particular nation and religion; the appeal of the romance is
rather to those who seek to find a stable position within the society.
Thus the replacement of epic by romance in the twelfth century
would seem to mean that anxieties about the continued existence of
the society had lessened, leaving in their place anxieties about per-
sonal rank and function.

That romance should replace epic as the most popular form in
this century is highly significant since it was a period when a large
number of other societal changes first became apparent, changes to
which scholars have given the collective name, "Twelfth-Century
Renaissance."[3] At the same time that the romance was coming into
existence, Western Europe was making its first steps toward some-
thing like a complex modern society. Trade was expanding rapidly,
cities were growing, and a prominent middle class was becoming
evident. Governments and the courts from which they were ad-
ministered were becoming dependent upon larger numbers of peo-
ple, some of whom had real prospects of attaining noble rank. The
early beginnings of universities were apparent. Literacy was
spreading, particularly among the laity, the inhabitants of the cities
and courts. There was also a significant increase in the amount of
leisure time available to large numbers of people. Thus the rise of a

new society, a society of cities and courts, goes hand in hand with the rise of romance. The romance was public entertainment, the chosen entertainment of the new culture, and it stands as a major expression of the new culture's values.

Although the earliest romances are all in the French language, a number of them originated in England or the English court. These Anglo-Norman works include some of the most famous and the most influential of the romance stories: *Tristan, Lanval, Amis et Amiles, Gui de Warewic.* It would be foolish if not impossible to try to distinguish between the Anglo-Norman and continental traditions during the earliest period, but within a hundred years two different bodies of romance literature had clearly emerged. Late in the thirteenth century, English began to replace French as the language of romances written in England, and by 1300 no more French romances were being written there, although some of the older ones were still being circulated. The fourteenth century saw the heyday of the English verse romance—now a distinct type from the contemporary romances of France—and, soon afterward, the beginnings of a decline, as prose began to replace verse. This trend continued into the sixteenth century, and eventually the verse romance gave way entirely to the various types of prose narrative that were the precursors of the novel.

In name as well as in nature, the romance was a popular literature. The word "romance," as used in France, originally meant the vernacular or spoken language as opposed to Latin, the language of culture. Applied to a book, "romance" meant one that was written for ordinary people, in their own language. When the word was borrowed into English, it meant either the French language or something written in French. A "romance" was the same as the "French book" that so many English writers, including Malory, mentioned as the source of their stories. Only later, as other kinds of writing began to appear in the vernacular, did "romance" come gradually to refer to a particular type of literature.

The typical medieval romance shares the characteristics common to other, later forms of popular literature. The most important of these characteristics is the emphasis on plot and action to the exclusion of everything else—rhetoric, idea, and character development included. The rhetoric of the romances is often poor, the philosophic content meager, and the characters simple and obvious. The emotional effects sought after are likewise obvious, often crudely so. Melodrama and sentimentality are much more common than anything that merits the names comedy or tragedy.

The term "popular literature," however, is subject to misunderstanding and especially so when used in connection with the medieval romance. It does not—indeed it cannot—refer only to literature read by the majority of the population, for there has never been a popular form that had an audience of that size or anywhere near it. Even television, which probably has the greatest mass audience ever assembled, cannot lay claim to such numbers, and books atop the best-seller list, in a day like ours of supposedly universal literacy, reach only a fragment of the population. In the Middle Ages the largest audience for any popular writing must have been quite small. But numbers are important only insofar as they assure continued support for the literature. In modern times success has come down to a matter of profit margin, but some popular forms—science fiction is an example—survive on a tiny profit margin. In this case, one suspects, the continued allegiance and enthusiasm of the readers counts most.

Nor does "popular" necessarily imply an uneducated or uncultured audience. Among the several popular forms in our history, the gothic novel, the murder mystery (at least in some varieties), and science fiction are all aimed at fairly sophisticated audiences. Often the writers and the most avid readers of these works include the leaders of the society and the literati. Writers of popular fiction have numbered among their ranks both Horace Walpole and Graham Greene.

Popular works are distinguished from other types of writing, including *belles lettres*, by their aims, their special relationship with their audiences, and their internal characteristics. Popular literature has entertainment as its primary purpose; it does not, as a general rule, challenge or enlighten its readers. Its specific function is to fill idle time in a way that satifies the preexisting desires or needs of its audience. It is escapist. It avoids most complications in order to concentrate upon those matters that are most directly relevant to its purpose, hence the emphasis upon plot (myth) at the expense of character and rhetoric. Popular literature is subservient to its audience: it seeks to know and serve the readers as they are instead of seeking to change them. It is usually written for profit (money, recognition, social advancement), though this fact does not necessarily mean that the writers are insincere. Some are, but others are passionate about their work.[4]

Medieval romances are comparable to today's popular literature. Even though they were set in the past, the problems that they confronted were those of their contemporary society, and the solutions were also ones appropriate to their society. For this reason it was an ephemeral literature. When its day passed, it lost its effectiveness and came to seem either dull or ridiculous. All this has been, is, and will be true for more recent forms of popular writing: rogue literature, the heroic drama of the Restoration, the sentimental and gothic novel, the nineteenth-century melodrama, the western, the murder mystery, the soap opera. It is to these types of literature that we should compare the romance if we wish to understand the reasons for its existence, its place in its society, and ultimately its meaning.

THE AUDIENCE

Medieval romance was a literature of the people, but it was not a literature of the common people. Its place was the court. That is where it originated, where its stories take place, and where its first audience was. In France, romance writers regularly dedicated their works to kings and queens, princes and barons. Because such dedications are more often found in romances than in *chansons de geste*, the scholar Edmond Faral believed that powerful lords had begun to understand the capability of writers to influence their reputations and had become eager to stand as patrons whenever they could.[5] In England, romances were conventionally addressed to "lords" or "lordings." No doubt the authors meant to flatter their audiences by the use of these terms, and the terms themselves are very general. But if the nobility had not been a part of the audience, in fact or in anticipation, the terms would have been inappropriate.

There are even some indications that the romances were unknown outside the court. In the prologue to the *Chronicle of England*, translated from French for the benefit of the unlearned nobility ("lordes lewed": that is, those who know no Latin or French), Robert Mannyng of Brunne says that he has avoided the language and verse forms of the romances because many who hear "that strange Inglis / In ryme wate never what it is."[6] The thirteenth-century French romance of *Octavian* provides another example. Florent, one of the sons of the Roman king Octavian, has as a baby been estranged from his father and raised by a commoner named Climent. When Florent comes to manhood, he kills a Saracen giant and, in consequence, is to be knighted by Octavian. Hearing of the ceremony, some entertainers of the sort that traditionally recited romances *(conteurs, chanteurs,* and *jugleors)* come to the court, expecting to perform and be rewarded. But when they arrive at the palace, Climent, who does not understand their purpose in being there, drives them off, beating them and breaking their instruments. Florent has to explain to his foster father that the minstrels have come to honor and serve him. Climent's misunderstanding of the minstrel's trade shows that he is an ignorant villein; by contrast, Florent's actions are a sign of his innate nobility.[7]

The earliest audience for the romances must have been in the more important courts, among the nobles and their entourages, but this is not to say that these courts comprised the only audience. Such a conclusion would fail to explain the vitality of the form, for there were not enough of the upper nobility to have supported the romance over such a long period of time. Nor is the conclusion borne out by the nature of the romances, which from an early date place great emphasis upon social climbing, a subject of little interest to those who already occupy the highest positions in the society. The so-called romantic fiction that these works were recited in taverns and marketplaces has arisen because scholars of the medieval romance refused to believe that its audience could have been composed solely of the Marie de Champagnes or Humphrey de Bohuns and the small circles that surrounded them.[8] For such an obviously popular form of literature, it has been impossible to believe that the audience consisted of only a few, even though the reliable evidence did not point beyond those few. The mistake here has not been in the scholars' basic instinct about the romance but rather in the tendency to think in majoritarian terms and with an exaggerated notion of the smallness of the court audience. A popular form of literature can be supported by an audience drawn from a modest percentage of the total population, and the medieval court supplied this percentage quite satisfactorily, especially if, by "court," we mean not only those who were actually members of it but also those who wished to think of themselves as members. In a time when the court was the prime symbol of social status and of society itself, the latter definition must have included quite a variety of people. Thus it is possible to discard the idea of commoners listening to romances in the streets and still recognize the popular qualities of the genre.

One of the more prominent segments of the romance audience comprised women of rank. Chaucer joked about this fact when he made his Nun's Priest swear that the story of Chauntecleer and Pertelote was as true "as is the book of Launcelot de Lake / That wommen holde in ful greet reverence" (*Canterbury Tales*, VII, 3212–13). Albert Baugh cites several other examples that likewise show the composition of the audience, including the lines from the lyric "The Fair Maid of Ribbesdale":[9]

> Heo hath a mury mouht to mele
> With lefly rede lippes lele,
>   romaunz forte rede.
> (She has a beautiful mouth, with lovely
> red lips for the reading of romances.)

Furthermore, a number of French romances are specifically dedicated to women.

This is exactly as would be expected, not only because medieval women of rank had plenty of leisure time for reading but, more than that, because the position of women in medieval upper-class society made them especially vulnerable to the appeals of romance fiction. They were in and of the society, and yet they had little chance to take an active part in it. While a man could work to achieve a place for himself, most women could gain a sense of place only through marriage or through fantasy. One might even suspect that the advent of the romance, with its emphasis on love, occurred when substantial numbers of women began to be included in the audience for the *jongleurs'* songs. It is no objection to this supposition that women in the romances play a distinctly subservient role, that their identity is completely dependent upon men, or that the literature was almost exclusively created by men. Women were subservient in the society, and no successful popular literature would have portrayed them in any other way. Since their social identity would be achieved through marriage or through some other type of association with men, a satisfying fantasy identification must also have been of this type. And as for the matter of authorship, it is still true that much successful women's literature is written by men. Nevertheless, one must suppose that the clearly male-oriented medieval romance provided less satisfying fantasy fulfillment to its female audience than some of the popular women's literature of later ages.

Most scholars agree that the audience for the English romance was less aristocractic than the audience for the French romance. Baugh, in fact, seems to take it for granted that the two audiences were completely different, although he believes that in both cases it was an educated audience.[10] John Halverson, in a comparative study of the French and English Havelok romances, has concluded on the basis of language and detail of the poems that the English work was intended for a bourgeois audience in contrast to the aristocratic audience of the French *Haveloc*.[11] Although these conclusions are mainly based on reactions to the style, tone, and language of the poems, such reactions are not to be denigrated, especially when the stylistic differences are so apparent. To turn from the French to the English romances is to go from one world to another. The English romances lack, almost totally, the grace, the sophistication, the development, and the courtly atmosphere of their French counterparts; the worst of them are the hastiest sorts of translation or crude popularizations. One often wonders why the English translators even bothered to write in verse. Their use of the obvious and jingling tail rime, parodied by Chaucer in *Sir Thopas*, is only one example of this difference in style.

Two relatively early English romances offer clear evidence of a difference between French and English audiences. In both *Arthour and Merlin* (late thirteenth century) and *Richard Coer de Lyon*, the authors (or author—since some think the same man wrote both) take time to explain why their poem is in English. *Richard Coer de Lyon*, the author says, is written for "lewede men" who know no French but wish to hear of noble deeds (ll. 21–28); the author of *Arthour and Merlin* explains:

> Freynsche use this gentilman,
> Ac everich Inglische Inglische can;
> Mani noble ich have yseighe,
> That no Freynsche couthe seye (ll. 23–26).

There are problems of meaning in both statements: "lewede" is an ambiguous word, and the difference between "gentilman" and "noble," if any, is unclear. Nevertheless, these points are certain: the writers take it for granted that the audience of the French romance is noble and educated; they understand that by writing in English they are addressing a wider audience (*not* an essentially different audience); they interpret the differences between the older and the newer audiences as being differences of rank and education as well as language.

There is no reason to suppose that the romance's audience in England or in France included substantial numbers of the middle or lower classes until quite late, the fifteenth century at least. On the contrary, there is every reason to believe that the romance was a literature of the nobility, of those who associated with the nobility, and of those who aspired to nobility. The indications, evident as early as the thirteenth century, of a broadening audience point not to the appreciation of romance by different types or classes of people but to the expansion of the original category. The courts were larger, and there were more people with pretensions to gentility. The common man of the Middle Ages probably had his literature, but it was an oral literature and is irrecoverable. The romance belonged to the courts.

Authors of Romances

Medieval records abound with references to all kinds of entertainers, professional and nonprofessional, some wandering from town to town and court to court, some hired temporarily or permanently by kings or well-to-do noblemen. The professionals seem to have appeared most often at splendid public occasions such as royal weddings, coronations, and feasts, where they made their living through gifts of clothing, food, or money. They played music, told jokes, danced, tumbled, did feats of magic, and performed dramatic entertainments; they also sang or recited tales. They had a bad reputation with churchmen and moralists, partly because of the loose lives that they led and partly because of the inducements to idleness and frivolity that they offered. They were known by a variety of names, including Latin *histrio* (originally meaning 'actor' but later applied to mimes, storytellers, and dancers) and *joculator* (originally meaning 'entertainer'). The latter is the source of French *jogler* (Modern French *jongleur*, Modern English *juggler*), which was the word usually applied to the reciters of the epics and, often, of the romances. Later, the French term *menestrel* (originally from Latin *ministerialis*, 'servant') came into use, perhaps referring specifically to a performer attached to a particular court but also, clearly, with a broader meaning as well. The English derivative *minstrel* referred to many categories of entertainers, probably most often to musicians of some kind, but it could mean a reciter of tales, as in the phrase "minstrels of mouthe" *(Guy of Warwick)*. For these, however, the usual English word was *gestour* (Modern English *jester*), originally meaning the reciter of a *geste* or 'story' (in poetry or prose). Other terms in use were *gleeman* ('entertainer'), a word that had been used for reciters of tales in the Anglo-Saxon period, and *disour* (a 'speaker'—primarily of jests and fabliaux, it would seem).

Many medieval writers mention these entertainers. John of Salisbury, Petrarch, and the author of the English *Speculum Vitae* seem to condemn them all, without exception. Thomas Cabham, subdean of Salisbury in the thirteenth century, condemns most of them but reserves some praise for the *joculatores*, "who sing about the deeds of princes and the lives of saints and bring consolation to men in sickness or hardship."[12] None of these writers, however, tells us much about the entertainers, and other medieval references, though frequent, provide no more than glimpses of the performers and their craft. They were an accepted part of the court, part of a backdrop that was taken for granted. Only rarely do we encounter details that seem to give life to this institution of the medieval scene, as when the author of *Kyng Alisaunder* mentions a *gestour* stopping to wipe his mouth.

One of the earliest and best-known stories of minstrel presentation is that of Taillefer, who sang for William the Conqueror at the Battle of Hastings. The story is told by four different writers in slightly different versions. According to Wace in the *Roman de Rou*, Taillefer rode before Duke William on the way to Hastings and sang of Charlemagne and the battle of Roncesvalles; in reward William granted him the first blow of the battle.[13] Wace says that Taillefer had been a member of William's court for a long time, but whether as a professional entertainer or not is unclear. The casual circumstances of the singing and the fact that Taillefer came to participate in the fighting suggest that he was not a professional or that minstrelsy was perhaps only one of his duties. Other passages in medieval literature indicate that minstrelsy, though it required training, was an accomplishment shared by all kinds of people, including beggars. In *Libeaus Desconus*, for example, a maiden arrives at King Arthur's court accompanied by a dwarf servant who plays various instruments and is a "noble dysour." The heroine of *Bevis of Hampton* learns minstrelsy in the course of her travels and uses it to make a living when she has no other means of support.

Nevertheless, professionals did exist, and some of them wrote romances. The names of approximately two dozen *jongleurs*, most of whom were also authors, come down to us in association with twelfth- and thirteenth-century narrative poems in French. Many of these are known to have been professionals, or else they are the authors of several works, implying that they were professionals. The names include Jean Bodel, Graindor de Brie, Gautier d'Arras, Bertrand de Bar-sur-Aube, Girard d'Amiens, Chrétien de Troyes, Marie de France, and others. Whole companies of *jongleurs* were organized at various places in France from the late twelfth century onward, including the famous *confrérie d'Arras*.

Scattered bits of information survive concerning some of these authors. In the prologue to his epic *Les Saisnes*, Jean Bodel, a professional *jongleur* who lived in Arras during the late twelfth and early thirteenth centuries discusses the *jongleurs'* art and divides their subjects into three "materes"—those of France, Britain, and Rome—divisions which are still generally accepted today. He contrasts himself with what he calls the "vilains jougleres" and with "these bastard jongleurs who go through the small towns with their long fiddles stuck in their tattered robes." Obviously Bodel, as an author, felt superior to the wandering minstrels, who, he says, do not sing the true story that he tells; he is also slightly contemptuous of the stories of the matter of Britain (i.e., the Arthurian stories), which are "vain et plaisant." The *Chevalerie Ogier, a chanson de geste* written about 1200, states that its author was a *jongleur*, Raimbert de Paris, who was the best of his kind. One manuscript of the poem adds: "He was a gentleman and all his family also; he wrote many songs of great heroism."

According to Edmond Faral, *jongleurs* like Raimbert and Bodel were men who traveled about and presented their songs to audiences of common people ("un public de gens du peuple"); in general, these were the performers—and sometimes the authors—of *chansons de geste*. In addition, there were "minstrels," who recited for the nobility ("un public de seigneurs cultivés") and who were permanently attached to some specific court; these were the performers and poets of the romances, or *romans d'aventure*. Faral's distinction is based primarily on a subjective appraisal of the level to which the poems are directed and is certainly much too rigid. Neither Bodel nor Raimbert fits precisely Faral's definition of a *jongleur*, Bodel having scorned the traveling singers and Raimbert having been himself a member of the nobility. Yet no doubt the two kinds of performers did exist, and a few authors of medieval narrative poetry are known definitely to have belonged to a class like that of Faral's "minstrels."[14]

One of these was Adenet le Roi, the author of *Cléomadès* and minstrel to Duke Henry III of Brabant, then later, after Henry's death, to his two sons, Jean and Godefroi. Still later he was attached to the court of Gui de Dampierre and wrote a *chanson de geste* for him. Adenet is mentioned in several records, often as a "menestrel," and is known to have accompanied his patron on the crusade of 1270. Another poet, the author of the thirteenth-century romance *Le Vair Palefroi* and several other works, is presumed to have been a minstrel or *jongleur* like Adenet because of his name, which he gives variously as Huon le Roi and Li Rois de Cambrai.[15] Bertrand de Bar-sur-Aube, the author of *Girart de Vienne* and probably of *Aymeri de Narbonne*, seems also to have been a professional singer of tales. A few of these *jongleur*-authors even passed their trade along to their sons. The prologue of the *Bataille Loquifer* speaks of one Graindor de Brie who wrote the poem, preserved it, and passed it along to his son when he died; the Anglo-Norman poet Thomas, who wrote the *Romance of Horn*, says that its sequel will be written by his son Gilimot.

Some of the authors of epic and romance, however, were not *jongleurs*, and almost all of them made it clear that they were not ordinary *jongleurs*. We have already seen one example of this in the case of Jean Bodel; another is Graindor de Douai, author of the twelfth-century epic *Chanson d'Antioche*, who distinguishes between himself and the "new jongleurs" singing the tale in his time. The prologue of the *Destruction de Rome* claims that its version of the story is unknown to the other *jongleurs*, who don't know a penny's worth of the history: the *true* history was found in a manuscript at Saint Denis, where it had been for 100 years. This is undoubtedly fiction, but it shows that the author did not want his poem associated with the usual products of the *jongleurs*. The bookish history that he invented implies some bookishness in him and, quite possibly, a reading rather than listening audience.

Other authors make similar remarks. Both Thomas and Béroul indicate that many versions of the Tristan story were in circulation in their day, and both consider their own versions to be superior to the others being told. Thomas says that he had heard the tale many times but never according to Breri, "who knew the gestes and stories of all the kings and counts that have been in Britain." Béroul claims that he remembers the story better than the storytellers who say that Tristan drowned Yvain. Obviously such statements had become conventional. In *Folque de Candie*, author Herbert le Duc says that he is no villein like the "villein-jongleurs who know no such songs, however much they chew and ruminate over them," and Chrétien de Troyes, in *Erec and Enide*, seems to separate himself from the professional *jongleurs* entirely: "This is a story about Erec the son of Lac, a story which is regularly corrupted and destroyed before kings and counts by those who make a living with their songs."

Some of these writers held positions at court or followed professions. Jean Maillart, author of the *Comtesse d'Anjou*, may have been a notary and, in any case, seems to have been employed in some trade besides that of a minstrel as evidenced by his statement that "I have other things to do." Chrétien, who makes it clear that he did not make a living by telling stories, may have been a herald-at-arms, for in the *Chevalier de la Charrete* he says of one such person, "This herald was our master." Gautier d'Arras, author of *Eracle* and *Ille et Galeron*, was probably an officer of Philippe d'Alsace whose name occurs in many public records and who was apparently a person of some importance. He seems to have held or administered land, and he is called in various records by the titles *miles* ('knight'), *dominus* ('lord'), *prepositus* ('prefect, overseer'), *minister* ('under-official, administrator'), and *officialis*.

A number of the romance writers were "clerks." This includes two Anglo-Norman poets, the author of the Arthurian romance *Fergus* who gives his name as "Guillarmes li clers" (William the Clerk) and the "Mestre Thomas" who wrote the *Romance of Horn*. The *jongleur* Bertrand de Bar-sur-Aube calls himself "uns gentis clers," and in the conclusion to the *Chevalier de la Charrete* we learn that this unfinished work was completed by a clerk named Godefroi de Leigni. The poet usually known as Herbert le Duc de Danmartin is called in one manuscript "Guibert clerc à Danmartin." Unfortunately, "clerk" is not a precise term. In most cases, it merely indicates that a man has had a university education, but that information alone can be of some use to us since it implies a bookish training that a *jongleur* would not ordinarily be expected to have. The claims of some authors, such as Hue de Rotelande, to be translating from Latin also imply an educated background, whether or not the claims are true.

It is possible that some of these writers were members of the nobility, but the evidence is unclear. Was Herbert le Duc a duke, or was this merely an honorary title like "le roi"? When Bertrand de Bar-sur-Aube calls himself a "gentis" clerk, how high a birth does that imply—or does it imply anything about birth? These are unanswerable questions. The level of education shared by the romance writers suggests that they were not lowborn, yet if many of them were important men by birth we would expect to have clearer evidence of the fact. Some perhaps came from the lower ranks of the nobility, some from the upper levels of the mercantile classes. A good number of them may have been court officials, either by vocation or as the result of appointments made to them by their patrons.

Even less is known about the writers of English romances than about the writers of French romances. For the eighty or ninety extant English romances written before 1500, the names of only a few authors survive: Thomas of Erceldoune, a certain William who translated *William of Palerne*, Thomas Chestre, Geoffrey Chaucer, Henry Lovelich, and John Metham.

Thomas of Erceldoune, or Thomas Rymer as he was also called, was a famous poet of the thirteenth century (he died about 1290) who, according to legend, produced a number of prophecies, including a prediction of the death of King Alexander of Scotland. A few public records refer to him, and several medieval English authors, including John Barbour and Robert Mannyng of Brunne, mention him. Mannyng seems to say that he wrote a version of the Tristan story in English. The only existing English version of that story is the Auchinleck Manuscript, where it *is* attributed to Thomas of Erceldoune, but it seems likely that the Auchinleck poem is citing Thomas as an ultimate authority, as French authors sometimes cited famous *jongleurs*. The English *Tristrem* closely follows the Anglo-Norman *Tristan* of Thomas, and the English poet-translator, not knowing any better, probably thought this Thomas was the same as the more well-known Thomas of Erceldoune. So, in addition to knowing nothing about Thomas of Erceldoune's life, we apparently have no romances written by him.

William of Palerne concludes with a statement that one "William" translated the poem from French "as well as his wit would serve him, even though it is feeble." William's hesitancy about his abilities as an author (a well-justified hesitancy) suggests that this may have been his first or only attempt at translation. Two other amateurish writers who produced romances, both in the mid fifteenth century, were Henry Lovelich and John Metham.

Lovelich was a London skinner who translated the *Estoire del Saint Graal* and Robert de Boron's *Merlin* into English verse. Metham was, according to his own account, a "symple scoler of philosophye" from Cambridge who translated various pieces from Latin for Sir Miles Stapleton of Ingham. Metham was nothing at all like a *jongleur*. Most of his translations are informative rather than entertaining (a palmistry, a physiognomy, prognostications), and his one "romance," *Amoryus and Cleopes*, is mainly a frame story providing an excuse to present miscellaneous bits of scholarly lore.

At the end of the English *Launfal* (late fourteenth century), the author gives his name as Thomas Chestre. Nothing is known about this man except the obvious fact that he was a hack writer. However, on the basis of style, several scholars have concluded that he may also have been the author of *Libeaus Desconus* and *Octavian*, two other Middle English versions of French romances and both found in the same manuscript with *Launfal*.[16]

Chaucer is the English romance writer about whom we know the most, and of those mentioned here he was probably the most like the French romance writers in terms of social status and professional commitment. Like Chrétien de Troyes and others, he was a court poet. He came from the upper middle classes (his father was a wine merchant), but early in his life he appears in the public records as a member of the entourage of Lionel, duke of Clarence. Subsequently he enjoyed the patronage of some of the most important men in England, including John of Gaunt, Richard II, and Henry IV. He wrote the *Book of the Duchess* as an elegy for John of Gaunt's first wife Blanche, and he dedicated the *Legend of Good Women* to Richard II's wife Anne. His well-known lyric, "The Complaint of Chaucer to His Purse," shows his dependence as a poet upon financial support from noble patrons. His writings attest to the breadth of his education although we do not know where he acquired it. Yet, while his background may have been similar to those of certain French romance writers, his work stands apart from theirs, both French and English alike, as a more personal and serious artistic expression. It is not a good example of popular literature, and, although he produced several important romances, he is not known primarily as a romance writer. His *Sir Thopas*, a scathing burlesque of the English romances, indicates his distance from the main tradition, especially from the slavish and amateurish English tradition of his time.

Concerning the other writers of English romances, we must

rely on evidence from the works themselves. Albert Baugh has carefully surveyed the evidence and provided us with the most sensible and best-documented conclusions that we are likely to get.[17] His ideas were a corrective to the notion, widely held up until that time, that the Middle English as well as the French romances were the products of itinerant minstrels, and his views have gained increasingly greater acceptance ever since they were put forth. While not rejecting the possibility that minstrels sometimes wrote romances, Baugh considered this the exception rather than the rule and argued for two related conclusions instead: that many of the romances originated in the study, "descended by a literary rather than a popular tradition," and that the authors were more often court poets or clerics than minstrels. His evidence consisted largely of statements from the romances themselves concerning the writers' sources, passages containing religious sentiments, and the marked tendencies in several of the romances toward Christian propaganda.

SINGING AND READING

At one time, public singing of songs and narrative poems—by professionals and nonprofessionals—was common, if we may believe the evidence of the romances. In the English *Lyfe of Ipomydon*, the hero learns to sing as part of his regular education, and in the *Romance of Horn* the whole Irish court, including the king's daughter and son, has been trained in singing lays: "At that time everyone knew how to play the harp well; the more noble the man, the more he knew of that avocation." In Thomas's *Tristan*, Ysolt composes her own "piteous lay of love" and then sings it. In the Icelandic translation of the missing portions of this romance, Tristan also sings lays on two different occasions, but his ability surprises the company, apparently indicating that Thomas did not expect noblemen to be trained in minstrelsy. He did, however, consider it a desirable accomplishment and even a mark of superior education and abilities.

The songs referred to in all these passages seem to have been short—shorter than most romances or *chansons de geste*. For example, in *Horn* and *Tristan*, several lays are sung in succession. (A typical lay runs between 500 and 1,000 lines in length.) Even a brief romance, on the order of 2,000 lines, would take a considerable time to recite, and no more than one would be likely to be performed on a single occasion. We lack good evidence that such poems were sung publicly, but there is no difficulty in imagining a medieval audience, at the court or elsewhere, listening with moderate attention to an epic or romance of 4,000 to 6,000 lines—a good evening's entertainment. Works longer than this create special problems. Many romances, particularly the earlier ones, are 15,000 to 18,000 lines long, and while such length does not preclude recitation, it would seem to require two or more sittings and an especially attentive audience. If such performances were common, it is remarkable that there are no clear instances of them among the hundreds of references we have to public entertainment in medieval France and England.

There was, however, another way of presenting narrative poetry publicly, and one that was sometimes used for longer works: by reading aloud from a manuscript. Baugh lists several examples of this. One of the earliest (thirteenth century) comes from *Havelok the Dane*, where Havelok's coronation is the occasion for a variety of public entertainments: tilting, fencing, wrestling, stone-putting, games of chance, bull and bear baiting, *gleemen* playing on tabors, the singing of *gestes*, and "romanz-reding on the bok." The romance reading is clearly distinct from the more traditional minstrel performance of the *gestes* as well as from other musical entertainments. It is not clear who performed the reading.

Reading aloud to small private groups had long been practiced in the Middle Ages, and there are additional examples of public readings.[18] The kind of reading mentioned in *Havelok*, however, may represent a transitional stage between the memorized performances of the *jongleurs* and the solitary reading habits of later ages. Two other English examples from the fourteenth century represent something closer to solitary reading. In Chaucer's *Troilus and Criseyde*, Pandarus finds Criseyde and two other ladies listening to a maiden reading from "the geste of the siege of Thebes." Interrupted by her uncle, Criseyde halts the reading, presumably to have it continued later, and she and Pandarus discuss the book briefly. She calls it a "romance," and he remarks that the version he knows contains twelve books. This is clearly an example of leisure reading aloud in private from a romance of substantial length but probably not as long as most Thebes romances. It is not read aloud out of necessity: we know that Criseyde can read because elsewhere in the poem she both receives and writes letters. Apparently she listens to it simply to make a social occasion of her leisure entertainment.

The other example is equally interesting. In John Barbour's poem *The Bruce*, while The Bruce and his army are on the march, they come to Loch Lomond and have no way to cross except in one small boat. The Bruce and some of his men, presumably his captains or personal entourage, are ferried across first and then encamp while the time-consuming task of transporting the rest of the army across proceeds. To pass the time, the king produces a manuscript of "Ferambrace" (probably the twelfth-century epic *Fierabras*, although there were English versions of this work in Barbour's time and "Ferumbras" is the usual English form of the hero's name), and he reads it aloud to his men until the whole army has crossed the loch (ed. Skeat, ll. 435–66). In this and the previous example, the easy availability of romance manuscripts is remarkable. It did not seem strange to Chaucer that a noble lady would have in her possession a copy of a long romance, and Barbour did not think it improbable that a king would carry a romance with him while campaigning.

A third example occurs in the romance *Eger and Grime*. As Grime is secretly leaving the court to fight an important battle, Eger distracts attention from his departure by reading a romance from a window so that the whole court can hear him.

All of these examples come late, after the appearance of the prose romance and at a time when literacy in the vernacular was widespread among the nobility and even the middle classes. The examples do not illustrate the practice of the twelfth and thirteenth centuries, but they do show that a trend had been underway that eventually resulted in the romance becoming a book, to be read much as books are read today. It is impossible to say when this trend began, but the proliferation of romance manuscripts beginning in the twelfth century probably indicates that it had already begun then, for manuscripts are meant to be read. On occasion *jongleurs* may have used them as aids to recitation or singing in the traditional manner, but we have no evidence to show that this was a common practice. It is hard to conceive of a *jongleur* singing, playing a harp or fiddle, and turning pages all at the same time. It is more reasonable to suppose that the appearance of romances in manuscript indicates the existence of an audience for written romances and that the songs of the public singers were different works altogether.

One reason that the importance of oral presentation has been exaggerated is the presence, in verse romances throughout the Middle Ages, of the so-called minstrel tags. These are introductory remarks and asides by the author which give the impression that he is addressing an immediate, listening audience; they include direct addresses to the audience, authors' statements about themselves and their audiences, and pauses in the narrative for rest or other activities. They have often been taken as evidence that the poems were intended for oral delivery—for example by Jean Rychner, who quoted a series of them to prove that the *chansons de geste* were sung by *jongleurs*.[19] The problem with such conclusions is that minstrel tags occur even in poems which few would suspect of being minstrel works, and this suggests that they had become purely conventional. A good example is the fourteenth-century romance *William of Palerne*, a fairly close translation from the twelfth-century *Guillaume de Palerne*, made "for hem that knowe no frensche." The English poem is unskillful and bookish-sounding—not at all the sort of work one would expect to hear from a minstrel—and yet, early in the poem, the author pauses, as a minstrel might, and says:

> Thus passed is the first pas of this pris tale,
> And ye that loven and lyken to listen ani more . . .
> Preieth a pater noster prively this time
> For the hend erl of Herford, sir Humfrey de Bowne (ll. 161–65).

Although the romance is over 5,500 lines long, no other such breaks or divisions occur, as we would expect if the poem had actually been written for oral presentation. Obviously, the minstrellike pause is conventional—and an excuse for the author to mention his patron's name.

One could easily multiply such examples. Here it is enough to note that minstrel tags may be suspected of being conventional even in the earliest romances. The *Romance of Horn* (twelfth century, Anglo-Norman) begins by speaking of an earlier work concerning the hero's father: "Lords, you have heard the verses from parchment, how the baron Aalof came to his end." This betrays a startling mixture of traditions, speaking as if to a listening audience on the one hand, but on the other hand referring to the work's antecedent as a parchment book. The latter seems to presume that the audience is familiar with books, and one does not expect that of the audience for an oral narrative.

Actually, the minstrel tags are only a part of a larger convention, the major part of which is the verse form itself. In its written form, the verse romance is an imitation of a minstrel's song, just as Plato's dialogues imitate conversations or the epistolary novel imitates an exchange of letters. Such imitations of form relate the works to a familiar and understood reality and are necessary in any literary tradition. In the case of the verse romances, the conventions say, in effect: "Like the songs of the minstrels, this is a story told to you, a group of noble persons, for your entertainment by one who seeks to serve you; it is a true story, passed down by word of mouth (or, later, by book)." Such conventions imply that an oral narrative tradition had in fact existed and that something like it (perhaps lays sung at court or public readings) continued to exist. The disappearance of the minstrels would mean the demise of the minstrel conventions. This occurred near the end of the fifteenth century, as prose romances completely replaced the poetic romances and the minstrel phrases ceased to be used, having lost their meaning even as a convention.

MANUSCRIPTS OF ROMANCES

The romance as we know it is a book, or rather a part of a book. There are several different types of romance manuscripts, and some changes in type are observable between the time of the earliest ones and the end of the Middle Ages. The earliest romance manuscripts in England are from the thirteenth century; with only a few exceptions these are French, but the number of English manuscripts steadily increased throughout the fourteenth century. About the end of the fifteenth century, printed books rapidly supplanted manuscripts through the efforts of William Caxton, Wynkyn de Worde, and others, although romance manuscripts continued to be produced in the sixteenth century and there is at least one, the Percy Folio, from the seventeenth century. For the most part, these are works of small to moderate size (usually quarto or small folio) and of modest appearance, with only a few illuminated capitals and rarely an illustration. This is particularly true of the manuscripts in English. Until the end of the fourteenth century the writing material was invariably parchment, but in the fifteenth century the majority of manuscripts were written on paper, which had by then become widely available in England. It is thus clear that, in general, books of romances were produced in the cheapest possible way, as one would expect for books that had a fairly large potential buying-public.

Karl Brunner has pointed out several significant facts about the romance manuscripts as a group.[20] Very few of them, he notes, contained only one romance when originally written. There is now a quite substantial proportion of one-romance manuscripts, but several of them show obvious signs of having been excerpted from originally larger collections. Even at that, the great majority of extant manuscripts are collections and usually ones with several different types of works in them. The manuscript devoted solely to romances is an oddity. Other kinds of works frequently found with the romances include saints' lives or other religious narratives and historical narratives, although there is no limit to the variety of materials found in these manuscripts. Nothing suggests that the manuscripts containing romances were mass-produced or even prepared according to a standard format. On the contrary, many of them were certainly prepared on special order or for a specific person or family.

The personal or family manuscript was common in the Middle Ages, but the type is probably best known to modern readers through the "Book of Wicked Wives" owned by Jankyn, the fifth husband of Chaucer's Wife of Bath. Such books often contain many different types of works united by a common theme or interest (antifeminism in Jankyn's case). The type is well exemplified by the unique *William of Palerne* manuscript (Kings' College Cambridge MS 13), which contains three romances, a history of England, a treatise on the kings of Cologne, and a poem on hunting—just the sort of works that a nobleman of the fourteenth century might wish to have in his possession—and shows signs of frequent use, with many scribblings in the margin. Another, earlier example is Royal MS 12.C.12, a highly personalized miscellany written in Latin, French, and English. It contains two romances: *Amis et Amiles* and *Fouke Fitzwarin*, a prose account of a famous rebel; in addition, it includes a service in honor of another rebel against the crown, Thomas of Lancaster, who was executed in 1322. Among the other contents are some typical household items: instructions for dyeing linen, charms against mice, recipes, prognostications of weather, rules for diet, arithmetic problems, and interpretations of dreams.

The closest thing to a standard format for romance manuscripts is that in which romances comprise part of a volume—often a large one—devoted to historical materials or to religious-didactic materials. There are many such manuscripts, both in French and English, and, along with a few volumes containing only romances, they include the most important of the extant romance manuscripts. Among these are Cambridge University Ff.2.38, a large fifteenth-century manuscript containing forty-three items (religious poems, saints' lives, nine romances), and Cotton Caligula A.2, another fifteenth-century manuscript containing thirty-eight items (religious poetry and prose, eight romances). The earliest of these major manuscripts in English is also the best known and most important. This is the Auchinleck Manuscript, a severely damaged collection of religious and secular poetry, written between 1330 and 1340, apparently in London. There seems to have been no overall plan for the book outside of placing the religious pieces at the beginning. The contents include seventeen romances, quite a number of religious narratives and didactic poems, four secular poems, a list of Norman barons, and an account of the kings of England. Originally the manuscript had numerous, rather primitive drawings, but all except seven have been cut out.

According to a widely accepted theory, this manuscript was the product of a small secular bookshop in London, where it was planned, copied, and partly written, perhaps on special order.[21] This theory presupposes the existence of such bookshops at an earlier date than had before been suspected and of a wider buying-public for books than had generally been thought. It is not clear who would buy such a book, but it would presumably not be a monastic library because of the strongly secular leanings of the work nor a family of rank because of the relatively crude workmanship. This seems to leave as the most likely possibility a London citizen or citizens of considerable wealth.

Much has been said concerning the possibility that several extant manuscripts were minstrel books, intended to be carried around and read from in public performances. Four English manuscripts have been mentioned in this connection because of their size, the quality of the handwriting, and the contents. All are narrow in width, of a size that might be carried in a pocket, and in general they are crudely written; the contents are similar to those of the large romance manuscripts. The possibility that these were minstrel books cannot be denied, but such conclusions are purely speculative. Other manuscripts of a similar format do exist, and not all of them contain the type of materials that a minstrel would be expected to recite. Books with a long, narrow shape may have been desirable for some other reason, such as ease in storage. In general, the arguments for these being minstrel books would carry greater weight if the manuscripts were older, but three of them are from the fifteenth century, when the likelihood of minstrel performance for romances is much reduced.

From its beginnings in the late twelfth century to its old age in the fifteenth century, the verse romance of England changed in many ways. The most obvious of these changes are in language (from French to English) and in length (from long romances to short ones), but there were also changes in the type of stories that were popular, in the romances' treatment of political and social issues, in their didacticism, and even in the dominant verse form. All these changes were expressions of more fundamental changes in the romance audience and in its patterns of thinking. As a result, the verse romance is not one type of work but many, and each type has its own characteristics, its own appeal, and its own history. One of the earliest types, the child-exile romance, was short lived, barely surviving the thirteenth century. Some types, such as the love romance, sprang up early and thrived until the end of the Middle Ages; still others, such as the didactic romance, came into existence only at the end of the period. In the following chapters, each major type will be discussed separately, roughly in the order of its appearance on the scene. In the earlier period, adventure stories—part of the heritage of the *chansons de geste*—predominate, later to be supplanted by an interest in love, in social issues, and even in moral questions.

2 The Child Exile

$\mathcal{A}$mong the earliest romances in England were those of Horn and Havelok. Anglo-Norman poems concerning both heroes were written about 1175 and 1200 respectively, and these were followed by Middle English versions in about 1225 and 1280. (Only about four other extant English romances are believed to have been written as early as the thirteenth century.) The two stories have been associated with each other from a very early time. The Middle English *King Horn* and *Havelok the Dane* occur together in a single manuscript (Laud Miscellany 108), in which they are the only romances, and both appear to have been copied from the same earlier manuscript. The *Laud Troy Book* mentions them side by side, and modern scholars consistently discuss them together because of the obvious similarities in their stories and their historical settings. In a vague and confused way, both stories recall the period of the Viking (Danish) invasions, and both stories were considered historically true in the Middle Ages.

Each story tells of a prince who, as a young boy, is alienated from home and inheritance, is sent into enforced exile in a land where he is unknown or where he has no social position, and must therefore reestablish his personal identity and win back his kingdom by means of natural strength and virtue. These are stories about growing up—growing up in a personal, military, social, and political sense—but growth for the heroes does not mean change as much as it means regaining something lost. At the same time, these are stories of empire building. Both heroes end as rulers over the land of their exile as well as their inherited land and have political influence that extends beyond the borders of their own personally created empire. In these romances, as in several later ones, there is a close identification between the individual and the state. The empire is the creation and embodiment of a single man, the hero; its continued welfare depends totally on his abilities and on the soundness of his claim to the throne.

The earliest Horn romance and perhaps the earliest of all the extant romances of England is the Anglo-Norman *Romance of Horn*, also called *Horn et Rimenhild*. It was composed about 1170 or 1180, during the reign of Henry II, by one Master Thomas, who was probably a clerk and possibly a professional singer. Despite having some *pro forma* references to the doctrine that rulers should serve the poor rather than the rich, the poem is clearly aristocratic in its sympathies and point of view. It describes court life in an elaborate and tolerably realistic fashion, placing great stress on rank and its prerogatives. All of this suggests that it may have originated in and for Henry's English court. The two main scenes of the action, Brittany and Ireland, had both come under Henry's control, by peaceful means, in the early 1170s, and the empire-building theme of the romance had a parallel in Henry's own deliberate (and successful) policies. Members of the court would be the ones who were most concerned with news from the crusades (Henry himself took the cross in 1187), and perhaps this explains why the *Romance* contains a much lengthier and more detailed picture of its Saracen villains than does its Middle English counterpart, *King Horn*.

King Horn is the earliest romance in English. It was composed about 1225, during the early years of Henry III's reign, but it derives from a different and probably earlier tradition than that on which its Anglo-Norman predecessor is based. It has been thought to be a poem of the court, but if so the court is a different one from that of the *Romance* because, in addition to being in English, *King Horn* lacks all the courtly description and courtly values of the earlier romance.[1] At the same time, however, there is no sign of antagonism toward the court, and it is probable that while *King Horn*'s audience had a different language and level of sophistication, its political allegiances were similar to those of the *Romance*'s audience. In the English poem, internal dissension is relatively more important, and this may reflect the increasing prevalence of baronial revolt during the early thirteenth century in England.

Horn Childe stands clearly apart from the two earlier versions. It seems to have been written about 1320, during the time of Edward II, and it shows the influence of the late thirteenth-century border wars against Scotland and Wales. The Saracens are entirely gone from this version, and the romance's world has been restricted to Great Britain. The scenes of action are Northumberland, southern England, and Wales; the only outside invaders come from Den-

mark and Ireland. Thus the half-fanciful world of the *Romance* and
King Horn has been replaced with a more familiar world: *Horn
Childe* contains many more place names than the other Horn ro-
mances, and they are real places. At the same time, internal rebel-
lion plays only a small part in this poem. *Horn Childe* shows us an
England fighting to maintain its integrity while constantly
threatened by various factions along its borders.

The earliest Havelok romance is the Anglo-Norman *Lai
d'Haveloc*, composed about the year 1200, near the end of Richard
I's reign or the beginning of John's. Its story is drawn from the
Havelok episode in Gaimar's *Estoire*, and in fact one of the manu-
scripts is a version of Gaimar in which the *Lai* replaces the episode.
This strongly suggests an audience interested in English history
and particularly in the origins of the English nobility and society.
The center of the action is northern England (Lincoln and
Grimsby), and this too may tell us something about the author and
audience, especially since the author's sympathies toward Denmark
seem as strong as or stronger than his sympathies toward England.
Curiously, King Arthur is portrayed as an enemy, an invader of
Havelok's native land. This probably means that Arthur was still a
Celtic hero, not yet fully adopted by the English—which seems
also to have been the case in Geoffrey of Monmouth's *History*,
written not long before this romance. The likely audience of the *Lai*
would be the French-speaking baronial families and courts, particu-
larly in the north where ties of loyalty to the old Danelaw were still
felt. The author's point of view seems distinctly baronial: he com-
bines approval of peasant life with a contempt for peasants, and he
insists that the true heir to the throne must be recognized by his
under lords.

Like *King Horn*, the Middle English *Havelok the Dane* comes
from a source independent of its French antecedent and evidences a
sharp shift in audience, though not in point of view. Its date of
composition is usually placed about 1280, early in the reign of
Edward I and shortly after the period of most intense rivalry be-
tween the king and the barons. The influence of this period prob-
ably accounts for the poem's detailed picture of unjust rule under
two usurpers, who may well be reflections of Simon de Montfort or
others like him. The romance has definite royalist sympathies but
at the same time attaches great importance to the rule of law. This
could point to a bourgeois audience, as has been suggested,[2] and the
scenes of village life are vivid enough to indicate the same thing.

The romance also shows us the rise to power of characters who are not nobly born (Grim's sons), and this is something not found in any of the other Horn-Havelok romances. None of this eliminates an aristocratic audience, however. It was, after all, the barons who created Magna Carta, already viewed in the thirteenth century as the foundation of English law, and sympathies for the middle class can come from outside that class just as easily as royalist sympathies can come from outside the royal family. The *Havelok* poet's answer to conflicts over the crown is a king of royal birth who rules according to law, and this ideal could appeal to anyone in the thirteenth century.

In social and political terms, the significant common feature of these five romances is their insistence on birth as a prerequisite for good and stable rule and the close association that they make between birth and virtue. These stories will not appeal to anyone lacking a firm commitment to the idea of the born heir. The Horn-Havelok romances are unlike many later ones in that the social climbing in them takes place in appearance only; the heroes are born to the state that they eventually achieve. This is probably why romance versions of these two stories, after being quite popular in the twelfth and thirteenth centuries, fell into disuse in a later, somewhat less monarchist age.

THE OLD KING AND THE KINGDOM

All of the Horn-Havelok romances begin with the fall of the old king, the father of the hero (or heroine). The *Romance of Horn* mentions the hero's father only briefly, but the others describe his kingdom and his eventual death in some detail. *Havelok the Dane* and *Horn Childe* also give accounts of the heroine's father, the king of the land in which the hero is exiled. *King Horn* even begins by announcing that it is a "song of Murry the king" (Murry—or Allof in one manuscript—is Horn's father), implying that the story is about the father rather than the son. Yet Murry is dead by line fifty-eight.

In a sense, however, these *are* stories about the father. His death and the fall of the kingdom are the initial problems confronted in the romances, precipitating the action. The hero's goal is to fill the place left vacant by the death of the father, to remake himself as the father and thereby to ensure that the kingdom will endure. Symbolically, the father, the son, and the kingdom are one.

The old king has two different types of virtues, familial and political, which conform to the twofold emphasis of the plot on the development of the hero as an individual and on the regaining of the lost kingdom. The father presides over a loving and happy home (see *Havelok*, 348–49; *Horn Childe*, 13–16), and the whole family is beautiful (*Havelok*, 344; *King Horn*, 10; *Romance*, 262–68). The father's political virtues are those associated with a stable rule. He is strong, brave, a good warrior, and a firm ruler, with many knights and swains (*Havelok*, 343; *Romance*, 252; *Horn Childe*, 10–12). His virtues are conventional ones, all relating to one thing, his ability to keep the ravages of war away from the kingdom and to assure his subjects that they need not fight to maintain their safety. Thus it is important that he be nobly born to avoid contention over succession to the throne, that he be strong and warlike to keep invaders out of the realm, and that his kingdom be broad to keep areas of potential conflict at a distance. Medieval man had long understood the importance of large kingdoms and also of alliances with neighboring kingdoms in keeping the peace, as we can see both in *Beowulf* and in the *Chanson de Roland*. This is the reason why both Horn and Havelok create greater empires than they find. These romances do not speak to a greed for land or conquest in the hearts of their audiences, nor to a sense of self-righteousness about national worth, nor to notions of manifest destiny. Their idealized kingdoms appeal quite simply to a desire for peace and protection.

The best and fullest description of a well-ruled kingdom comes at the beginning of *Havelok the Dane* (ll. 27–105), where we are told of the heroine's father, King Athelwold of England, a maker and enforcer of good law, loved by all because of his good works. He had outlaws and thieves imprisoned and hanged, refusing to accept bribes to free them. In that time merchants could go about their business all over England without injury. He let no one, not even the clergy or the nobles, harm orphans. Anyone, even the strongest knight, who did wrong to widows was imprisoned. Anyone who raped a maiden was castrated. Athelwold himself was the best warrior that ever was, he was generous with his goods, and he always fed the poor.

This list of the benefits of strong rule seems to tell us much about popular political expectations in the late thirteenth century. The king is seen as subject to a series of specific obligations, the first of which is an obligation to law. Medieval Europe, and England in particular, was very law-conscious: law was the soul of the body politic. It was the thirteenth century that first created the Magna Carta and then set about turning it into a constitution by means of successive reconfirmations. The coronation oath of the king stressed his legal obligations to his subjects, and these obligations, as expressed for example in the charters of liberties issued by several twelfth-century kings, were viewed as having existed since Anglo-Saxon times, just as *Havelok* seems to portray them.[3] One might well say, therefore, that the opening of this romance provides a summation of the popular view of the "laws of King Edward," to which legal documents of this period frequently appeal. Other royal obligations apparent in the passage from *Havelok*, such as duty to the church and duty to aid the weak and needy, are likewise commonplaces of medieval political thought. Most interesting for the study of the romance, however, is the passage's stress on the king's duty to protect his realm both from enemies abroad and from disruption and crime at home, and the idea that such protection can result only from strongly, even harshly applied power.

The old king and his kingdom in the Horn-Havelok romances have only the common defect of mortality. When the king dies, the kingdom which, according to the assumptions of these romances, is totally dependent on him and his abilities will fall. The alarm is sounded early. Aalof in the *Romance of Horn* is no more than introduced before we hear that he was brought to his end; later we are told of the many difficulties which he had confronted in achieving and maintaining his throne. At the beginning of the *Lai d'Haveloc* and of *Horn Childe*, the kingdoms are already under attack. In its usual unimaginative but efficient manner, *King Horn* immediately alerts us to Murry's downfall by explaining that he was "king in the west, as long as it lasted" (ll. 5–6). The ideal kingdom described at the beginning of *Havelok the Dane* contains the seeds of its own downfall in its very perfection, and the good rule in England and Denmark immediately succumbs upon the deaths of their kings.

INVADERS AND TRAITORS

The fall of the old kingdom and the continued conflicts of the plot are brought about by two different kinds of evil forces, invading armies from outside the kingdom and treacherous individuals within it. The romances do not establish much of a connection between the invasions and the internal dissensions, nor do they question the causes, beyond passing them off as instances of common human vices such as brutality and greed. Like most popular literature, the Horn-Havelok romances maintain a strictly black and white vision of morality. Villains are identified right away and with no uncertainty. In *King Horn*, for example, the hero's two companions, one of whom will remain faithful and one of whom will be a traitor, are introduced this way: "One of them was named Child Athulf and the other Fikenhild. Athulf was the best and Fikenhild the worst" (ll. 25–28). The author of Havelok often curses his villains and compares them to Satan or Judas. Elsewhere enemies of the hero are compared to dogs.

Usually the first opponents to make an appearance and also the first to be vanquished are the outside invaders. The fact that they are foreigners is enough to indicate that they are evil, but they are often associated with traditional enemies of the nation or the faith as well. In the two earlier Horn romances, the attackers are Saracens. Saracens, of course, were never a threat to England, and the fear of them in the romances was partly a carry-over from the *chansons de geste*, strengthened by the crusades, which caused the English romances, like those of France, to use the term "Saracen" for any non-Christian enemy. In part too, the English popular mind had completely confused the Viking invaders of a century before with the Moslem enemies of France, who still seemed to be a threat. In *Horn Childe* a Danish *here* (the old Anglo-Saxon word for the Viking army) invades Horn's kingdom, and a second attack originates in Ireland, long a bastion of the Vikings.

Domestic villainy is seen as subtler, more persistent, more dangerous. The sequence of action in the Horn story, where the hero fights first to demonstrate his strength and valor, then to bring vengeance on the murderers of his father, and finally to conquer evil companions with whom he has been associating since the beginning, seems to say that internal dissension is the ultimate threat to a state. This attitude may have something to do with the fact that, while there were frequent threats of invasion to England during this period, none resulted in the conquest of even a part of the kingdom. In its treatment of domestic villainy, the Horn story also contains a certain crude wisdom regarding personality. In most literature villains are alter egos of the hero, and in the Horn story

that connection is suggested by the brotherlike relationship be-
tween the hero and villains as children. Once the hero has subdued
his environment, has brought under control the forces outside of
himself, he must then conquer the evil within himself before he can
rule well. The final conflict in the Horn story is set in motion when
the villain attempts to marry the heroine and seize her kingdom,
that is, to do by force what the hero is attempting to do in more
conventionally acceptable ways. Similarly, the first act of villainy
consists of putting an unpleasantly sexual connotation on the meet-
ings between the hero and heroine: the villain tells the heroine's
father that Horn is sleeping with her—a charge that we know to be
untrue. In one sense, therefore, Horn's defeat of the villain repre-
sents the control of his own lusts.

The single most important trait of the domestic villain is
treachery, which was the ultimate political vice in medieval society.
Since the very fabric of feudal government depended on the making
and keeping of oaths, the existence of men who would solemnly
vow to do one thing and then do something else not only threatened
continual trouble but also promised to destroy the social system
itself. The villain in the Horn romances has a name which in itself
suggests this quality: he is called Wikele in the *Romance*, Fikenhild
in *King Horn*, Wikel in *Horn Childe*—all cognate with Old English
ficol, "deceitful." When we first see these characters, they are usu-
ally making oaths that we perceive to be false. The Wikele of the
Romance, before his act of betrayal, sits at dinner with Horn, flatters
him, and makes exaggerated promises of good faith (ll. 1823–45).
By contrast, Horn is conspicuously faithful to his alliances. When
Wikele asks to be made a present of Horn's white horse, Horn
declines because it was a Christmas gift from his close friend
Haderof and offers another horse instead, thus enraging Wikele,
who immediately begins plotting his treason. Faithfulness to prom-
ises is a central theme in the Horn story, as in many other ro-
mances, for the major tests of the love between Horn and his lady
are their promises, after the villain's lies have parted them, to be
true to one another for seven years.

Two of the more brutal villains of the medieval English ro-
mances are Godrich and Godard of *Havelok the Dane*, both chosen
by their dying sovereigns to serve as regents during the minority of
the two kings' children (the hero and heroine of the romance) after

swearing to care for the children, educate them, and pass the king-
doms on to them at the appropriate time. But Godrich plots to
secure England for himself, forcing the young princess to marry a
rustic laborer (Havelok) against her will, thus presumably putting
her out of the line of inheritance for the crown. He also imprisons
the princess in a castle where she is dressed in poor clothing and
deprived of food. Later Godrich falsely informs his English follow-
ers that Havelok, now king of Denmark and leading an attack
against Godrich, has been burning churches, imprisoning priests,
and strangling monks and nuns. When Godard gets control of Den-
mark, he throws Havelok and his two little sisters in prison, where
they are kept in poor clothing, cold, and without food. When the
children complain of this treatment, Godard replies by carving the
throats of the two girls and cutting them up in pieces. In a less than
convincing moment, he then hesitates over killing Havelok and
finally has him sent off to a peasant's cottage to be bound and
gagged (with a dirty rag) and eventually drowned. The punish-
ments meted out to Godard at the end of the story are brutal in
accordance with his crimes. First he is flayed over all his body with
a sharp knife; then he is bound backwards to an old diseased mare
and driven to the gallows, not by the road but over the plowed
fields. Finally he is hanged. "I don't care who pities him," says the
author; "he was false" (l. 2511).[4]

Two of these romances describe, in some part at least, the
effects of the invaders' or the villains' rule on the old king's good
kingdom. When the pagans in *King Horn* conquer Suddene, they
begin to kill the people and tear down churches (heroes often build
churches when they get to be kings); the only people allowed to live
are those who give up their faith. In the *Romance*, while Horn is
absent reconquering his own land, Wikele uses money from Brit-
tany's treasury to build a castle (an act of oppression), thus alarming
and antagonizing even his own brother. In *Havelok* (ll. 260–79), Earl
Godrich, in addition to building castles, requires oaths of fealty
from the whole kingdom, replaces the old justices and sheriffs with
his own appointees, and has the poaching laws strictly enforced.
These are all well-recognized ways for a medieval lord to accrue
power and wealth to himself. The romance expresses a strong anti-
pathy to centralized government, not entirely consistent, of course,
with the attitude expressed in the earlier description of the old king
Athelwold's rule.

BEAUTY AND POWER: THE HERO AND HEROINE

The center of the fantasy world is the hero. Besides being the most important person in the romance and the only one whose character is much developed, he is also the least realistic. He is unbelievably strong or handsome or brave, or all of these, and he acts in ways that are startling and inconsistent with the otherwise commonplace course of events in these stories. But because the audience must identify with the hero, some point of contact must be arranged, some means by which the listener or reader can see himself in this oversized, exotic figure. Naturally, the romancer's task is made easier by the fact that audiences are quicker to identify with what they want to be than with what they think they are; nevertheless, not any idealized character will work as a fantasy hero, and perhaps the most critical part of the romance writer's art consists in finding and emphasizing those traits in his hero that attract the audience's sympathies. The Horn-Havelok romances do this by balancing off the heroes' exceptional strengths against some ordinary human weaknesses—weaknesses that are temporary or the result of circumstances, weaknesses that can be overcome but that make possible a bridge between audience and hero.[5] For Horn and Havelok the most important weaknesses result from their youth and exile.

When the old kingdom falls, the hero is still a child, too young to make any effective resistance to his enemies. In all versions of the stories, he comes under the guardianship of a paternal figure who raises him to manhood. Great stress is placed on his youthful help-lessness. At the opening of the *Romance*, Horn and his companions are found in a garden hiding from the Saracens who have just overrun the kingdom. In *Havelok the Dane*, after Havelok's sisters have been murdered, the young hero pleads desperately with Godard to spare his life, promising to give up his inheritance and do homage to the new regent. The hero's weakness also arises from the fact that he is in exile. Since he is in a foreign land, his inherited rank means little, and he must make his way by means of work and natural abilities. Horn, in the two earlier romances, works as a serving boy for the king, and Havelok supports himself by becom-ing a porter.

Great pity is extended to the heroes at the outset of all these romances, by the villains who seize their lands as well as by the kings who receive them in the lands of their exile. In fact, the authors' desire to show their heroes as helpless, pitiable waifs, completely at the mercy of their enemies, along with the plot necessity of having them survive their childhood experiences creates a recurring improbability in the Horn-Havelok romances. This improbability we have already noticed when Godard ruthlessly murders the infant princesses and then unaccountably relents and delegates the murder of Havelok to one of his serfs. The villains invariably recognize the threat posed to them by the continued existence of the hero, but, for reasons that the authors attempt to obscure or hasten over, they go about the murder in such an elaborate way that the hero escapes. It is, of course, a common situation in popular adventure literature.

Counterbalancing the hero's temporary weaknesses are his unusually great natural virtues. He is skillful, quick to learn, good looking, and brave; neither Horn nor Havelok has any trouble winning battles. But Horn's greatest virtue is his beauty. He is the fairest young man in the world: "No fairer one could be born, nor rain rain upon, nor sun shine upon; there was none fairer than he was. He was as bright as glass, he was as white as the flower, rose-red was his color" (*King Horn*, 10–16). As we have seen, the Saracens take pity on him for his beauty, but its main effect is to make all women fall immediately in love with him. In the *Romance*, Horn attends a banquet when he is sixteen and captivates all the women of the court; in all three versions, the heroine falls in love with him at first sight or before. In fact, there are indications that Horn's beauty was thought of as supernatural, for in both the *Romance* and *King Horn*, when he comes to speak with the heroine, he glows so that he lights up the room (*Romance*, 1053–54; *King Horn*, 385–86).

Havelok's main virtue is his enormous strength. As a young man, he so distinguishes himself by his ability to perform manual tasks such as lifting, chopping wood, and carrying water that his fame spreads throughout England. In *Havelok the Dane*, he has to leave his foster father's house because he is eating more than the rest of the family combined, and he travels to Lincoln where he gets a job as a porter by pushing aside as many as sixteen other applicants for the task (ll. 931–44). Havelok's greatest display of strength comes in a stone-putting contest held as part of some village games (ll. 1022–58). On the first try, he throws the stone twelve feet beyond the farthest previous try, and then, while everyone is nudging his neighbor and murmuring over this display, he loses interest in the game and remarks, "We're wasting too much time at this." Throughout both of the Havelok romances, feats of raw strength continue to be characteristic of the hero. Instead of conventional weapons, he fights with axes or stones. In a spectacular scene in *Havelok*, he beats off sixty attackers with a door bar, killing most of them (ll. 1766–867). Besides being strong, however, he is gentle, considerate, and chaste.

While the hero's weakness makes it possible for the reader to identify with him, the virtue makes it desirable. Characters such as Horn and Havelok embody the ordinary man's desire to be infinitely appealing to women or to be strong enough to be unassailable. Such virtues may be found in all classes, but in these romances they are directly associated with the inherited nobility of the heroes. When Horn arrives in Ireland during his second period of exile, his beauty instantly causes him to be treated as a nobleman and accepted into the court, even though he has disguised himself and is acting the part of a servant.[6] The Irish king jokes that his son would do well not to go wooing with Horn as a companion. And indeed the Irish princess falls in love with Horn just as the heroine had earlier. This love at first sight is a perception of his true nature, that is, of his nobility. His "nature" is also the reason why, in the *Romance* and *Horn Childe*, he effortlessly surpasses all his companions in a long list of skills associated with the life of the nobility, from learning and warfare to chess and the singing of romances. In the Havelok story a key element of the plot turns upon the association between the hero's strength and his nobility. The villainous king who is serving as the guardian of the heroine deliberately misinterprets her father's instructions to marry her to the "highest and strongest" (that is, the most noble and the best leader) in the kingdom and forces her to marry the presumed commoner Havelok, who is tall and physically strong. When the two interpretations prove to be embodied in the same person, the evil king's intentions are frustrated.

Havelok, however, has an even clearer and more spectacular evidence of his natural nobility in the form of a beam of light (a "fragrant" light in the *Lai*) that emanates from his mouth while he is asleep. (In *Havelok* he also has a "royal mark" on his right shoulder.) Everyone who sees the light immediately interprets it as evidence that he is a king's son and the true heir to the Danish throne, and the light is also the means by which several plot reversals are set in motion. As Grim and his wife come to carry out Godard's instructions to drown the boy, for example, the wife sees the light in the bedroom and saves the hero's life. Later, the light tells the heroine that she has married a man appropriate to her station. Resentfully spending her first night with Havelok, she becomes aware of a brilliance in the room after he has fallen asleep. Her cry of surprise wakes him: "Sire," she says, "you are on fire. Alas, you are all aglow" (*Lai*, 445–46).

The heroines of the Horn-Havelok romances are, like the heroes, paragons of virtue and beauty in the conventional manner; they are also young and defenseless. These are expected characteristics, marking only the heroines' desirability, their appropriateness as future wives for the heroes. In general, they are shadow figures, important only as companions to the men. So it is with a sense of surprise that we occasionally become aware of their sorrows or frustrations, as when the heroine of the Horn story struggles to arrange a tryst with him against the opposition of his guardian or when the heroine in the Havelok romances is forced into marriage and then into bed with a man she believes to be far below her social status.

The symbolism of the heroines, seen not so much in what they are as in what they do, is extremely interesting. Neither Horn nor Havelok is a lover or pursuer of women in any sense; instead the women, in one way or another, come to them. Horn's sweetheart (Rigmel in the *Romance*, Rimenhild in *King Horn*, Rimnild in *Horne Childe*) falls in love with him, makes all the advances, and insists on marriage while he is still recalcitrant in several obvious and not-so-obvious ways. In this she displays uncontrollable passion rather than resolution or purpose, and this passion is one shared by all women who see Horn. Havelok's young wife (Argentille in the *Lai*, Goldeboru in *Havelok*) is forced upon him against the will of both, but she quickly becomes content with the marriage as soon as she knows that he is royally born. The beautiful princess is a privilege that accrues to the hero because of his nobility and natural virtues. She is also a means by which he comes to political power, for he eventually gains one of his kingdoms through his marriage to her.

Even before that, however, she brings to him power and access to power. Horn's progress toward his former noble position begins when the heroine, desiring him to be worthy of marriage to her, arranges for her father to knight him, and immediately afterward he embarks on the series of battles that will end in restoration of his crown. His aim, in the earlier battles at least, is to make himself worthy of her. In *Havelok* the connection between the heroine and the hero's rise to power is less direct but still obvious. After their marriage they return to Havelok's childhood home, fleeing the king, and there Grim's sons, who are to be Havelok's generals in his later battles, swear allegiance to him and his new wife. In the *Lai*, the hero does not know of his noble birth, and it is Argentille's discovery of his flame that leads them to a prophetic hermit who tells them that Haveloc is noble. Argentille also helps Haveloc by teaching him how to win an apparently lost battle against an enemy king.

In the Horn story, a ring symbolizes the romantic alliance between the hero and heroine. Indeed, the ring was the best remembered and often the central motif of this story, especially in *Horn Childe* and the later ballad versions. The ring is closely identified with the heroine and with her love for Horn, serving as a bond between them during the time that they are separated. Like her love, it is a present from her to him, made just as he is forced to leave her father's kingdom and embark on his second period of exile. Rimnild, in *Horn Childe*, informs Horn that the ring will change as her love for him changes: when her thoughts turn to another, the stone will grow pale, and if she loses her maidenhead it will become red (ll. 568–76). The ring conveys power. Riminhild tells Horn that if he looks on it in battle, he will never be afraid or defeated (*King Horn*, 571–76). This prophecy is fulfilled on three separate occasions as Horn, going into combat, looks on the ring, thinks of Riminhild, and then promptly and effortlessly annihilates whole armies of his enemies. In the *Romance*, Horn defeats a pagan champion (the murderer of his father) after gazing on the ring and thinking of Rigmel.

These incidents make it clear that Horn's physical strength and courage as well as his political power are dependent upon the heroine and her love. So, too, is Horn's very identity. When he goes into exile the second time, he assumes a pseudonym and does not take back his true name until he returns to the heroine's land. This occurs after the seven-year period during which they promised to be faithful to one another has elapsed and at a time when the heroine is being forced by the villain to marry another king. Horn arrives at the marriage feast in disguise, comes before the heroine, and reveals his identity to her by means of riddles and by dropping the ring into a cup of wine from which she drinks. The heroine and her ring enable him not only to win her kingdom but also to make himself known as the true heir to his father's kingdom. Argentille, in the *Lai*, is the means by which Haveloc comes to know himself and his birth. Symbolically, beauty and love, strength and influence, identity, birth, and privilege are all bound up in the image of the heroine.

Why are women the source of all this virtue and power? The answer lies in the basic symbolic meaning of the Horn-Havelok stories and helps to explain the essential reasons for their appeal. In essence, these are stories about the individual and societal importance of family. The problem with which they begin is the destruction of the hero's family. For the hero, this means loss of protection, nation, social status, and personal identity; for his kingdom, it means loss of stability, law, sometimes even of religion. The plot carries the hero through various substitute families, all somewhat unsatisfactory because they are not his real family. Havelok literally becomes a member of Grim's family, is raised with Grim's children, and thinks of Grim and his wife as father and mother. Similarly, Horn, during his first exile, is taken into the king's household and given to a nobleman who educates him and generally serves as a foster father. Good and faithful servants populate all of these romances, each one of them having ties to the hero that resemble those of either a father or brother—Herland, Haderof, Hardre, and Wothere in the *Romance;* Athulf and his father in *King Horn;* Wihard, Arlaund, and Hatherof in *Horn Childe;* Grim and Sigar Estal in the *Lai;* Grim and Ubbe in *Havelok.* The story's resolution comes about when the hero regains the family lost at the beginning, reestablishing the old ruling family through his marriage and sometimes being reunited with his mother as well. Once all threats to the family end, so does the romance.

The heroine is essential to the re-creation of the old family. If good rule, social position, and personal identity all depend on a man's ability to fashion a family in the image of his childhood family, then his wife-to-be is the source of all that is important to him. This is the sense we get from the Horn-Havelok romances. Birth is virtue, marriage is essential, and woman is power.

Specifically, the power resides in the woman who is closest to the hero's childhood or childhood home, hence the somewhat sisterlike characters of the heroines: Horn and his sweetheart are raised in the same household; Havelok and Goldeboru have exactly parallel family histories; in all the romances the hero's lady is the first eligible woman with whom he comes in contact.

TRIALS AND ADVENTURES

Unlike many other romance heroes, Horn and Havelok undergo adventures that are not primarily military in nature but rather socio-economic. There are battles in these romances, but they occupy only a small fraction of the narrative, and it is only in the longer poems, the *Romance of Horn* and *Havelok the Dane*, that we get detailed or lengthy descriptions of combat. Furthermore, these heroes do not have any great difficulty winning their battles. Instead, the military supremacy of the heroes is taken for granted while the tension and suspense of the plot develop in the other, nonmilitary scenes. The central problems of the plot have to do with the hero's identity, his relationship to various persons (including the heroine), his social position, and his livelihood.

Horn's adventures typically involve social confrontations or ceremonies, especially in the *Romance*. As a child he is brought before the king to give his name and lineage. As a young man he is forced into an interview with Rigmel during which he must discourage her amorous advances because he is not yet ready to receive them properly, yet he must do so without insulting her. Later he must clear himself of Wikele's false charge against him. In Ireland he undergoes a series of social trials (hawking, hunting, chess, harping) with the children of the Irish king. Even the reunion with Rigmel takes place in a formal, social context: the feast celebrating her marriage to Modin is taking place in the court, and Horn, coming before the assemblage in disguise, has to reveal his identity by means of the ring and a riddle. What is being tested in all these episodes is the hero's understanding of rank and social proprieties in difficult situations. Thus it is not surprising that, as a boy, Horn serves an apprenticeship in roles such as cupbearer or carver for the court. He passes the tests by responding to various characters in ways befitting their true (not their pretended) natures. So, for instance, he insults Wikele and Modin and throws an insolent porter

off a bridge, but he treats the Irish princess who has fallen in love
with him with delicate civility. This is true of other characters as
well. The good ones immediately perceive Horn's nobility and
treat him accordingly.

Havelok's trials are mainly physical and economic. He is raised
by Grim as a fisherman, then later goes to work as a porter, lifting
bundles, chopping wood, and carrying water.[7] He first distin-
guishes himself in such exercises as wrestling and stone-putting. In
battle he displays physical strength combined with a practical incli-
nation to use whatever weapon is available (stone, ax, door bar).
Where the Horn romances test the hero-king in his abilities to
maintain social proprieties and order, the Havelok romances test
him as a provider and defender.

Both heroes undergo a symbolic social progress from servant
through various more elevated but obviously useful roles, to king.
In Brittany, the hero of the *Romance* is first a cupbearer, then a
knight and military commander, and finally the king's enforcer; in
Ireland he serves as a court servant and then as a champion against
the invading Saracens before he is offered a promise of the crown
(which he rejects). In *King Horn* there is a less complex development
from meat carver for the court, to knight, to commander, to king.
Haveloc in the Anglo-Norman romance is first a fisherman, then a
sculleryboy and porter, and then a commander before becoming
king. In *Havelok* the hero finds himself in the family of a serf (Grim)
who takes up fishing; then he becomes a porter, a champion, a
commander, and a king. The theme of social progression is rein-
forced in other ways. As a child Horn claims to be of low birth, and
he adopts the disguises of a poor palmer, a fisherman, and a min-
strel or harper. As a young man, the hero in the *Lai d'Haveloc* is
given the name Cuaran, which, we are told, is the Breton word for
sculleryboy, and in *Havelok the Dane* he seems to be disguised as a
merchant when he returns to Denmark to conquer that land. How-
ever, the disguises and the progressive social roles alike are appear-
ances: we know from the beginning that the hero is heir to the
throne, and we are constantly reminded of his nobility.

In addition to the hero's social progress toward the kingship and
the tests of his kingly abilities, a second clear pattern emerges from
these plots: the reestablishment of personal identity. In one sense,
of course, the establishment of his identity and hence his heredity is
necessary in order for him to become king, but identity is impor-

tant in its own right as well, especially in the Horn story. In all five romances, the loss of the hero's hereditary rights is tantamount to a loss of self, for the hero finds himself displaced into a land where he is not known and a society where he has no rank. Sometimes he does not know his own family—or he seems not to. He undergoes a change of name and appearance. When Horn goes into exile for a second time, for example, he takes a pseudonym (for no apparent reason) and retains it until just before he leaves Ireland. Then in returning to the heroine's kingdom, he passes through several disguises before being recognized and securing the kingship for himself. In the *Lai*, Grim changes the hero's name upon his departure from Denmark, and Haveloc is known by still another name when he goes into service with the king. There are several scenes in the Horn romances where the hero's name or identity is the subject of conversation. The Irish king in the *Romance*, who was once a companion of the hero's father, remarks that Horn resembles Aalof greatly. Later this king's daughter sings part of a lay about Horn while Horn himself is present; then he sings the rest of the lay and does it so well that she thinks this must be Horn himself. In these scenes, and even in the recognition scene with the heroine where puns on his name are used to reveal his true identity, the hero displays a reticence about his name, as if revealing it would place him in danger. (In some cases it would; in others it would not.) It seems that the name and true identity cannot be made known until the hero is ready to take his rightful place as king.

Stories such as those of Horn and Havelok have potential appeal to all who exercise or depend upon the royal power because, besides offering assurances that the power is strong and good and divinely ordained, these romances personalize that power through the identification of the audience with the royal hero. By pitying the helpless young hero, by seeing him in the role of social outcast, by following his confrontation of identity problems similar to its own, the romance audience could realize feelings of familiarity with the king, even feelings of affection for him, while at the same time being assured of his superiority and righteous strength. Such feelings and assurances should have been particularly welcome in the expanding courts of the twelfth and thirteenth centuries, to the many officials and servants, the *ministeriales*, whose roots were among the common people but who lived in close dependence upon the king. To those subject to such appeals, the romances also offered the fantasy that a person could be born to privilege and power and yet not have this fact recognized by the world, perhaps not even recognize it himself. In the land of these romances, the barriers between king and serving boy and porter—hence between king and clerk and page—were lowered.

By balancing strengths and weaknesses, however, the child exile romances did compromise the seeming invincibility of their heroes. This was not the case with another type of early romance, a type whose heroes deserve to be called supermen because of their extraordinary feats of combat. These romances offered even more wish fulfillment than did the child exile romances, they were even more popular than the child exile romances, and their heroes did not have to be royally born.

3 *The Best Knight in the World*

Most of the great heroes of romances were the creations of French writers during a period of somewhat less than 100 years, roughly 1150–1250. In addition to Horn and Havelok, the list includes Lancelot, Yvain, Perceval, Lanval, Tristan, and the three figures with whom this chapter deals: Ipomedon, Bevis of Hampton, and Guy of Warwick. All of the stories have ties with England. In fact, except for Chrétien de Troyes (the author of romances about Lancelot, Yvain, and Perceval), all of the authors probably lived in England.

Although later ages remembered the Arthurian stories best, medieval audiences seem to have given the most attention to those knights whose exploits surpassed all bounds of reasonable human endeavor and encroached on the fantastic and the supernatural. These are the heroes who kill 300 opponents single-handedly, who battle dragons, and who conquer whole empires aided only by badly outnumbered forces. Unlike some other medieval heroes, their travels seldom carry them to the lands of faerie; they operate in a world that is as close a representation of the real world as any found in the romances, but their deeds are exaggerated beyond natural proportions. They are the medieval supermen.

In plot, their stories, and especially *Bevis of Hampton*, are similar to the child exile romances. In all of them the young hero sets out to improve his social status, acquires fame and power in a series of combats, and eventually wins both kingdom and heroine. Though born a person of some rank, he is always suspected of being low-born, and his social progress is marked by a series of disguises and false identities. The heroines and villains are very similar to those in the Horn-Havelok stories, even in being as skimpily developed, and faithful servants abound here too. However, the superheroes struggle not to regain a lost kingdom but to forge for themselves a new identity and position, one not rightfully theirs by birth. In this sense they are involved in real rather than merely symbolic social climbing, so these heroes tend to be lower born than Horn and Havelok. They do not have the marks of nobility, either natural (beauty) or supernatural. Furthermore, we do not find the close linkage between kingdom and personal identity here. The kingdom is not such an important matter, and Guy, clearly the most famous of these three heroes, never actually wins one, although he is offered several. The real aim of these heroes is to achieve recognition as being special and good, and their rewards come when, as they travel about in disguise, they hear dukes and kings in far-off lands speak admiringly or resentfully or fearfully of them. But it does seem to be important that their special identity, once established, be perpetuated, and so these romances give much attention to the fate of the hero's lands and children after his own death. Whereas the Horn-Havelok stories conclude with the hero's marriage, these romances continue the narrative up to or past his death— considerably past it in the case of Guy of Warwick. As all this implies, the role of the heroine is somewhat different too. She still represents land and rank, but she is not so clearly a symbol of power. After her marriage to the hero, she becomes closely identified with him, as is implied by the fact that she always dies when he does or immediately afterward.

The geography is different too. The scene of action for Horn and Havelok is a small group of closely related kingdoms, but here it is the world. The crusades have profoundly influenced the superman romances, and in them it is insufficient to extend the hero's power over a kingdom; instead, the scenes of his conquests include the Mediterranean area, both the Western and Eastern Empires, Africa, and the Near East. Christianity becomes an important issue, both Bevis and Guy being identifiable in some sense as champions of the Faith. There are more adventures, and there is greater variety among them, even though their increased numbers make them more repetitious. The action in these romances is physical and military rather than social and economic. Even when they are fighting for status or the Faith, these heroes achieve by physical force, typically in single combat. This is not, however, a sign that the authors and audiences were interested in strength and warfare for their own sakes. As in the child exile romances, the battles are perfunctory, having symbolic value only: they are the comic book sort of fight, in which the result is more important than the process.

The Anglo-Norman *Roman d'Ipomédon* is the story of a young

prince who sets out to become the best knight in the world in order
to win the lady he loves. It was composed by an author who called
himself Hue de Rotelande and who later wrote another similar
romance named *Protheselaus*. Hue probably lived in a small town
near Hereford and wrote both poems during the 1180s, that is,
about forty years after the Second Crusade (in which Anglo-
Normans took part) and a few years before the beginning of the
Third Crusade (led by Richard I of England and Philip Augustus of
France). Although Hue claimed that both his stories were
translated from Latin histories, in fact he made them up. The plots
bear similarities to folklore and to other romances but no more so
than would be expected in any work of this kind. Hue dedicated his
poems to Gilbert Fitz-Baderon, lord of Monmouth, and this indi-
cates what one would otherwise guess, that the original audience
was a baronial court. It must have been a fairly sophisticated court
too, one capable of identifying with a continental hero, for the
action takes place in the Norman kingdoms of Apulia, Calabria,
and Sicily (although there is no evidence that these lands were
actually known to the author or the audience). The romance also
shows an attitude toward court similar to that found in Chrétien's
romances and betrays no sign of antiaristocratic sympathies. Dur-
ing the fourteenth and fifteenth centuries Hue's story was twice
translated into English verse and once into English prose. One of
the verse translations *(Ipomadon)* follows the original faithfully and
is almost the same length; the other *(The Lyfe of Ipomydon)*, while
directly dependent upon the Anglo-Norman poem, is much short-
ened and conventionalized through omission of incidents, minor
characters, and detail.

　　The story of Bevis of Hampton first appears in an Anglo-
Norman romance, *Boeve de Haumtone*, which was composed about
the year 1200 and which even more clearly than *Ipomedon* shows the
effect of the crusades on the popular imagination. It tells of an
English boy sold into slavery in Egypt who subsequently becomes
a champion of Christianity throughout the Moslem world and the
most prominent hero of his time in Europe. The Anglo-Norman
original is an extremely varied and sophisticated work championing
the cause of Anglo-French Christianity. It was later translated into
a more exaggerated and culturally narrow-minded English version,
which shows the influence of *Guy of Warwick* (written later than
Boeve de Haumtone but before the English translation) and perhaps of

Ipomedon as well. Some antiroyalist sympathies also creep into the Middle English version. Apparently, an English translation of *Boeve de Haumtone* was made about 1300, and this became the basis for a variety of manuscript versions that differ somewhat in episode and detail, although none deserves to be considered a separate work. The Middle English translator added several episodes: one of these is a dragon fight, which we are informed is a feat performed only by Bevis, Lancelot, Wade,[1] and Guy of Warwick; another is an interesting and rather surprising battle in the streets of London, in which Bevis kills 5,000 men. Printed editions of the Bevis story continued to appear down into the nineteenth century, making it one of the longest-lived of all medieval romances.

By far the most popular of these romances, however, was *Guy of Warwick*, which tells of a young knight who tries to win the world for love and then, having done that, tries to win the world again for God. The Anglo-Norman original, *Gui de Warewic*, was probably composed between 1232 and 1242. It is one of the most complicated and emotional of the medieval romances and obviously appealed to a broad audience, both in its own and later times. Its sympathies are clearly though not vehemently antiroyalist, and it is unusual among the really popular medieval romances in portraying some sincere Christian sentiments. Like the Horn-Havelok stories it is set in late Anglo-Saxon times, during the second great wave of Danish invasions, and although the history is inaccurate it is less so than in any other nonhistorical romance. The scene of action includes much of Europe and extends into Africa and the Middle East. English translations of the poem exist in three manuscripts, containing two separate versions, both of which follow the original closely.[2] After the Middle Ages *Guy of Warwick* enjoyed an even more vigorous old age than Bevis of Hampton and was still a prominent piece of popular literature in the eighteenth century.[3] To many readers both in the Middle Ages and since, *Guy of Warwick* has seemed the prototype of chivalric romances.

THE ENEMY

Superman stories deal with problems of control, mainly control of one's environment, and they appeal to audiences who share (or fear) a sense of impotence. Superheroes in the twentieth-century comic book and other popular literature are primarily eradicators of crime. In the medieval superman stories, most of the heroes' enemies are noblemen from other lands, men identified only by name (or rank) and homeland. From this is seems clear that the threats against which author and audience felt a need for protection and which called for the abilities of an extraordinarily strong hero were rank and geography. The first of these is easy to explain in the medieval context. To all except the possessors of great political and military power, the excesses and abuses of rank were a continuing danger throughout the Middle Ages and would have seemed particularly so to the lower nobility and the members of court who were daily called upon to anticipate the plans and whims of their feudal superiors.

When the hero's enemies are not noblemen themselves, they nearly always have direct connections with the nobility. One recurring motif in these romances is that of the underling or relative of a king who conceives a dislike for the hero and maliciously attacks him. Among Bevis's opponents are a porter at Hampton, ten foresters who assail him while he is returning from a hunt, two knights who deceive the king of Egypt into betraying the hero, and the jailers of the king of Damascus. Ipomedon has to fight his lady's steward, and on two different occasions Guy is opposed by seneschals. All three heroes have to fight the relatives of men whom they have previously defeated in battle. These enemies gain power solely through their association with men of rank: the foresters and seneschals would not be threats if they did not have the protection or authority of the king. Other opponents are symbolic of the king, such as the lions that attack Josian (the heroine in *Bevis of Hampton*), or of power itself, such as the giants whom all three heroes must confront.

It is not surprising that most of the enemies have power over foreign lands even though those lands themselves often meant little to the romance audience. This is, in part, a case of transference: the threat of foreign power is psychologically easier to deal with since domestic power is seen as the source of good as well as evil. Domestic power *is* the ultimate issue, for in all of the superman romances the final battle is fought at home. Ipomedon ends by defeating the Indian knight in the kingdom of his lady's father, then by battling and subsequently recognizing his own brother, with whom he is reconciled. *Bevis of Hampton* concludes with a confrontation between Bevis and the king of England, who, however, restores the hero's rightful heritage without a fight because he is afraid of Bevis (Anglo-Norman version). Guy's last combat is in defense of England, but the romance actually concludes when Guy's son Reinbrun has his lands restored by the English king just after Reinbrun has gone through a battle and reconciliation with the son of Guy's closest friend and protector.

Nevertheless, the geography of these romances has significance in itself: the world is seen as an enemy to be conquered. This is apparent from the fact that virtually all of the heroes' opponents are identified with real places—cities, provinces, kingdoms, empires— and that many of them are known only by their rank and homeland. Their titles are enough to establish them as enemies; we do not need to know anything about their character, and they do not have to commit any evil deeds or threaten the hero. The feeling that the world is a thing that the hero must subdue is particularly obvious in the early action of *Ipomedon* and *Guy of Warwick*. Once Ipomedon has decided to distinguish himself, he leaves Calabria (the province bordering his own native Apulia) and performs chivalric deeds in France, Germany, and Arabia. We are told no more about this phase of his adventures. His next military undertaking is a great tournament in Sicily, in which his opponents come from all over Europe. Guy, with similar motives, leaves England and travels to Normandy where he defeats noblemen from Pavia and Saxony in a tournament and then performs deeds of chivalry in Germany, Lombardy, France, Normandy, Brittany, and Spain. No further information is given regarding these adventures either. When Guy discovers that his deeds do not yet satisfy his lady Felice, he leaves home once more and goes even farther abroad.

The crusading spirit is obvious in both these sequences of action, yet neither hero's undertaking is precisely like a crusade since their main goals are to gain a personal reputation and win a lady. It is equally obvious that these lands are nothing more than names to the authors of the romances, for no information is given regarding the countries themselves, except that some of them are Christian and some are "Saracen." Otherwise, Arabia and Sicily are just like Normandy, and all are identical with England in terrain, dress, custom, and social organization. Sometimes, in fact, the romance writers betray their geographical ignorance in startling ways, as when Bevis goes boar hunting in Egypt and on his return to the city is attacked by some foresters. We can frequently see that the writers have no idea how far away from each other these lands lie or what sort of natural obstacles lie between them.

For over one hundred years the insularity of England—and of France—had been disappearing, and now came the crusades, which made new and far-off lands seem even more relevant to life in the Northern European courts. Medieval man had become part of a world stretching from Ireland to India, and, as in our own day, he could exert control in that world only by allying himself with established sides or causes. The romances show that the sides he took were those of native country or province (the homes of the superheroes are not Italy and England but Apulia, Hampton, and Warwick) and religion. Yet this large and important world remained a mystery to him—witness the romance's continuing confusion between the ancient Viking invaders of England and the Saracens—and mystery must have heightened the anxiety with which he lived.

In keeping with these observations, we find that one of the most striking aspects of the superman romances is the emphasis on size and number. All of the heroes fight giants, who are identified with distant places such as India and Ethiopia. When a romance writer wants to say that his hero faced a difficult battle, he says it with numbers. Guy goes into battle accompanied by 100 men and in the midst of the fighting is assaulted by 1,000 enemies. Bevis leads an army against a force from Babylonia comprised of fifteen kings, each leading 15,000 men. The actual numbers are unimportant and soon forgotten by the author. At one point in the English *Bevis of Hampton*, the hero confronts fifteen opponents who soon after are said to number fifty, having unaccountably multiplied like Falstaff's assailants. What is significant is only that the numbers be large and that the forces be lopsided. The true enemies are size, number, and space.

The geographical names in these romances give us an indication of the way the world appeared to medieval audiences. Most of the action takes place in the familiar lands of England, France, Germany, or Italy, the most recurrent place names being Normandy, Brittany, Lorraine, Almain (Germany), and Lombardy. Beyond this nucleus of kingdoms lie the lands known by name only: Greece, Arabia, India, Egypt, Damascus, Hungary, Turkey, Russia, Africa. A few of the names appear to be fictional (Monbrant in *Bevis;* Coisne in *Guy*), but most come from report, not from the imagination. The progress of the action generally carries the hero from nearer places to those farther away, and the climactic battles, though fought near home, typically involve exotic opponents such as King Leonins of India *(Ipomedon)*, the Babylonians in *Bevis of Hampton*, and the Viking champion, Amorant of Ethiopia, in *Guy of Warwick*.

COMBAT

Description of physical and military combat comprises an inordinate amount of these long romances, and, like the enemies, the combats are interchangeable and repetitive. This is what makes the superman romances such tedious reading today, but the repetitiveness must have had something to do with the appeal of the romances in their own day. Therefore it is useful to pay some attention to the details of some typical battles.

Although the hero's enemies are often whole armies and kingdoms, his battles are generally fought against individual opponents, one at a time. This is necessary not so much because the romance writers desired to keep their heroes' exploits within reasonable limits but because these are stories about the individual man. The audience was less interested in armies fighting armies than in one man sallying out against the world and subduing it by force.

The one-against-many trick is managed in a variety of ways. In describing general engagements, the writers usually pass over the confrontation of armies and concentrate on the hero and a few other key figures in such a way that the battle becomes a little story with a plot of its own, involving elaborate cause and effect sequences, treachery, revenge, noble speeches, self-sacrifice, and a host of other motifs. The tournament also lends itself readily to the purposes of these romances, for its formalized and regulated combat easily breaks down into a series of individual jousts. One gets the impression that jousting was constantly in progress in all corners of Europe and that princesses hardly ever chose a husband any other way than by holding a tournament. Then there is the custom of using champions to fight the battle, a practice whereby the issues of conflict are presumably settled just as irrevocably as with an army and lives are saved into the bargain. The superheroes are always volunteering to champion causes in single combat, usually against giants.

Despite the variety that the romance authors introduce into their combats, it is hard today to understand the medieval audience's taste for this sort of thing. There is violence enough in them, but of a conventionalized and not very elaborate nature. Physical combat in words is not as exciting as actual tournaments, and the authors, apparently understanding this difficulty, sought to spice up their accounts with revenge motifs and melodrama. Most of the battle descriptions themselves seem rather tired. They do not have anything like the realism, bloody detail, or imagination of the combats in the older epics such as the *Chanson de Roland*. What they do have is a ritual of threat and conquest. In Bevis's encounter with the Saracen standard-bearer Rudefoun (Anglo-Norman version, ll. 567–86), to take a typical example, the whole first half of the description is devoted to detailing the ways in which Rudefoun symbolizes threatening power: he is the representative of a king and leads 100,000 men; he is villainous and a pagan; he is ugly like a boar (aside from dragons, boars are the most threatening beasts in romance literature); his lance with silver fastenings indicates that he is backed up by wealth. Defeating this enemy, however, is easy: it is done in a single stroke. The fact that Bevis defeats him is what is important, not the way in which it is done. The short scene concludes with symbolic confirmation of the victory. The opponent who threatens with a lance is killed with a lance, and Bevis then hurls at him two insulting terms ("son of a whore, scum") that have earlier in the romance been used of Bevis himself.

Although such gloating over victory is not particularly characteristic of combat in the superman romances, some kind of confirmation is always present, sometimes in the enumeration of the enemy dead after a battle, sometimes in the rewarding of the hero for his valor. Likewise the threat to the hero can be posed in many forms. A common sequence has the enemy warrior overcoming a companion of the hero or endangering, perhaps wounding, the hero himself. Endless minor variations can be worked on the same themes.

As the story progresses, the hero's battles become more difficult and the descriptions of them become longer, but their essential nature does not change. All the battles do the same things and follow the same pattern. This is true even of fights with giants and beasts, fights which are constructed by expansion and slight modification of the usual pattern. Bevis and Guy both fight beasts.

In the original Anglo-Norman version Bevis defeats two lions and a boar (in the English version he first delivers a challenge to it!), and Guy subdues two dragons. The English translator of *Boeve de Haumtone* added a dragon fight to his romance, apparently in imitation of Guy's, to which he compares it, because he thought it was the ultimate achievement possible for such heroes as these.

Guy's great dragon fight was one of the things that made his story memorable for medieval audiences, and the author gives it a prominent place in the action (it is Guy's last battle before his marriage to Felice) even though it is neither the longest nor the most important of his combats. As in all the other battles with beasts and humans alike, the first thing that the romance tells us about the dragon is its menacing nature. It has been ravaging Northumberland, killing men, women, and horses. It is black, ugly, and huge (after it is dead, measurement proves it to be thirty feet long), with a bull's neck, lion's claws, impenetrable scales, and wings. Guy refuses all help and fights the dragon alone with spear and sword. The first assault has no effect on the beast, and Guy prays for aid. The second assault results in the loss of part of Guy's corselet, and three of his ribs are broken. In the third assault he kills the dragon by carving it open upward from the navel. It is the wounding, the direct bodily threat to Guy, and not the prayer that leads to the defeat of the dragon. The only differences between this and battles with human opponents are some details of the beast-enemy's appearance and the weapons with which it fights (claws and tail instead of lance and sword).

The kind of repetition found in these battles and elsewhere in the romances is more than a casual feature of this and other forms of popular literature. The plots of medieval romances, as of modern romances, murder mysteries, westerns, and similar genres, are constructed by formula and comprise variations on a few basic themes. The reason is that when stories attract their readers by offering fantasy solutions to recurrent social and psychological problems, they make a commitment to the audience to confront the same problem repeatedly and to offer the same satisfying symbolic solution. In a sense the early episodes in any sequential popular work are an advertisement for what follows. The audience, pleased by the beginning, expects more of the same and will take its business elsewhere when its demand is no longer met.

The Hero: Disguises and False Identities

Shortly before his death, Guy of Warwick, who has been traveling about the continent dressed as a poor pilgrim, returns to England, which is then being threatened by a Danish invasion. The Danes have proposed a single combat between their giant Colebrant and anyone who will volunteer to fight for the English, but no one comes forward. Athelstan, the English king, wishes that Guy were there. That night an angel appears to the king in a dream and tells him to go to the north gate of the city, where he will find a champion. In the morning he goes where the angel has directed him and finds Guy outside the gate, still disguised as a pilgrim. When the king seeks his help, Guy declares himself too poor and weak to undertake such a battle, but all the English bishops and counts prevail upon him strongly, and he finally accepts the challenge. Dressed in armor and mounted on a horse, he now appears as a magnificent and powerful knight. He kills Colebrant and drives the Danes from the land, but when offered a reward he refuses, saying that all thanks are due to Christ. Pressed to reveal his name, he finally agrees to tell it to King Athelstan if he will accompany him alone outside the city. When the king does so and learns that his benefactor is Guy, he offers him half the kingdom, but the hero asks only honor and protection for his son. Then he leaves.

This is one of the great fantasy rituals of popular fiction, a self-aggrandizing, even narcissistic fantasy. The hero is desired by name and needed in fact. No one else will do and he knows it, but he is reticent, and this makes him the more hotly pursued. He appears humble and timid, but we relish his power. After the great fight, those who will be forever indebted to him desire something more than his services; they want his name—which means they want the man himself. But secrecy still protects the fantasy. Only we (and the king) know; the world does not. The dual role of poor pilgrim and glamorous knight and the use of a disguise contribute greatly to this orgiastic dream of self-importance. As we have seen in the cases of Horn and Havelok, disguises and dual identities can serve several functions in romance, enabling the hero to undergo symbolic social transformations and aiding in audience identification with him. But another and ultimately more important use seems to have been the discovery of the superman romances: cos-

tume-changing, role-playing, and discreet revelations of one's se-
cret self are exciting fantasy materials in themselves.

In the Horn-Havelok romances the reader can identify person-
ally with the hero and also politically with the kingdom he estab-
lishes. In the superman romances the case is different. There are no
good or bad kingdoms, and while political and social attitudes are
sometimes apparent in these stories, there are no politico-social
messages. The emphasis is on the hero, and the reader is asked to
identify completely with him. We therefore see him less objectively
than we see Horn and Havelok. The hero is not described and has
virtually no characteristics of any kind, including unusual strength
or good looks. He is what he does. Instead of telling us that Guy is
strong, the author tells us that he killed a dragon which no one else
could kill; instead of saying that Guy was handsome, the author
says that many women desired him.

These heroes are not social climbers. Rank is an issue in these
romances, but the context is completely different from that in the
exile romances. Instead of undergoing a symbolic progress through
the social ranks from servant to king, the superheroes have two
different kinds of concurrent identities, one low and humble, one
high and flamboyant. They are not even trying to become kings.
Ipomedon is already prince of Apulia (a kingdom of little conse-
quence to readers in England) and all he needs to do to reclaim his
right is to reappear in the kingdom in his own person. Bevis be-
comes king of the fictional land of Monbrant—while his sons are
kings of Egypt and England respectively—but soon after becoming
king he dies and his title passes to his eldest son. Guy never rules
any kingdom at all although several are offered to him. The aim of
these heroes is personal prestige ("pris"); they are trying to be
"better" than anyone else. Ipomedon and Guy both set out to
become "the best knight in the world" so that they can win the
hands of their ladies. Bevis, as Josian tells her father late in the
romance, becomes the best man in Christendom: "*N'i ad meilur home
en cristientez.*"

The dual identities comprise a fantasy of appearance and real-
ity. The humble man is what the world sees, the appearance; the
superman is what the hero (and the reader) knows himself to be.
Both manifestations are exaggerated to an extreme. Bevis, really the
son of an earl, tends sheep (*poverement vestu e poverement chaucé*) so
that his mother and stepfather cannot find and kill him, and soon

afterward he is sold into slavery. But after a fifteen-day stint as a shepherd he goes to court where he beats the emperor of Almain with a mace, and, once sold into slavery, he is accepted into the court of Egypt as the future heir. Guy, the son of a seneschal, is first seen serving the young girls in court. Felice rejects his offers of love because he is a "*valet.*" In Constantinople Guy refuses marriage with the eastern emperor's daughter because he is, as he says, the son of a "*povre vavasur.*" He travels about as a pilgrim in poor clothing, riding on a mule, and twice uses a pseudonym to cover his true identity.

The most elaborate and interesting use of disguises is in Hue de Rotelande's poem. Ipomedon refuses to reveal his name and heritage right up until the end of the romance, and he behaves in a peculiar, attention-getting fashion. At the court of Calabria, he asks to be taken into service and dispense wine to the court, still wearing his elegant mantle. Everyone laughs at him until he presents the mantle to the butler, a deed which all the court says was "*gentle,*" that is, noble. He is called "*l'estrange valet,*" a title which means both 'young foreigner' and 'strange servant.' (In like manner the heroine is known throughout the story only as "*la fiere pucele*"—'the haughty virgin.') Ipomedon continues to draw attention to himself by his obsession with hunting, combined with an apparently cowardly refusal to perform chivalric deeds.[4] Despite this, the lady falls in love with him.

Later, when the heroine has called a tournament in Sicily to choose a husband for herself, Ipomedon reappears in a second disguise. Arriving in the kingdom with a resplendent entourage and joining the court under a covenant that he will serve the queen in her chamber and kiss her once every day at her bedside, he is called the "*dru*" ("drewlereyne" in the English versions), that is, the queen's 'sweetheart.' Again he spends all his spare time hunting, making no preparations for the tournament, and is laughed at by the court. However, when the first day of the tournament arrives, he goes to a hermitage in the woods under the pretext of hunting, changes into armor, and returns to win the day. On the three days of the contest he appears first as a white, then as a red, then as a black knight, each time bearing down all his opponents and each time revealing his identity only to Jason, the lady's cousin.[5]

When the tournament is over, he disappears, only to show up again much later in Sicily as a fool in old and rusty armor who, seemingly in jest, takes up the challenge against an ugly knight attempting to force the lady into marriage. He fights this battle after a secret change into black armor.

Ipomedon's disguises—servant, sweetheart, fool—are in keeping with an image of him as a ridiculous seeker after status in the court, one who has high ambitions of associating himself with real power and position but who has neither the birth, courage, nor ability to accomplish what he aims at. In contrast is the gaudy image, achieved by secretive changes of costume, of the colorful and conquering knight who does not seek but is sought. Just as he has a variety of disguises, so also Ipomedon has two different "high" identities: one as Ipomedon, the true heir by birth, the other as the best knight in the world, the man who has earned his position by fighting for it.

LOVERS, FRIENDS, FAMILY

The role of the heroine in the superman romances has some interesting and distinctive characteristics. In *Ipomedon*, which by its own account is a story about love, the hero falls in love with the heroine before he has even seen her, in a manner that we have come to associate with "courtly love" and that is radically different from love in the Horn-Havelok romances. Marriage with her is Ipomedon's original goal, and all the major action of the poem is directed toward winning her. Hue de Rotelande was hardly the inventor of this pattern, but it was new in his day. It is clear that the lady symbolizes Ipomedon's achievement, and with the marriage to her he gains power and land over and above what he has inherited, but he does not have to win her. She falls in love with him, gradually but hopelessly, on seeing him as the strange valet, but he still has to prove himself before he can have her. In *Bevis of Hampton*, Josian falls in love with the hero first, just as the heroines do in the child exile romances, but the actual winning of her is difficult. During the course of the romance she is married to two other men, and questions are raised about whether she has kept her virginity (that is, whether she has kept herself for Bevis) although it turns out that she has, even during a marriage that lasted for seven years. Guy, like Ipomedon, is the one to fall in love, and he labors mightily to win the reluctant Felice. But once he has proved himself the best knight in the world and the marriage to her is accomplished, he leaves her for other adventures, this time in the name of God rather than the name of love. His departure from her is permanent: she does not see him again until minutes before his death.

Although the lady is the hero's initial goal in these romances, the final goal is proof of the hero's self. In *Ipomedon* and *Guy of Warwick*, the lady is the knight's excuse for becoming great, as if it had never occurred to him to seek power and self-aggrandizement until he had some other reason to do so. A desire for self-power of course is an unattractive quality, and in the medieval context it was a deadly sin. For this reason it was psychologically necessary to adduce some further reason—whether love, God, or social beneficence—for the hero's pursuit of fame, but even a casual glance at the romances shows that these further reasons are specious. No passion at all is attached to the heroines; we are told that they are beautiful, and that is all. *Guy of Warwick* is not really a religious story, despite the shift from service of Felice to service of God, and Guy's battles after his change of heart are no different from the battles before. *Ipomedon*, in which all the battles are supposedly fought for love, actually shows that love is a hindrance to the hero's progress, for in the roles of a lover, as strange valet, sweetheart, and fool, Ipomedon is laughed at, while in his warrior roles, well separated from his lady, he achieves the wished-for ideal. As if to explain the perverse effects of love on Ipomedon, his tutor at one point advises him that love often aids a man in becoming a famous knight—with the emphasis clearly on fame, not love.

In fact, all three of the romances display an ill-hidden resentment toward the heroines by deliberately and unnecessarily tormenting them in various ways. Nothing in the plot forces Ipomedon to conceal his identity from his lady when he is fighting in the tournament or later when he is opposing King Leonins, and his secrecy keeps her in mental anguish throughout the romance. When Guy leaves Felice she begs him not to go, and when he does go, after only fifteen days of marriage, she contemplates suicide. (The only reason she does not kill herself is that she is carrying his child, begotten on the first night of their marriage.) Again, when Guy is about to die, he sends for Felice only at the last minute so that she arrives just in time to see him expire. Bevis's lady, Josian, is clearly punished for her first two marriages even though they are made under duress and even though she keeps her virginity while married. After the first marriage, the hero comes to her dressed as a pilgrim and tells her that Bevis has married another woman; after the second she is condemned to death for killing her husband but is rescued at the last minute. (In the English versions she is tied naked to the stake.) The fact seems to be that the heroines are necessary to the hero in some ways—they provide an excuse for his search for fame, and they bear him sons who will perpetuate his name—but that in other respects they interfere with his real pursuits. As a result the romances have a decidedly mixed attitude toward heroines.

Of the three heroines, Josian is the most tormented, and it seems significant that this romance also displays some hatred toward the hero's mother. The mother has conspired with the emperor of Almain in the killing of Bevis's father and has tried to kill Bevis as well. Later when Bevis is called a *"fiz a putain"* he admits the charge although he resents the other names directed at him, and he himself calls his mother a whore. Eventually he wars against the emperor, who is killed (not by Bevis himself) in molten lead, and the mother falls from a tower and breaks her neck. Bevis, we are told, is not sorry for this. What makes this seem significant in terms of Josian is that her trials end after the death of the mother, thus suggesting that the resentment expressed toward her is really resentment against the mother, who gave birth to the hero on the one hand but killed the fantasy-father on the other. This motif has parallels in some of the love romances.

Josian is the most active and best developed of the heroines. Felice and La Fiere Pucele do little other than wait for their men to come and get them; they are love-objects almost exclusively. Josian participates in the adventures of the romance and even has some adventures of her own, including, as we have seen, one in which she kills a man (her second husband, whom she strangles with her girdle on their wedding night). It is unusual for a romance heroine to have adventures of her own, and it indicates that in addition to her role as lover-beloved, she fits into another important character class, that of companion-friend. There are many of these characters in all three romances, and much of the action involves them. Not infrequently the stories leave the heroes for a time and follow the adventures (military, like those of the hero) of the friends. These friends fight battles alongside the heroes, fight battles on their own, travel about disguised as paupers or pilgrims, and are rewarded with kingdoms at the end. They are sometimes responsible for killing major enemies of the hero, especially when, as in *Bevis of Hampton*, those enemies are relatives of the hero or otherwise closely associated with him. The heroes are continually saving the friends just as they are about to be killed, and there is almost always at least one scene in which hero and friend, both in disguise, battle each other before discovering, in the midst of the fight, their true identities.

The classic scenes involving friends are the reunions. A typical example occurs in *Guy of Warwick*: Guy and his companion Heralt, along with two other unimportant companions, are ambushed by henchmen of one of the major villains. The two expendable companions are killed, and Heralt avenges the deaths of both. Then Heralt is wounded and rescued by Guy, but Guy, thinking that his friend is dead, takes him to an abbey for burial and leaves him there. After some further adventures, Guy encounters a poor pilgrim traveling by the sea and asks who he is. The pilgrim says that he is a knight who has lost his lord. "Who is your lord?" asks Guy. "Guy of Warwick," replies the pilgrim, and Guy recognizes him as Heralt. They weep for joy, embrace, faint, and continue their travels together.

While often threatened, wounded, lost, or left for dead, the friends always reappear for the requisite tearful reunion. In fact, even when they are a generation older than the hero, they always live at least as long as he does so that these reunions can occur. Heralt even survives Guy to serve as fighting-companion to the hero's son Reinbrun, whose adventures occupy the last third of the romance. The idea seems to be that close friends, united with the hero by participation in his trials and conquests, are eternal. To a large extent this is also true of the enemies: the same ones keep coming back. The friends form an important link between the hero and the world, from which he is essentially isolated. Being the best knight in the world is a lonely occupation; the friends, who are always alive out there somewhere, moderate the isolation and provide the human contact that, as the action shows, is unsatisfactorily provided by the heroine and the hero's own family.

The friends, in fact, constitute a symbolic family. The hero's tutor, one of the more ubiquitous types of companion in these romances, is a substitute father. (The hero's real father is never a fighting-companion.) Heralt begins as Guy's tutor, Bevis has his tutor Sabot, and Ipomedon has Tholomeu—who, however, is just an advisor, not a fighting-companion. Then there are the contemporaries of the hero, symbolically and sometimes actually his brothers. In *Ipomedon* these include Jason, the lady's cousin, and Cabanus, who turns out to be Ipomedon's real brother. In *Bevis of Hampton* there is Terri, the son of Sabot, and Escopart, a Saracen villain-friend who is defeated by Bevis, then after being baptized becomes his servant and fighting-companion, and finally betrays him. The most unusual of the companions is Bevis's horse Arundel, whose adventures parallel those of the human friends just as the beast-battles parallel the battles with humans. (The English translator seems to have been somewhat embarrassed by Arundel's role, for after Bevis, Josian, and Arundel have all died at the same time, he asks us to pray for all of them, adding "if men are permitted to pray for a horse.") Guy's close friend is Terri of Worms, and Guy performs a variety of services for him, including the winning of Terri's lady and the restoration of his lands. The hero's children sometimes fill the roles of friend and companion too.

The main function of the hero's children, however, is to perpetuate him, to confer a sort of immortality on him—immortality being the ultimate desire of those whose fantasies revolve about fame and self-importance. The heroes themselves die, but they leave after them sons who carry on their achievements or rule the kingdoms they have won. (Romance heroes never have daughters.) Ipomedon's sons inherit the kingdoms of Apulia and Calabria, and the adventures of one son, Protheselaus, are continued in a later romance. When Bevis dies, the lands he has conquered remain in the hands of his sons and Sabot's sons. Guy's death is followed by a long narrative, made a separate poem by one of the English translators, in which his son Reinbrun, after a series of fairly ordinary adventures, gains the lands which are rightfully Guy's but which he never ruled in person. Some of these heroes also have monuments erected in their honor.

SERVICE TO MAN AND SOCIETY

Although the true purpose of the hero's battles is to eliminate symbolic threats and bring him fame and power, other more socially acceptable reasons are invariably given, particularly before the major battles. The real, underlying wishes of the hero are covered over in part by his constant humility (the chief Christian virtue), in part by providing him with causes. Some of these causes are, superficially, the main subjects of the romances, but on closer inspection they turn out to be inconsistent with the action or with other major themes of the romances.

The causes are always ones with which the audience cannot take issue. They include God, justice, and the underdog, but the most frequently adopted cause is love—which suggests that one reason for the new courtly love literature in the twelfth century is that love had become intellectually respectable. After all, it is not obvious that striving to win a wife or mistress should be considered a good cause, but new social pressures on the individual to marry plus the fact that "love" was also being used to describe the bond between man and God had made wooing a serious thing. Similar social and philosophic developments may also have led to the increasing sympathy for underdogs that we see in the romances. Ipomedon's main cause is love; Bevis's is Christianity; Guy's is love at the beginning, then after his change of heart, God. But there are many other causes as well. No fight is allowed to occur without a sufficient justification.

Explanations of these justifications are sometimes lengthy and complicated, and they tell us much about the basic attitudes of the romance writers. During Ipomedon's travels, for example, he discovers a war in progress between the kings of France and Lorraine. He decides to side with France, apparently because Lorraine has twice as many soldiers, but there are reasons for siding with Lorraine as well, and the choice is difficult. The fact that Ipomedon allies himself with an older brother and one who has succeeded to the kingdom in his own right is an indication of Hue de Rotelande's royalist sympathies. Elsewhere in the story Ipomedon always sides with women or with victims of aggression; this is not an inconsistent alignment for women are always presumed to be victims. The great tournament in which Ipomedon distinguishes himself is held by the heroine who must choose a husband because Calabria is threatened with invasion and the barons insist that they must have a male ruler in time of war. Christian sympathies also add to the sense of threat, for one of the more powerful barons has suggested that the lady marry the king of Spain, a heathen. (This is the only mention of pagans in the romance, but it seems to be of some importance because the king of Spain is the first opponent Ipomedon defeats in the tournament.) Later, Ipomedon must on three separate occasions rescue his lady's handmaiden Ismeine from relatives of the ugly knight.

Bevis, who usually fights against Saracens but not always for Christians, also acts as a defender of women and an enemy of impurity. All of his major opponents want the heroine Josian for themselves; his minor opponents include a giant who eats Christians, two lions who kill Josian's chamberlain and threaten Josian, and some nameless invaders of Seville, which is at that time ruled by a woman. Unlike Ipomedon, Bevis never has a difficult choice of sides, and this is not because his faith guides him: more often than not he fights on the side of Saracens—who of course become Christians in the end, but so too do the enemies, the ones who are left alive. Instead, his allegiances are made on the basis of self-interest (against assaults on Josian, his future wife), personal revenge (against the foresters who insult him), defense of the violated (against the invaders of Egypt and Seville), and antagonism to sexual desire (against his mother who betrayed his father when she "desired other company").

Guy of Warwick is characterized by elaborate explanation of the sides that the hero takes in his many adventures, as it is also characterized by long and complicated developments resulting from his participation in each of these conflicts. He begins as a champion of beauty, attempting to win the hand of "Felice la bele" and then participating in a tournament for the hand of the princess of Almain. Most of his early adventures involve women in some way, but his allegiances are determined by other factors. In part two of the romance, when he is supposedly fighting for God, the action is precisely of the same sort except that women are not so frequently involved. Religion is almost never a consideration in his choice of sides. Instead, he has a marked propensity for personal revenge, self-defense, and the lower as opposed to the higher nobility. The romance makes it clear that Guy fights in service to the good, but the good cause is often difficult to determine. When it can finally be ascertained, it turns out to be the side first harmed, the side with the woman on it, the Christian side, or the side represented by the man of lower rank. In this last respect, *Guy of Warwick* shows some favoritism for mildly disruptive social attitudes, as it does in making its hero the son of a simple seneschal and as *Bevis of Hampton* does, less obviously, in pitting its hero against the king of England.

Whether it is because the heroes' stated causes are different from their real aims or because of natural contradictions between the various sympathies of the romances, all three of these stories contain some poorly resolved psychological conflicts. In *Ipomedon* the conflict is between love and chivalry, and it is made the subject of several comments by the author and by characters in the romance. As has already been pointed out, Ipomedon has two identities, one as the admired and self-sufficient fighter, the other as lover-fool. The two seem irreconcilable, yet love is the reason for fighting: he has no other reason that the author cares to admit. Ipomedon would clearly flounder between the two roles if it were not for the helpful arrangement according to which he is always one person or the other, fighter or lover, never both. Though a crisis of identity never comes because of this literary schizophrenia, Ipomedon nevertheless frets in his lover role, disliking the image he projects in it except when he is hinting at his other and superior role, and he is constantly uncertain what to do. Various statements made in the romance highlight the dilemma. The lady thinks that love destroys chivalry, but Tholomeu tells the hero that love can help him become a famous knight. The author remarks that love makes people act without reason. The contradictions, like most really troublesome ones in romance literature, are resolved by being forgotten.

The underlying conflict is between the independent man, the one who needs no one and is needed by everyone, and the man dependent on others, particularly on women. Ipomedon's love relationships extend to many women other than his lady, including the queen whom he serves as *dru*, the handmaiden, Ismeine, whom he is condemned to defend against a series of assailants and whose embarrassing advances he must tactfully resist, and his mother who gives him a ring (a symbol of love) that will reveal his true identity. But whenever he acts dependent upon women, as the strange valet, the *dru*, and the knight in rusty armor, he is ridiculous. At the end, Tholomeu's theory is accepted, and Ipomedon, first fighting more fiercely after thinking about his lady and then revived from his wounds by his mother's ring, conquers his last enemy, the ugly and foreign knight who would force the lady to his will. But this knight symbolizes the hero himself as lover, as is shown by the fact that they wear identical armor and by the knight's claim, on being defeated, that Ipomedon has been killed. In fact, most of Ipomedon's enemies have been himself. In the tournament he has fought first on the inside, then on the outside. The given reason is that he has taken the weaker side on both occasions; the real reason is that he was fighting himself. And his major opponent on the third day, Duke Adrastus of Greece, comes dressed in red armor and is assumed to be the Red Knight (Ipomedon's disguise of the previous day). Is love a help or a hindrance to chivalry? Is chivalry a help or a hindrance to love? There is no clear answer. Ipomedon manages to achieve both in combination, dies symbolically by killing the ugly knight, and is replaced by the new, the married Ipomedon, about whom we know nothing except that he had sons and died.

In *Bevis of Hampton* the apparent conflict is between love and religion: Bevis, a fighter for the Faith, loves a woman who is pagan. But this conflict is so superficial that the author does not even bother to give it any attention. Christianity is just a polite excuse for battles actually fought in defense of self and personal prerogatives. Bevis is superior to the other characters because he is a Christian and virtuous, but he is superior to Christianity too. There is nothing humble or Christian about him except his professed faith. Christianity means only our side against your side.

The most fascinating character in this romance is the giant named Escopart. He is a servant of Yvori of Monbrant, Josian's husband, and therefore, as Escopart himself points out, a servant of Josian. He fights Bevis, loses, and agrees to become his man and be baptized, baptism being the main and sometimes only mark of Christians in the romance. Escopart's baptism is a truly funny scene and a bit surprising in the casualness with which it treats a Christian sacrament in the midst of the Middle Ages. First he is too big for the font, so a special one is built for him; then, when he is immersed, the water is too cold and he jumps out immediately, calling an end to the ceremony, for, he says, he is "too much of a Christian already." Escopart is an important alter ego of Bevis, a giant who was once a dwarf (as Bevis has risen from humble origins to become a conqueror), a Christian warrior who was once a pagan (Bevis grew up in Egypt), and a servant of Josian. The comic baptismal scene is a release of unadmitted frustration against the hero's need to be humble and Christian: Bevis is also too big for the font.

Like Ipomedon, Bevis's basic problem is his relationship with women, but here the question is not whether the relationship interferes with his desired independence but whether the relationship is allowable at all, on moral and personal grounds. Bevis is a fighter whose adventures begin when he is victimized and almost killed by his lecherous mother. He spends the rest of the romance engaged in the winning and defense of another woman, Josian, but he finds that there are many objections to her: she is a pagan, she calls him a villein, she has been twice married, and her virginity is questionable. Bevis overcomes each objection through proof of his own superiority, but doubts about the woman persist. Bevis does not initiate the relationship with Josian and in fact resists effectively for some time. Unlike Ipomedon and Guy, he never betrays any passion for his lady, right up until the end. When he finally agrees to extend his love to her and kisses her (nothing more than that, the author assures us), two of the villains carry the news to her father that Bevis has slept with her. As a result the father sends him on a mission that is supposed to end in Bevis's death but instead only results in seven years in a vermin-filled dungeon. The French author gives no reason for this imprisonment, and the English translator indicates that Bevis's mistake was in letting his imprisoner, previously defeated in battle, go free. The plot sequence, however, shows the reason is that Bevis has violated his warrior's purity by the kiss. The uneasiness between Bevis and Josian does not go away until after they are married and she becomes a childbearer rather than a lover. Even then the two are together very little.

Guy of Warwick's dilemma is between Felice and God, but, once he recognizes the conflict, it is easily solved in favor of God. He agonizes not over what he should do but over what he has done: he has killed and destroyed for love. There is a fairly sophisticated meaning here, and the author is aware of it. Guy, pursuing happiness ("Felice"), has victimized others and has shown no gratitude toward the true source of happiness, God. That is to say, there is a conflict between the end and the means, and the result is a feeling of sin and guilt. Guy solves his conflict and his guilt feelings by changing causes, or at least he appears to do so. Felice, like other heroines of romance, is not desired for herself or even for her beauty, although the beauty is essential. She is desirable because she means power, rank, prominence, and heirs. When Guy leaves Felice, he is already the best knight in the world, he has been offered kingdoms, and his wife has conceived a child—a son of course—on the first night of the marriage. By leaving Felice, Guy misses out only on sex and married life, neither of which supermen tend to pursue with vigor. At the end Felice is still around for the emotional death bed scene and to die immediately after her husband. Despite all this, Guy's feelings of guilt seem convincing.

The popularity of the superman romances attests to the late medieval interest in the individual, in the self, and it was probably this same interest that prompted the clergy's fulminations against self and pride over the next several hundred years. Already in *Guy of Warwick* we can see the moral reaction starting to grow. Some later romances show the reaction even more clearly, for popular romances are not all of the wish-fulfillment type, many, in fact, having pretensions to literary seriousness, just like much popular literature of our day. The earliest type of "serious" romance was the historical romance. Like the superman romance, this claimed to be historically true, dealt with superheroes, and was usually very long. Many plot motifs, attitudes, and conventions are common to the two types as well. The major differences are that historical romances had heroes who were recognized as real historical figures and their attention was directed primarily to political, rather than personal, themes.

4 *History and Politics*

omances claiming to be true accounts of historical per-
sons and events were in vogue from the time of Henry II
until the end of the fifteenth century, when they were prominent
among the works printed by Caxton. Throughout this period the
most popular historical and pseudohistorical narratives proliferated
in new versions and in copyings of the old ones. With the exception
of works like *Guy of Warwick* and *Bevis of Hampton*, no other type of
romance survives in so many manuscript versions as some of the
historical romances, probably because no other type took itself so
seriously and thus so readily justified the labors of scribes. For the
same reason, these are usually long romances, a fact which does not
always distinguish them clearly from other types during the early
days when all romances were long but which does set them apart in
the fourteenth and fifteenth centuries. As an example, we can con-
trast the 28,000 lines of Henry Lovelich's *Merlin* (early fourteenth
century) or the 14,000 lines of *The Gest Historiale of the Destruction of
Troy* (1350–1400) to the 2,000-line length which was common for
most of the later verse romances.

Although the historical romances are numerous, the stories told
in them are relatively few and center about five major heroes: Hec-
tor (Troy stories), Alexander, Arthur, Charlemagne (or Roland),
and Richard the Lioned-Hearted. Romances dealing with the first
four of these figures exist in both French and English, the French
poems being earlier, of course. Historical romances are basically
war romances. They contain elaborate and lengthy descriptions of
combat, and love plots have a minor place in them, if they occur at
all.

Medieval writers on historical subjects, the romance writers
included, made two standard claims for their work: that it was
accurate and that it taught useful lessons. The claim to accuracy
was, in fact, a claim to faithful recapitulation of sources that seemed
reliable. Writers like William of Malmesbury and Robert of

Gloucester took this claim seriously, sometimes to the point of slavishness, but the romance writers knew the difference between their work and true history, and their romances show that they knew it. Serious historians in medieval England wrote in Latin prose, used a group of sources that derive ultimately from Bede and the *Anglo-Saxon Chronicle*, and represented these sources in a truly accurate way; romance writers wrote in the vernacular and in verse, used sources that go back to the pseudohistory of Geoffrey of Monmouth, and followed their sources only when they felt like it. But they still made the claim to faithfulness, backing it up with fictional references.

History was considered useful, in addition to being entertaining, because it offered examples of good and evil behavior to be followed or shunned by the reader. History, it was held, acts as a mirror, reflecting the actual events of the past but enlarging, diminishing, or modifying them to reveal (or hide) truth.[1] Accuracy was important, but insight was more important. Historians were among the major medieval exponents of the purely accurate, but they were interpreters too, and especially moral interpreters. This stress on interpretation played right into the hands of the romancers, who were not a bit concerned with accuracy but were interested in portraying model heroes for their readers to admire. The line between a model for right actions and a wish-fulfillment hero is faint, and the romance writers had no interest in drawing it more boldly.

William of Malmesbury indicated that, to his mind, one important use of history was to instill nationalistic fervor in the common man by showing him examples of brave national heroes from the past,[2] but the romance in England shows no particular tendency to focus on English heroes. In France, nationalism had shown up early in the *chansons de geste* dealing with Charlemagne, but Englishmen had more trouble finding a national champion, real or fictional. Arthur was a Briton who fought against the ancestors of the English themselves, the Anglo-Saxon kings were largely forgotten, and the English kings since William the Conqueror were French by ancestry and language, if not by sympathy. Right down through the fifteenth century, the sense of national identity and pride fails to show up clearly or in a sustained fashion in English romances. Instead, the emphasis is on internationalism. The only real English king among the heroes of historical romance, Richard I, was a champion of Christendom, not of England, and his exploits occurred far away, in the Holy Land. The other important heroes were Trojan, Greek, or French. Perhaps it was this very internationalism that enabled Englishmen to forget on which side King Arthur fought and eventually to adopt him as their own national hero, a process that occurred near the end of the Middle Ages. That Arthur had no particular standing as an English hero earlier than this is indicated by the fact that English romances about him were almost nonexistent until the end of the fourteenth century, and throughout the Middle Ages he remained a more popular figure in French romance than in English.

The earliest Arthurian romance composed in England dates from the end of the thirteenth century, almost 100 years after the first Arthurian romances in French. This, the earlier version of *Arthour and Merlin*, relies on early French chronicle versions with additions from the Vulgate romances and narrates, in some 10,000 lines, the story of Arthur's ancestry and birth, rise and fall. The romance ends with Arthur's forces victorious and the pagans in flight. The story stresses magic and the supernatural very heavily, Merlin being almost the most prominent figure, and contains long descriptions of Arthur's battles. A later version of *Arthour and Merlin*, composed in the fifteenth century, contains only the part of the story having to do with Merlin and Uther Pendragon and does not get to Arthur at all. The *Merlin* story from the French Vulgate Cycle was also translated into English verse in the early fourteenth century by Henry Lovelich of London, and about the same time a translation of Chrétien's *Yvain*, named *Ywain and Gawain*, was made. From the late fourteenth century there is a fine Arthurian piece, the Alliterative *Morte Arthure*, which is based on Wace and concentrates on Arthur's tragic fall. The other Arthurian romances in English verse are not historical romances and will be dealt with in chapter eight.

Benoit de Sainte-Maure, a Norman poet whose patron was Henry II, wrote the earliest romance version of the Troy story about the year 1184. Benoit based his 30,000-line poem, the *Roman de Troie*, on two independent Latin prose accounts of the Trojan war (by Dares Phrygius and Dictys Cretensis), both of which were well-known in the Middle Ages and were considered to be reliable firsthand narratives. Though claiming to have translated faithfully from his Latin sources, Benoit actually rewrote the story considerably, adding, among other things, the earliest known version of the Troilus and Criseyde (here called Briseida) story. This poem enjoyed great popularity in France, but in England the Troy story became even better known through a Latin prose translation and abridgement of Benoit, the *Historia Destructionis Troiae*, written a century later in 1287 by the Sicilian Guido delle Colonne, who claimed that it was a true historical account based on independent sources.

There are three English verse romances on the Troy story. The earliest of them, *The Seege of Troy*, got its story from Benoit, Dares, and another work, the *Excidium Troiae;* the later two both copied directly from Guido. The *Seege* also differs from the others in being a short romance, only about 2,000 lines, in which space it runs whirlwind-fashion through all the major events from the search for the golden fleece to the final destruction of Troy. Written in the early fourteenth century, this poem survives in four manuscripts of a century or so later, each of which varies so much from the others that the poem has long been considered a minstrel romance. Sometime during the later fourteenth century, a writer from the northwest Midlands composed the best of the English Troy romances, a 14,000-line translation of Guido known as *The Gest Historiale of the Destruction of Troy*. This is one of the alliterative revival poems. From the end of the fourteenth century we have another long (19,000 lines) Troy romance in verse, the so-called *Laud Troy Book*, based more loosely on Guido and perhaps on Benoit as well.

The stories of Arthur and of Troy were international ones: their heroes and events were associated with European civilization, not with any particular nation, and versions of the stories, including both "histories" and romances, appeared in many lands and many languages during the late Middle Ages. This is also true of the story of Alexander the Great, which had enjoyed currency in Western Europe since the ninth and tenth centuries when two Latin translations of the biography by Pseudo-Callisthenes became available and accounts of various marvels associated with Alexander began to work their way into vernacular literatures. Several romance versions in French appeared in the twelfth century, among them the Anglo-Norman *Roman de Toute Chevalerie* by Thomas of Kent. Subsequent retellings such as the *Fuerre de Gadres* and the *Voeux du Paon* added new fictional episodes to the legend. In the fourteenth and fifteenth centuries several English and Scottish authors used these three works as the basis for various verse and prose romances, some of which survive only in fragments. The best known of these is *Kyng Alisaunder* (also called *The Lyfe of Alisaunder*), an early four-teenth-century poem of 8,000 lines, which tells the whole story of Alexander from his conception to his death, following Thomas of Kent. A somewhat longer (11,000 lines) romance, *The Scottish Alexander Buik*, which translates the *Fuerre de Gadres* and *Voeux du Paon*, was composed just before the middle of the fifteenth century.

In contrast to the Arthur, Troy, and Alexander stories, the large body of literature dealing with Charlemagne was specifically French in sympathies and popularity. These stories, which recount mainly the Christian-Saracen wars in defense of France, exist in numerous French epics and romances, mostly of the twelfth cen-tury, and did not spread much into other European vernacular literatures. The exception, however, is English literature. In the fourteenth century (primarily the later fourteenth century) a sizable number of shorter English romances dealing with the national French heroes but stripped of their nationalistic spirit appeared in versions which do not seem to have circulated much because none of them now exists in more than a single manuscript. Although there is no way to be sure, one might guess that the Charlemagne stories enjoyed what popularity they had in England because some segments of the upper classes, and even perhaps the well-to-do middle classes, wanted to identify themselves with French tradition and culture, just as they continued to do in much later times. If this was the case, we might conclude that English versions of the tradi-tional French romances started to appear in the late fourteenth century because at that time some families with French roots were no longer at ease with the French language.

Three romances of adventure from the Charlemagne cycle seem to have been well known in England in their French versions. These are the *Chanson de Roland, Fierabras*, and *Otinel*. All are stories dealing with the defense of France against Saracen invaders; in the latter two, the heroes are both young Saracen knights who partici-pate in the invasion of the West but later accept baptism and be-come Christian champions, fighting against their own people. All three of these romances exist in manuscripts that we know were either written or circulated in England. The *Fierabras* is the ro-mance that Robert Bruce read aloud to his troops during the cross-ing of Loch Lomond. All three romances continued to be copied and read throughout the Middle Ages.

English versions first appear in the Auchinleck Manuscript (1330–1340), where the Otinel story is told in two separate poems: *Roland and Vernagu*, translated from the *Estoire de Charlemagne*, itself a French translation of a popular Latin prose work, the *Chronicle of the Pseudo-Turpin;* and *Otuel a Knight*, drawn from the *Otinel*. Another English Otinel poem, *Otuel and Roland*, appears in the Fillingham Manuscript, written during the last quarter of the fourteenth century. *Otuel and Roland*, which is really the last part of the Auchinleck Manuscript's *Roland and Vernagu*, uses both the *Estoire* and *Otinel* as its sources. Also in the Fillingham Manuscript and another manuscript of the late fourteenth century are two versions of *Fierabras*, known respectively as the *Fillingham Firumbras* and the *Ashmole Sir Firumbras*. New English versions of all three stories were written about 1400: *Duke Roland and Sir Otuel of Spain* (from the *Otinel*); *The Song of Roland*, which uses the *Chanson de Roland* with some additions from *Pseudo-Turpin;* and *The Sowdon of Babylon*, translated from a shortened Anglo-Norman retelling of the *Fierabras* and from the later *Destruction de Rome*, which is a preface to the *Fierabras*. In addition, one other English poem of about 1400, *The Sege of Melayne*, for which no source is known, tells a story of the warfare between Charlemagne and the Saracens. Most of these poems come down in fragments, some of them badly mutilated, and, with the exception of the *Sowdon of Babylon*, none of them is over 2,000 lines long.

Two important historical romances seem to be original in their English versions. One of these is *Richard Coer de Lyon*, an early (about 1300) and long (over 7,000 lines) romance which tells of King Richard I's exploits on the Third Crusade, prefaced by many fanciful and sometimes astounding fictions about his birth and early life. The popularity of this work is attested to by the existence of seven different manuscripts and a printed edition (by Wynkyn de Worde) from the fourteenth, fifteenth, and sixteenth centuries. The relationships among the manuscripts are complex, suggesting that the history of the text has been equally so.

The other originally English historical romance tells the fictional story of Titus and Vespasian, a Roman son and father in the time of Nero, who are both suffering from disease and, in separate incidents, are cured through miracles of Christ. In gratitude, they receive baptism and lead an expedition to conquer Jerusalem, held by the Moslems. There are actually two poems on this subject, one in alliterative verse and the other in couplets, both composed near the end of the fourteenth century. The alliterative version, usually called *The Siege of Jerusalem*, is short (1,300 lines), the couplet version, *Titus and Vespasian*, much longer (5,200 lines).

In many respects, these long pseudohistorical works are the least satisfying of all the medieval romances. It is true that, as a group, they are more sophisticated and contain more variety than many romances, but they often lack cohesion, focus, and—above all—imagination. The longer ones in particular seem deliberately drawn out. In them, it is not enough that some armies, some battles, and some councils be described: every army must be enumerated, every single combat on every battlefield must be pursued to its conclusion, every speech in every council must be quoted in full. The writers seem to have no sense of proportion and no powers of selection. All these things may be characteristic of better-educated writers—and many features of these romances indicate that the authors were well educated. They tend to pick subjects that are "worthwhile," and the importance of the subject dictates prolixity; they write with their minds and not with their instincts. At the same time, being worried about keeping their audience's attention for their important subjects, they may work hard to spice up their stories. There are abundant signs that these writers tried to do this, and at times they succeeded. There are moments of excitement and genuinely moving scenes in all or most of these romances, and there is interesting detail as well, but for the most part they are unimaginatively conventional despite their greater seriousness and sophistication.

WARRIORS OF GOD

Although the historical romances may seem to comprise an ill-sorted collection, it probably seemed a natural group to the medieval audience, for, with only a couple of exceptions, the heroes of these romances belonged to the ranks of what were known in England as the Nine Worthies. These were the foremost kings of history (foremost from a medieval, Christian point of view), all noble, all good, and all in some sense "warriors of God" (Ernst Curtius's phrase). The Worthies were, according to an episode in the *Morte Arthure*, Alexander, Hector, Julius Caesar, Judas of the Macabees, Joshua, David, Arthur, Charlemagne, and Godfrey of

Bouillon. This list agrees substantially with those found throughout European literature, and it agrees exactly with one other medieval list from England. Three of the kings are pagans, three Jews, and three Christians. What they have in common apart from the fact that they were famous throughout the Western world is that they were all viewed as having been, in their own time, the champions of order and civilization against the forces of chaos and evil. They are God's warriors in the sense that they defend the closest thing in their day to God's worldly kingdom. Thus, Alexander and Caesar become heroes to Christians just as Isaiah and Virgil became Christian prophets by seeing through their glass somewhat less darkly than did their contemporaries. The Worthies are, in the military-political arena, what the prophets and poets are to religious revelation and learning.

Four of the nine kings are central figures in English historical romances, and another, Godfrey of Bouillon, is the subject of French historical romances and some English prose romances. In other words, almost all of the Worthies became the subjects of romance except for the Jewish heroes, and it is easy enough to understand why these lacked popular appeal: Jews were suspect or despised throughout this period (as is abundantly illustrated in *The Siege of Jerusalem*) and, perhaps even more important, medieval Europe looked mainly to Greece and Rome for its cultural heritage. The two historical romance stories that do not involve the Nine Worthies—the story of Richard I and the story of Titus and Vespasian—are very similar to the ones that do. They are crusading stories; the heroes champion order as opposed to deceit and lawlessness and are men of historical note (Titus and Vespasian are identified with the Roman emperors of those names). The Titus-Vespasian story, in particular, is quite similar to that of Alexander and has no elements which cannot be paralleled from the other historical romances. Richard I, of course, is the obvious English substitute for Godfrey of Bouillon, the hero of the First Crusade.

Crusading is really the main activity of these romances, although it appears in various guises. The siege of Jerusalem, Alexander's expedition to the East, and the attacks on Aigremore and Atalie in the Fierabras and Otinel stories are all described in ways that parallel the account of Richard's crusade. The same is true of Arthur's expeditions into Saxony, Lorraine, and Italy *(Morte Ar-*

thure) since his major opponent, the Roman Emperor Lucius, though presumably a Christian himself, is allied with various Saracen powers. Alexander is pictured as a Western leader (lord of Greece, Achaia, Egypt, Libya, Sicily, Lombardy, Champagne, and Rome) who calls together his knights from all these lands to bear "weapons of defense" and go with him against the pagan Darius. The *Chanson de Roland* also fits into this tradition of little crusades, and there is in fact a theory that it was originally composed as propaganda for the crusading policies laid down at the Council of Clermont (1095).[3] The rest of the historical romances—the Troy stories, *Arthour and Merlin*, and much of the Charlemagne material—narrate defensive actions rather than armed expeditions, but the issue in them is still the defense of ordered, God-inspired civilizations against the threats of the surrounding world. All the historical romances show that the world which surrounds the island of Western civilization is pagan, lawless, monstrous, and dangerous and that this alien world, left to its own devices, can be expected to make constant invasions into the bastions of civilization. The counterinvasion, the crusade, then becomes a way of expanding and strengthening civilization and striking at the source of the threats to it.

MARVELS AND MAGIC

The outside world is the wilderness, where dangerous and unheard-of beasts may dwell and where the laws of God, nature, and man do not seem to apply. The Troy stories generally begin with the adventures of Jason seeking the golden fleece ("Out in the Orient orible to here . . .": *Gest Historiale*, l. 151), an episode filled with strange creatures, strange customs, strange tasks set for the hero, and an enchantress (Medea) for good measure. Heroes, on leaving their homelands, typically encounter unexpected and irrational behavior on the part of aliens. As King Richard returns from a reconnaissance mission to the Holy Land, for example, he is captured and made to undergo a strange combat (an exchange of blows somewhat like that in *Sir Gawain and the Green Knight*); then, when he kills his opponent, he is thrown in prison without food—unheard-of treatment for a king. A similar violation of the respect due to established rank occurs at the beginning of *Otinel* when the then-pagan hero of the romance appears in the French court and verbally abuses Charlemagne, to the astonishment and amusement of Roland and the other knights.

The unpredictable and dangerous nature of this alien world is best illustrated in passages like those in *Kyng Alisaunder* that describe the wonders of the East, a favorite theme of much medieval literature. As Alexander passes through India, he encounters 300-foot-long fish in the Ganges, a race of pygmy soothsayers who hunt griffins and dragons, a mountain so high that the sunlight never touches its northern slopes, amazons, cannibals, men with scales and the heads of dogs, and a black race with only one eye and one foot. Alexander's men are parched and are attacked by hippopotamuses (grisly beasts, larger than elephants). Other heroes meet with similar, if less spectacular, wonders. In the *Morte Arthure*, the Emperor Lucius's army includes giants, witches, and warlocks, and his camp contains "mervayllous bestez," including white mules, elephants, "elfaydes," and "arrabys." At the outset of his travels, no further away than Normandy, Arthur finds a giant who eats children and cares nothing for laws (ll. 994–97).

Medieval readers were fascinated by the possibility that such creatures existed, as witnessed by the popularity of Mandeville's *Travels*, the bestiaries, and the "Letter of Alexander to Aristotle." Whether readers actually believed in the existence of these monsters or not, the "wonders" have a coherent underlying philosophy, according to which nature as we know it results from the enforcement of the principles of order, reason, and the mean. It is reasonable and moderate to be six feet tall and have two eyes; anything more or less, though possible, is an excess and in that sense a violation of natural law. Every monster, every strange attribute, every horrible custom of medieval "wonders" literature can be explained as an extreme, a violation of the mean, or an irrational combination of things. To the medieval audience, gigantic size, cannibalism, and lawlessness all go together as deviations from the moderate, and they are frightening both in themselves and because they suggest the possibility of such deviation. To deal with them, one needs a hero who, in some senses at least, is himself a deviation from the mean.

The hero is superior to ordinary men in strength and courage, but the heroes of historical romances are never supermen like Guy of Warwick. They are more complex, more human, capable of error. Hector can espouse a view of revenge with which the author clearly disagrees (*Gest Historiale*, ll. 2212–14), and Arthur can rashly accuse one of his knights of cowardice and then have to retract his words (*Morte Arthure*, ll. 1920–45). These heroes may be individualistic, extreme, or even peculiar in their behavior, the best example of this being Richard Coer de Lyon. Richard has no sooner been crowned king than he disguises himself to participate in a tournament. This is romantic behavior for a young knight like Ipomedon but astonishing behavior for a king. In addition, Richard is rash and somewhat deceitful. Despite all sorts of attendant dangers and political complications, he readily goes to bed with a young princess who has assisted him, when only a short time before he has killed this same princess's brother with a fist blow, after covering his fist with candle wax to make of it a lethal weapon. Then there are Richard's eating habits: at one point he kills a lion, tears out its heart, and eats it raw (though with salt)—hence the name "coeur de lion." Another time, while he is in the Holy Land, he inadvertently eats Saracen flesh and likes it so well that he continues the practice.

Richard's effective leadership on the crusade as well as his rash and brutal habits seem to have something to do with his unusual birth. According to the romance, his mother was Cassodorien, princess of Antioch. She married King Henry of England after he had sent messengers into all lands to find the fairest woman alive. The messengers encountered her and her father at sea, there because a vision had instructed them to go to England. The marriage has obviously been arranged by supernatural power—by God one would have supposed, since Richard is to become the champion of Christendom—yet there is the peculiarity that Cassodorien cannot stand to be present while the sacrament is administered: she swoons and runs from the church, and when her weakness is discovered she flees the country in haste. Supernatural birth or devil-birth is an old theme in folk legends, and such stories have sometimes been told of other historical persons, for example, Godfrey of Bouillon. The appearance of the devil-birth theme in *Richard* is certainly an appeal to the popular imagination at the expense of Christian propaganda. The birth legend indicates that Richard comes from a combination of nobility with beauty and of God's power with the devil's, this strange and unholy mixture being necessary to a leader of his sort. This is a way the romance writer shows how the hero is superior to the average man and yet consoles the audience for its lack of such magical power. Richard becomes God's champion but he has much of the devil in him too, as we are reminded by his violent acts and cannibalism. (In his brother John, the romance implies, the balance shifts the other way, toward the devil.) He has been foreordained for his position and is just as much a victim of his destined place in the scheme of things as those in humbler positions are. He did not choose to be king or the protector of Christendom. He becomes a sacrifice to the general welfare.

The magical birth of the hero, which confers on him the powers of the whole supernatural realm, the evil as well as the good, is the romance's answer to the supernatural marvels of the imagined alien world surrounding and threatening the relatively safe island of civilization. Since the issues involved in the conflict between civilization and the alien wilderness are only partly religious, the powers of the hero can only be partly explained by reference to religious doctrine and models. The hero whose power came directly and only from God would be a saint, and something rather different from a saint is required to combat the worldly or diabolical forces of lawlessness supported by physical or military might.

Besides Richard Coer de Lyon, two other heroes of English historical romance are notable for their unusual and magic-influenced births. They are Alexander, in *Kyng Alisaunder*, and Arthur, in *Arthour and Merlin*.[4] Both Alexander and Arthur are bastards. Officially, Alexander is the son of Philip of Macedon and his wife Olympias, but in actuality (the romance informs us) Neptanabus, an accomplished astrologer and magician, is the father. Neptanabus gains access to Olympias's bed by means of a ruse and appears to her disguised as Jupiter Ammon, "the fals god." Neither Philip nor Olympias is aware of Alexander's true heritage, but rumor and oracle continue to hint at the truth until one day the young Alexander pushes Neptanabus into a pit, and the dying magician admits that he is indeed the real father. Neptanabus has chosen Alexander's moment of birth carefully, so that he will be strong, brave, a good warrior, and "master of londes." The hero's birth is accompanied by storms, earthquakes, eclipses, and the sea turning green—all of which Philip interprets to mean that Olympias has brought forth an evil offspring.

Illegitimacy, traditionally associated with suspicious and possibly unnatural origins, characterizes the birth of Arthur in most or all tellings of his story. In *Arthour and Merlin* the account of his birth is preceded by a long history of Merlin and his magical birth, which results from a union between the devil and a young virgin. After consummation of the act, the girl is blessed by a hermit, and when Merlin is born he defies the devil's intentions by being good—although he is black. He later arranges the begetting of Arthur by magically disguising the hero's father, Uther Pendragon. The magical powers of both Arthur and Alexander themselves become clear later in their lives when they perform deeds impossible for other men: Alexander rides the horse Bucifal, and Arthur pulls the sword Excalibur from a stone.

One other use of the supernatural occurs in these romances, but it is a conventional and easily understood one. This is the intervention of divine power to effect a necessary conversion or to indicate which side of a conflict is the right one. Otinel, for instance, is converted to Christianity when the Holy Spirit descends on him in the form of a dove, and the conversion of Titus and Vespasian is brought about through healing miracles performed by St. Veronica's handkerchief (vernacle), which then miraculously flies off to a place in the church where all can see it. In *Roland and Vernagu*, a heavenly light confirms that the relics in Constantinople are true ones, and grapes bear fruit in March to show that God is with Charlemagne. In *The Sege of Melayne*, a wooden rood miraculously remains unburned in a fire, thus demonstrating to the Saracens the truth of the Christian faith. Although these are not instances of magic in the same sense as the other examples, they are indications that the historical romance depicts, in essence, a worldly struggle conducted by other-worldly powers, a struggle between ultimate right and ultimate wrong, in which humans are both the victims and the potential beneficiaries.

LawKEEPERS AND LawBREAKERS

The central theme and motivating force in these romances is the law, conceived of not as a temporary, local, and practical matter but as a universally prescribed mode of behavior, necessary to the welfare of all mankind. Down to the present day, law remains an important subject of popular literature, having been the major theme of the western and still one of the major themes of the murder mystery. The Middle Ages did not mean quite the same thing that we mean by law, but popular opinion then held it in respect equivalent to our own, as the history of the period attests.[5] We think of the law as a set of rules agreed upon by a particular group of people and enforced specifically for the benefit of that group; to the medieval mind, there was only one set of laws, prescribed by God. The word itself could mean either a religious or secular code of behavior, but medieval man did not confuse worldly law with godly life. Law prescribed the way one was supposed to live in order to secure peace and certitude while on earth, but it had its ultimate authority in God. Thus, medieval audiences could not conceive of pagans having different laws or customs that satisfied their needs in the same way that Christian laws satisfied the needs of Christians. There was only law and absence of law. If other people behaved in different ways, then they were wrong and no satisfactory civilization could be maintained under those circumstances. As the *Chanson de Roland* bluntly put it, "Paien ont tort e chrestïen ont dreit" ("The pagans are wrong, and the Christians are right," l. 1015). Most romances were unconcerned about matters of religious doctrine, but the romance writers were Christian, believed in God-given law, and understood the importance of laws in making life livable for everyone. This is the reason that they were so interested in the Christian-pagan wars.

Just as the laws of nature failed to function in alien lands, so the laws of society could not be trusted there either. On foreign and especially on pagan soil, one could expect to find established rank ignored, visitors or messengers treated with disrespect, women and children slaughtered without a qualm. Such irregularities called for equally uncivilized countermeasures, and so the heroes of the historical romances engage in the same tactics used by the enemy, although of course the heroes do it only to protect themselves or because the enemy did it first.

In medieval romance as in medieval society, the essence of law was the vow, or promise. Lawful behavior was doing what you said you would do—or not doing what you said you would not do—and the foundation of civilization was considered to be the compacts, spoken or tacit, made between men. The medieval faith in such compacts was often touching in its simplicity, but since there was nothing else, as medieval man saw it, to rely on for social stability, the faith was necessary. Breaking one's vow, the failure to live up to one's word, whether to a king or to a commoner, was treason.

English law would later distinguish between high treason, betrayal of the state, and petty treason, betrayal of an individual, but in the romances all treason is the same: a rupturing of the essential social compact. Even what we would call simple lawbreaking, including the breaking of unwritten laws such as the obligations of hospitality, could be called treason because, as a member of society, one had in effect agreed to observe these laws. The most serious type of treason, of course, was betrayal of the vows of fealty between lord and vassal, but nearly equal to that in seriousness was the betrayal of the bonds between two vassals of a single lord.

Arthour and Merlin provides a good example of the central importance of the fealty and treason theme in the historical romances. In essence, this romance (in both its earlier and later versions) depicts a period of political and social anarchy and the subsequent reestablishment of order through the efforts of the supernaturally empowered Merlin and a hero-king. The beginning of the story shows how the treason of the steward Fortiger (Vortigern) as well as that of his lord King Constantine (who had taken vows as a monk and then abandoned them) leads to more and more treachery. The result is that England comes to be jointly ruled by a heathen foreigner and an upstart steward. Rebellion ravages the land, and thousands of marriages are contracted between Christians and pagans. Not only are the holy marriage bonds disrupted, but the laws of nature cease to function as expected, for when Fortiger tries to build a castle for himself on Salisbury Plain, the workmen return each morning to find the previous day's construction mysteriously thrown to the ground.

The Alliterative *Morte Arthure*, which has promised to tell a tale about heroes of old who were "lele in theire lawe," places great emphasis on issues of faithfulness and treason. At the outset of the story, Arthur's right to rule is challenged on the grounds that he has violated his oath of fealty to Emperor Lucius of Rome. The suspicions about Arthur are allayed only when he points out that his ancestors ruled Rome long before Lucius did and so, of right, the emperor ought to be paying homage to *him*. King Aungers then shows that the Romans are the true lawbreakers, for when they occupied Scotland they rode riot through the land, raping the women and confiscating property "wyth-owttyne resone or ryghte" (l. 295). Later we see that Lucius himself is no respecter of law, for during his invasion of France he burns cities, cuts down forests, "confoundez" the commons and clergy, and takes their goods—all violations of "fraunchez," the legal protection that subjects enjoy as part of their agreement with their feudal lord (ll. 1239–54). Arthur, by contrast, establishes law in the lands that he rules (ll. 3088–93).

The villains in these stories are all traitors or betrayers of the law, among them some of the best-known traitors in Western literature. Ganelon violates his bonds of brotherhood with Roland and hence betrays Charlemagne. Modred usurps Arthur's kingdom, in violation of his oath of fealty. The "traitors" Antenor and Aeneas promise to defend Troy but instead hand it over to the Greeks. Pilate *(Siege of Jerusalem)* is the "betrayer" of Christ. In *Richard Coer de Lyon*, treachery against Richard is widespread. The sultan of Babylon, for example, having arranged by oath to settle his differences with Richard in single combat, attempts to trick and defeat the hero with enchanted horses—a bit of deceit that no longer seems very terrible because of its unrealistic circumstances and the lack of faith that we place in such compacts. But the major villain in *Richard* lives closer to home and uses less exotic tricks. This is King Philip of France who, throughout the story, tries to arouse enmity against Richard or else abandons him in hours of need even though the two kings have sworn brotherhood to each other. And then there is Richard's evil brother, John, who at the end of the romance makes an ineffectual grab for Richard's throne.

By contrast, we can identify the heroes by the scrupulousness with which they obey rules even in the most compromised of circumstances—or sometimes by the fact that they are the victims rather than the perpetrators of treachery. This is particularly noticeable in the two Charlemagne romances that have converted Saracens as the heroes. Fierabras, even before his conversion, hates traitors and behaves in ways that reveal his innate nobility. Although he becomes a Christian under duress, after having been defeated and severely wounded by Oliver, he refuses to abandon his new faith once he has promised to accept it. (In this case, prior commitments to family, nation, and religion can be ignored because they were made to pagans.) Likewise, in the Alexander romances, the hero's essential goodness shows through in his conscientious adherence to social rules. Like the rest of these heroes, Alexander is a fighter, and a brutal one, when the circumstances justify it. He breaks the neck of Neptanabus simply because he has heard rumors (true ones, fortunately) that Neptanabus has deceitfully fathered him. On a later occasion, he lays waste a whole city because the inhabitants ("ful of iniquite," as the author assures us) refused to answer him when he asked to be allowed entrance. Nevertheless, when King Darius sends one of his Persian followers to kill Alexander, this devastator of cities not only releases but actually rewards the would-be assassin because he was only doing his duty to his own lord (ll. 3962–4055). That Alexander is a preserver of law and order is made plain by the events at the end of the romance, for after he dies (by treachery) the land falls into sorrow and strife:

> Thus it fareth in the myddelerde,
> Amonge the lewed and the lerde!
> Whan the heved is yfalle,
> Acumbred ben the membres alle (ll. 8016–19).

VIOLENCE

The historical romances are set apart from the rest by a number of clearly marked characteristics: by their concern for factual accuracy (at least in theory), by their length and variety, and by the self-conscious intellectualizing of the authors. They are the most serious and the most moralistic of the romances; they are also the most violent. Unlike the superman romances, where the incessant battles repeat themselves in generalized rituals of threat and response, here the battles are vivid, imaginative, and bloody. It is not surprising to find violence in the medieval romance; the surprising thing is that we find it concentrated in one type of romance. Apparently, the psychology of the historical romance is different from that of the others.

The length of the historical romances results mainly from the frequent speeches and fights. True, the plots are complex and there is much incidental material of all kinds, but if the talk and the fighting were gone the romances would waste away to a fraction of their former size and presumably lose much of the appeal that they had for medieval audiences. Speech making and fighting may sound like strange companions, but in fact they are very much alike. Both are specific responses to specific situations that involve a threat or problem of some kind. Both are formal, socially recognized modes of self-assertion. Romance speeches are not conversa-

tional, do not offer psychological insights into the characters
speaking them, and are never true dialogues. Typically they are
challenges, answers to challenges, arguments, debates, or councils
(mass debates). The purpose of the speeches is the same as for
battles: to demonstrate the superiority of one side, one person, or
one way of thinking. As in the fights, the opponents are in clearly
defined emotional states, and the conflict often becomes violent. In
reality, the speeches are verbal warfare, and the battles are physical
arguments.

The verbal and physical violence is a response in kind to the
unreasonableness, barbarity, or lawlessness of the opponent. Be-
cause the enemy invades our land or fails to observe the laws of
rank, because he slaughters maidens or treacherously refuses to
make his true identity known, because he eats children or refuses to
be baptized, we are justified in devastating his lands, burning his
cities, massacring the women and children, and committing all
kinds of barbarities of our own, including—as in *Richard Coer de
Lyon*—cannibalism. The writers of historical romances produced
many conventional descriptions of battle, but they also sought va-
riety at times. *Richard Coer de Lyon*, one of the more sadistic of the
romances, shows a fascination with war machinery and its use—
catapults, arbalests, mangonels. In the *Sowdon of Babylon* a character
is decapitated by a portcullis, and there is a description of Neymes
killing one of the Saracens with a burning brand. Even relatively
timid romances such as the *Gest Historiale*, which regularly omits
much of Guido's battle description, are filled with streams running
blood, corpses in the mud, and sword blows that cut combatants
apart from the head to the waist. When vengeful justice warrants,
as in the executions of Clytemnestra and Aegisthus for the murder
of Agamemnon (ll. 13018–34), the *Gest Historiale* keeps all the grue-
some details.

When religious wars are involved, the violence may increase
dramatically, as in the *Siege of Jerusalem*, which revels more than any
other romance in gory detail. Approximately one-third of this
poem consists of descriptions of fighting and includes such scenes
as a woman being hit by a stone from a catapult so that the baby she
was carrying is thrown up like a ball over the city walls; another
mother tearfully roasting and eating her child while Titus is trying
to starve Jerusalem into submission; and an enemy warrior hit so
hard on the head that his brains run out at his nostrils. Again, the
principle of retribution is at work: violence is justified because the

Jews have betrayed and tortured Christ and because they persist in their treacherous behavior. As Vespasian begins the siege of Jerusalem, he sends messengers into the city to announce his intentions. The Jews bind them, cut off their hair and beards, strip them naked to the waist, put blacking on their faces, and send them back to Vespasian with cheeses tied to their necks. In answer to this kind of treatment, the Romans later dig a ditch around the city and fill it with corpses from the first battle so that the stench will fill Jerusalem and pollute the water supply. When the Romans catch Caiphas and the scribes, they flay, draw, and hang them, spreading honey on their wounds and tying dogs, cats, and apes to Caiphas to torment him as he dies. This is revenge for the "treason" of betraying Christ. Violence in the name of Christianity did not embarrass the writers of these romances. When Richard Coer de Lyon prepares at one point to behead 60,000 Saracens for concealing the whereabouts of the cross, an angel appears before him saying, "Seynyours, tuez, tuese."

The emphasis on violence, the view that the surrounding environment is hostile, and the reliance on totalitarian leaders are all features of a recognizable pattern, that of the defensive society that must protect itself at all costs from real or perceived threats to its integrity.[6] The historical romances present and encourage political views that are conservative, even paranoiac, and authoritarian in orientation; the history and literature of the late Middle Ages demonstrate that such views were in fact common. Defensive views are also pessimistic views, and this explains why so many of the romances of this group end with the defeat or death of the hero. The implication in those cases is that this is the world as it is, not as we wish it to be. These stories were held to be true because they showed not the fantasy but the real world—a world in which you held on to what you had because it might any moment be taken away and in which your ultimate hopes were fixed upon that mysterious and somewhat frightening authority figure who would fight on your side and, for a while at least, bar the doors a little more firmly and chase the forces of disruption a little farther from the gate.

ROMANCES OF REBELLION

Another and smaller group of romances gives a different view of history and politics. Among the early romances both in France and

England there were a few in which a wronged hero rebels against established authority, sometimes successfully, sometimes not. These have been called "epics of revolt" or "outlaw romances," and the type is fairly well known today from the Robin Hood stories, which come down to us primarily in ballad form but which bear strong similarities to the medieval rebel literature of the romances. Although these stories show lands ruled by an authority that is corrupt, weak, or selfish, they express political attitudes identical in all major respects to those of the historical romances. By siding with rebels against an unlawfully constituted or maintained rule, they complement rather than contradict the stories that fantasize about strong and lawful protector-kings. They never challenge the existing system or social myths; instead, their heroes attack temporary evils or inequities in an attempt to make the society work as the myths tell us it should. The rebel romances, therefore, are not revolutionary (true revolutionaries are much rarer in popular literature than in real life); they are stories of acceptance and integration and in fact are generally more optimistic than the historical romances because they usually imply that social ills can be remedied.

The tradition of rebellion is very old in Northern European society, and its roots go very deep. It was exemplified by the Norsemen who refused to accept the authority of Harold Fairhair in the ninth century and by the rebellion of Simon de Montfort under England's King Henry III. The principle that the law is greater than individual rulers underlies the Magna Carta and all of late medieval political thought. In fact, independence is so important an element of the European tradition that it is surprising we do not find more rebel romances. Probably the demands of an increasingly organized society discouraged rebel romances, just as the Church establishment discouraged literature that was not at least nominally Christian.

The classic of medieval rebel literature is the Old French epic *Raoul de Cambrai*, a powerful story about the tragic effects of injustice and broken vows. The hero, Raoul, is an unjustly disinherited young knight, rash and immoderate by nature, who turns outlaw and tries to win lands for himself by warfare. The results are evil beyond expectation: friend is turned against friend; the innocent are killed while those responsible for the injustice remain unharmed; violent feuds spring up and continue into the second generation; and the story ends in a state of general and unresolved rebellion. Far from promoting or siding with rebellion, this might even be considered an antirevolutionary work. Its sympathies are aristocratic, its criticism of the outlaws plainspoken.[7] Raoul is a sympathetic character (after he dies, his heart is cut out and found to be exceptionally large), but he cannot control his passions and he consistently acts against reason and the best advice. The political message of *Raoul de Cambrai* is that kings should respect inherited rights and act with foresight and consistency but that, even if they do not, subjects are ill-advised to take up arms.

The rebel romances of England are not like *Raoul:* they express a more direct resentment toward authority, but they also have more obscure political messages, and they end happily. In spirit, they are similar to some of the English political songs that survive to us from the Middle Ages, poems like the "Song of the Husbandman," the "Song on the Execution of Sir Simon Fraser," the "Song of Lewes" (by a partisan of Simon de Montfort's rebellion), and "On the King's Breaking His Confirmation of Magna Carta." Such songs are found in several manuscripts and are usually either complaints about the state of things or emotional exultations over what is taken to be a victory for truth and justice. These songs are philosophically akin to the historical romances in their insistence on the rule of law and their vengefulness against those who violate it or who oppress the people. Although these poems generally take the side of the "common" people against the rich and powerful, it is quite clear from their many topical allusions and their frequent use of French and Latin that they were written by and for the well-to-do. The "Song of the Husbandman" is a complaint not of a farmer in our sense of the word but of the owner of a farm. The "Song of Lewes" sides with one group of the nobility against another. And many of the political songs sound like the products of clergymen—who were often, of course, the younger members of noble families. "Common people," in these poems, means the ordinary nobility.

England's three surviving rebel romances betray this same bias toward the out-of-favor, disinherited, or ill-used nobility. The earliest, *Fouke Fitzwarin,* is the story of a Welsh nobleman who carried on a personal rebellion against King John of England. The romance survives in an Anglo-Norman prose version of the early fourteenth century, but all those who have studied it agree that it is a version, sometimes almost word-for-word, of an earlier Anglo-Norman poem. It comes down to us in a single manuscript, written in French, Latin, and English, which was likely a collection put together for a noble family in England. The second rebel romance is *Gamelyn*, a Robin Hood type of story about a disinherited younger brother who becomes an outlaw. This was written about the middle of the fourteenth century and exists in twenty-five manuscripts of the *Canterbury Tales*, apparently because Chaucer intended to write his own version of the tale and his manuscript of it got intermingled with the other tales. The third of these romances, *Athelston*, has a plot about a king who mistakenly follows the advice of an evil baron and has to be corrected by one of his good advisers. Since the nominal hero is the king, this cannot be considered a true rebel romance, but in other respects it bears strong resemblances to the type. It is very much a political romance, and the name of its central character, King Athelston, is probably meant to be vaguely connected with the historical King Athelstan, victor at the Battle of Brunanburh against the Vikings in 937. There is, however, no similarity between the Athelston of the romance and the actual King Athelstan. *Athelston* was composed during the latter half of the fourteenth century.

Like the French romances and the political songs, the political romances of England are motivated by a sense of injustice, a sense that we have somehow been deprived of the position and privilege rightly due to us. Christian philosophy fostered this feeling, not just among the nobility but among all members of the society, by its egalitarian view of man, by its emphasis upon other-worldly values, and by its derivation of the whole human race from the same ancestors. If we are all descended from Adam, then hereditary rank is a kind of historical accident which has bestowed increased privilege on some at the expense of others. This is the essential idea of the popular fourteenth-century rime that John Ball used as the text for his sermon during the 1381 Peasants' Revolt:

> When Adam delved and Eve span,
> Who was then the gentleman?

All medieval men would have been sensitive to this notion, however much they may have accepted the established realities.

In the romance, the general sense of injustice became translated into specific violations of hereditary or acquired rights. A good example is *Fouke Fitzwarin*, a rambling, episodic romance that expresses a lighthearted but nonetheless clearly defined antagonism toward unjust authority as represented by King John of England. Fouke, the hero, is leader of a small band of outlaws who defy and baffle King John in a series of entertaining, sometimes humorous episodes in an attempt to win back Fouke's rightful heritage—successfully, it turns out. The whole first third of this story is essentially a justification of Fouke's claim, which is traced back to the time of William the Conqueror. As the romance explains it, the claim is sanctioned alike by God, legal authority, military conquest, and heredity. The narrative that justifies the family claim and explains why others possess the lands is complex in its details but simple in terms of right. No doubt as a concession to contemporary opinion that the family was baseborn, we are told how Fouke's father, as a young man, entered a tournament dressed like a "borgeis" in borrowed rusty armor and mounted on a carthorse. But we, the readers, know that he is nobly born.

The most serious challenge to Fouke's claim comes from King John, whose motivations are both personal and sinful. John is portrayed as an unfavored son, wicked by nature ("qe tote sa vie fust maveys et contrarious e envyous"), who nourishes a hatred for Fouke ever since a childhood quarrel over a game of chess. Right up until the time that John, under duress, returns Fouke's lands, he remains vindictive and deceitful, breaking oaths, killing and looting as he rides over the countryside, and persecuting Fouke's wife out of lust for her. (John's lust for her, along with her beauty, good reputation, and extensive holdings in Ireland, was one of Fouke's reasons for marrying her in the first place.)

By contrast, Fouke follows a strict code of conduct, of which we are frequently reminded. Unlike the would-be adulterer John, he refuses a profitable marriage with the daughter of the Duke of Carthage when it is offered to him—because he is a Christian and already married. He will not fight for Saracens (not until they are converted, anyway), and he refuses to harm "loyal" people. In case a reader may have heard other reports of Fouke, the romance introduces a character named Piers de Bruvile, who assembles "all the dissipated sons of noblemen in the country and the other good-for-nothings" and goes about robbing all the loyal subjects. While out on his raids, Piers goes by the name of Fouke Fitzwarin, and thus Fouke gets a bad reputation. The problem is solved when Fouke catches Piers and his companions in the midst of a raid and beheads them all.

Fouke's code is based strictly upon assessments of the nature of his opponents. According to the value system of the romance, acts are not good or evil in themselves, but are good when done to the evil and evil when done to the good. In one episode Fouke and his brothers come to an island and kill six villeins who masquerade as noblemen but betray their base nature by raping, abducting, and imprisoning young women; the heroes then proceed to massacre the other local inhabitants because there was nothing but "thieves" on that island. Fouke's main principle is that he will harm only the king and his followers; all others are "loyal" and have rights that are to be respected. This gentlemanly treatment is reciprocated by most of the people of England and even by the King of France, who at one point is prepared to protect Fouke against John. An interesting incident involves Fouke's capture of several of the king's merchants. When Fouke asks them who will bear the responsibility if they should lose their goods, they explain that they themselves must bear the responsibility if the loss occurs through their own negligence or cowardice but that the loss falls on the king if it happens by natural disaster or by people's force ("en peril de mer ou par force de gentz"). Hearing this, Fouke confiscates the merchants' cloth, dresses his followers in it according to their deserts, and dismisses the merchants after feeding them generously.

The sense of alliance or camaraderie among all the people in opposition to an unjust king and the implication that the combined power of the law-abiding subjects is superior to that of individual rulers is characteristic of much late medieval thought. Despite social differences, the law binds people into one, represented by the hero who, like the average subject, is a victim (Fouke is abused of his lands unjustly, typically outnumbered in battle, etc.). There is a natural, emotional tie felt between the hero and all who represent the right, whether they are kings or the commoners who abet Fouke's cause throughout the romance. On a symbolic level, the tie is represented in the disguises adopted at various times by Fouke and his brother John de Rampaigne—monk, merchant, collier, minstrel: a rough cross section of the society. Only two classes of people are automatically undesirable: pagans and villeins, both of which are moral much more than social states. Yet the moral states are also natural ones. The evil are born that way, and they persist in their treachery; there are no reformations. Yet they can be defeated by the *force de gentz*, partly because that force is so strong and partly because the evil are also stupid (to evade John's knights, Fouke nails the shoes of his horses on backwards), selfish, and treacherous toward one another.

REMEDIES FOR MISRULE

The romance of *Gamelyn* clearly belongs in the same category with *Fouke Fitzwarin*, even though it makes no claim to historicity. The conflict is between the established forces of the law and a group of outlaws, who are, however, the truly law-abiding ones. The major villain in *Gamelyn* is an eldest son who breaks his oath to his dying father and deprives the youngest son (Gamelyn) of his share of the father's lands. Allied with the evil brother is an array of authorities and officials including churchmen, a sheriff, and some justices; eventually the villain himself becomes sheriff and attempts to pervert the law (by bribing a court of justice) and get Gamelyn hanged. As in other romances, the villains are evil by nature and must be killed in order to reestablish true justice at the end of the story. And there are also the good authority figures in whom the romance places its ultimate trust, for they lay down the pattern of true justice (the father) and bring about the story's happy ending (the king).

Nevertheless, *Gamelyn* expresses an antagonism toward authority unmatched in the other rebel romances, especially where officials of the church are concerned. The appeal of the romance, in fact, lies in its vindictive put-downs of these evil officials. The most memorable scene is one in which Gamelyn, chained to a post by his older brother but subsequently released by a faithful household servant pretends that he is still bound in order to test some abbots and priors. He pleads with them each in turn to release him, but they arrogantly refuse. Gamelyn then throws off his fetters and, with the help of the servant, begins to beat the churchmen with a staff. The author expresses ironic contempt for the abbots and priors: the pummeling of them is described as the "sprinkling of holy water with an oaken staff" and as "absolution." The servant Adam encourages the hero:

'Gamelyn,' saide Adam, 'do hem but good;
They been men of holy chirche, draw of hem no blood.
Save well the croune and do hem non harmes,
But brek bothe her legges and sithen here armes' (ll. 521–24).

Gamelyn's antipathy toward the Church is not limited to this scene alone, for later when he is an outlaw we are told that he would harm no one "but abbots and priours, monk and chanoun" (l. 781). His vengeance on his brother reaches its climax when, after the brother has bribed a court to sentence Gamelyn to death, the hero occupies the judge's seat himself and passes sentences of hanging on his brother and all the justices.

Gamelyn is a model of loyalty and faithfulness to his word. He rewards his followers generously, helps save a franklin's sons from death, falls prey to his eldest brother while trying to help him keep his word, and risks his own life to keep his oath to another brother, Sir Ote. In recognition of this lawful behavior, the king makes him chief justice of the kingdom at the end of the story. Gamelyn displays the same camaraderie toward the common people and the underprivileged that is seen in *Fouke Fitzwarin*, but here the sense of class conflict is stronger. Gamelyn's followers are consistently servants. The "lewede" men naturally take his part, and he eventually becomes king of a preexisting band of outlaws. His closest friend and ally is Adam Spencer, a name that indicates his multiple role as innocent man with God-given rights, servant, and Christ-like distributor of sustenance to the common people. Gamelyn, too, is a dispenser, both as outlaw king and when, in an earlier scene, he opens up his brother's larder to wine and dine "all maner men" for seven days and nights. His common-man role is continually emphasized by his actions, his associates, and his choice of weapons in battle: pestle, staff, and bare hands (in a wrestling match).

Gamelyn is only one of a number of indications that fourteenth-century Englishmen were becoming impatient with the political and military establishment. The evils of existing institutions were being repeatedly attacked in satirical works, of which the *Canterbury Tales* and *Piers Plowman* are the best known. The Wycliffite movement and the Peasants' Revolt are significant examples of similar dissatisfaction breaking to the surface in the society. *Gamelyn* illustrates the potential vigor of antiestablishment sentiment, especially sentiment directed against the Church, yet at the same time it demonstrates an ultimate faith in the institutions themselves. As in the other literature and reform movements of the fourteenth century, the romance maintains that social evil is the result of evil individuals or inadvertence on the part of the powerful, not of defects in the system itself. So King John is only one bad king in a line of otherwise benevolent monarchs, and the treachery of an oldest brother can always be righted by appeal to a higher authority.

The principal of higher authority, in fact, is essential to the medieval political romance, as it was to the society. The rebellious peasants could behead the archbishop and the king's treasurer in 1381 and yet innocently place their trust in the king himself. Attacks on the Church were directed at monks, priests, or friars—even at specific orders—but less often at the Pope and never at the Church itself. *Gamelyn* carefully restricts its attack to an unspecified perversion of primogeniture while leaving Church, king, and primogeniture themselves untouched.

An excellent example of ultimate faith in the system despite a consciousness of the evils that it tolerates is seen in the romance of *Athelston*. Here, instead of an evil landholder-sheriff, we have an essentially good but misguided king as the source of the trouble. Athelston has sworn oaths of brotherhood with three companions, Wymound, Egelond, and Alryke, and when he becomes king of England, fulfills his oaths my making Wymound and Egelond earls and Alryke archbishop of Canterbury. Egelond and Alryke remain faithful, but the envious Wymound seeks to enlarge his own lands and influence by accusing Egelond of seeking the king's death, and the king is taken in by this accusation. The ease with which this happens is an expression of the almost absolute faith placed in oaths by medieval thought, if not by medieval men. The effects of Wymound's treachery (and of the king's gullibility) are serious and extensive: Athelston becomes an enemy to his own sister (Egelond's wife) and nephews, kicks his pregnant wife (killing his own unborn heir) when the wife takes Egelond's side, and brings England under interdict when he opposes Alryke's attempts to judge the accusation rationally. But Athelston, though he and his land suffer the effects of treason, remains faithful himself, so much so that, when it becomes clear that Wymound is at fault, Athelston will still not betray his promise to keep the accuser's identity secret.

The solution in this romance comes about by appeal to God.

Archbishop Alryke arranges a trial by fire, in which all the accused—Egelond, his wife, and their children—are to walk a path of burning coals. When they do so without being harmed, it becomes apparent that they are falsely accused, and the same test subsequently applied to Wymound proves his guilt. He then admits his treason and is drawn and hanged. The ordeal as a method of determining guilt had long been abandoned when this romance was written, so its appearance in *Athelston* indicates not a contemporary practice but a surviving faith in man's ability to judge good and evil on an absolute scale.

The reliability of this faith is one basic message of both the historical and political romances of England; another is the reliability of the existing political establishment in warding off evil and preserving the peace. These are not troubled works; they deal with conflict but not with doubt. Doubt and unanswered questions, however, do characterize another type of medieval romance, one that treats of personal rather than political relations and one that, for later ages, became almost synonymous with the romance itself—the romances of love.

5 Love Stories

From the time of their common origin in the twelfth century, medieval romance and the courtly love tradition have always been inseparable, love being a part of many romances and central to certain types of them. The kind of love seen in the romances is similar to the *fin amour* of the troubadours and minnesingers in general character, but there are some differences too, the major one of which is the relative unimportance in most romances of the furtive, adulterous love affair. This occurs, but the typical love affair of the romance leads to marriage.

In courtly love literature, which probably reflected the social problems of its time,[1] the lover has two aims: sexual fulfillment and social advancement; in the most interesting and most discussed courtly love literature, these aims conflict and cannot both be achieved. The impossibility of achieving them increases the lovers' passion and leads to pathetic if not tragic conclusions. But in the popular romances of England, the social theme predominates. Even in the more passionate romances we never get descriptions of sexual relations and seldom of physical contact between lovers—only descriptions of longing, scheming to meet, etc. The one description of Tristan and Ysolt lying together is when they are sleeping innocently with the sword between them (after having made love earlier, we are told). Medieval romance is seldom erotic, and, when it is, the eroticism is symbolic or implied.

The most obvious similarity between the love of the romances and that of the troubadours is the tendency toward love at first sight. Romance lovers fall in love at first sight (or even from reports about their ladies) because their real desires demand only a few facts: the woman must be wealthy, noble, and beautiful. (In the most self-aggrandizing romances she must be very wealthy, very noble, and the most beautiful woman in the world.) She is won by military prowess and social virtue because those were supposedly the normal means of advancement in real life. The love for her is passionate, occupying all the lover's energies, because she symbolizes everything that is important to him. All of these characteristics of courtly love can be seen in the child exile and superman romances; other courtly love characteristics—such as the desire for sexual intercourse and the tendency toward adultery—are found only in the love romances, if at all.

The hero's desires become sensual when he takes the symbol for the object itself, when he considers the attainment of the woman as an end and not merely as a means to power, wealth, and fame. Adultery becomes a problem because the woman who best symbolizes power, wealth, and fame is already married—to the lord of the romance hero. Other problems result from the incestuous overtones found in many romances. It is natural for one desiring marriage and all the benefits that marriage confers (integration into the social order, stability, heirs) to think of that marriage in terms of the one he knows best, the marriage of his own father and mother. In a real sense, his desires are directed toward an image of his own mother and best fulfilled by a relationship with Oedipal overtones. This is an inevitable pattern, but, however inevitable, it creates feelings of guilt. To alleviate the guilt, the romances typically do one of two things: either they translate the love desires and relationships so completely into symbols that their Oedipal features are obscured, or else they end by destroying the guilt-laden hero. What the love romances have in common with one another, as opposed to the combat romances, is that they accept romantic relationships as an end in themselves and clearly show the effects of the resulting guilty feelings.

Passionate and sentimental love first appears in a group of romances composed in French during the twelfth century, and these include some of the most widely traveled as well as the longest-lasting romance stories. Some of these romances originated in England, and most of them were later reworked into English versions. Although their origins lie earlier and elsewhere, the earliest extant versions of the Tristan story and *Amis et Amiles* are in the Anglo-Norman dialect, as were probably the lays of Marie de France. Three other stories, those of *Floris and Blauncheflur*, *William of Palerne*, and Lancelot, come down to us in continental French versions, from which they were translated into Middle English verse. In the case of these, it is the English versions that will be considered here. Because of the diversity of these romances, they will be discussed separately, but in all of them it will be seen that the concepts of love are intimately related to attitudes toward self, family, and social fulfillment. Their appeal is obviously to an audience that had come to see sexual relationships as a means to self-achievement, self-knowledge, and identity but was troubled by many of the implications of this view.

THE LOVE POTION

In its own day as well as our own, the story of Tristan has stood apart, not necessarily as the most popular of the British romances—that depends on one's definition of "popular"—but as one that elicited a different and more serious attitude from those who handled it.[2] Judging from the number of extant manuscripts and from its persistence in popular literature for centuries afterward, *Guy of Warwick* was more often read than *Tristan*, but in the long run *Tristan* has survived better. In its original versions, the Tristan story brought forth imaginative efforts not expended on other medieval romances; it also appealed to more thoughtful authors, inspired nonromance poetry such as Marie de France's *Chevrefoil* and *La Folie Tristan*, and was talked about with a respect not granted to *Guy of Warwick* or the others.

A written version of the Tristan story seems to have been composed somewhere around the middle of the twelfth century, and from this "primitive" form of the narrative, no longer extant, four or five fairly distinct secondary versions developed. There is evidence that two or more of these different types were known concurrently to audiences of the twelfth century and that they competed in their claims to being the most accurate. Two lines of the tradition are represented by Anglo-Norman poems of the late twelfth century, one by a man who gives his name as Thomas and another by an author named Béroul. Both poems now exist only in fragments, and Béroul's in only one manuscript. Thomas's story, however, is known in its entirety because it became the basis for several other versions, including Gottfried von Strassburg's *Tristan und Îsolt* and a prose translation of 1226 made by a Norwegian friar named Robert. In the Auchinleck Manuscript there is a Middle English version that derives ultimately from Thomas, lacking only the end of the story and a few other short passages. The story told by Thomas is the most important one for the British tradition as a whole, and the discussion here will focus upon it.[3]

The central feature of the Tristan story is a hopeless and uncontrollable love between the hero and Ysolt, the young and beautiful wife of Tristan's lord, King Mark. The sole cause of their love, according to the story, is a magic potion, intended for Ysolt and Mark but accidentally drunk by Tristan and Ysolt while he is taking her to be married to the king. The lovers are victims of a mistake, and, as seen by the authors of the romances, their love is neither good, beautiful, nor necessary. Thomas, Béroul, and Friar Robert all in their own ways condemn the love while favoring the lovers. (Béroul also condemns King Mark and the counselors who attempt to make him aware of his wife's infidelity.) Thomas and the authors who follow him treat the love potion simply as a device, a convenient means of explaining why a man and woman who originally were only mildly interested in each other should fall helplessly in love just as the woman is about to be married to someone else. To Béroul the potion is an excuse for the lovers' immorality. Its effects come upon them against their wills, and both of them insist that without it they would have remained virtuous. Furthermore, in Béroul's poem, the effect of the potion lasts only three years, and when it wears off both lovers formally repent their sins and vow to live clean lives henceforth.

Not only is this not a good love; it is not fated either. No outside power makes Tristan and Ysolt fall in love. They do not want or plan to fall in love; their love is motivated by nothing that we see in the character of either, and it constantly interferes with the other and more serious aims of hero and heroine. This strange and powerful concept—all-consuming love by accident—is more than a psychological alibi; it masks what is probably the most important conflict found in medieval romance.

The story does not begin with the love affair but rather with the wars of Tristan's father, and it does not end with the conflict between Tristan, Ysolt, and Mark but continues to tell of Tristan's marriage, an unsatisfactory one because it is haunted by his former passion. The main characters appear in many guises, each guise represented by a separate character. There are three Ysolts: the heroine's mother, the heroine herself, and Tristan's untouched wife, Ysolt of the White Hands (mother, lover, and wife). There is also a second Tristan, Tristan the Dwarf, who is not a dwarf but an unfortunate husband fighting to regain his abducted wife. Even these meager details should make it evident that the story involves a fragmenting of self-images. Problems of self-image are basic to the story, and the opening section presents them in a bewilderingly complex way. All the versions devote a considerable amount of time to this section; in fact, the Middle English version is half over before the marriage of Ysolt and Mark takes place.

The opening section tells of Tristan's doubtful origins—his conception (out of wedlock), his birth, and the deaths of his parents—and raises lingering questions. Is he legitimate or not? Who are his parents (Tristan does not know until he is a young man) and what is their status in their homeland? Although Tristan is in fact the son of King Mark's sister and a foreign nobleman, one character calls him "churl" and his mother a whore, claiming that the young hero has no rights in Brittany. The hero's family connections remain in doubt as he grows up. He is adopted and educated by a seneschal (socially a step downward), and later events carry him to England where he is, by implication, adopted by King Mark.

There are five different father figures in this section of the story, all of them bearing somewhat different relations to the hero and all of them unsatisfactory in some way. The true father acts immorally and is defeated in battle. The seneschal, who is affectionate and who instills noble skills in Tristan, is poor: he appears at Mark's court in rags. Mark, who is the noblest and most powerful of the figures, is an enemy to Tristan almost from the beginning, albeit an enemy whom the hero cannot directly attack. The other two father figures are the men Tristan slays, thereby making himself, in each case, an heir: by killing an evil duke, the murderer of his father, he wins Brittany, which he bestows on the seneschal; by killing Morholt (whose role as a monster-father is suggested by his demand for sixty handsome boys in tribute), Tristan wins the right, never again mentioned, to succeed King Mark.

At the end of this preliminary section, Tristan has won his place in the world, but at great cost to himself. With the exception of Mark, whose role as a father is carefully obscured, even the substitute parents are gone (the seneschal does not appear in the later sections), fallen victim to their own inadequacies or to Tristan himself. The battle in which Tristan slays Morholt has two apparently different but actually related effects on the hero: the tip of his sword has broken off in the giant's skull, and Tristan has received an incurable wound. Both sword (a phallic symbol) and wound represent Tristan's now-damaged manhood. In striking at the image of his father, he has had the blow rebound on himself, and the broken sword becomes an emblem of Tristan himself: he will later be identified by it. Symbolically he has faced the dilemma side-stepped by the exile romances, a dilemma caused by the desire to inherit place on the one hand and the desire to win it on the other. He has done both, but he is overcome by an unexplained guilt, symbolized by the wound which stinks so that no one can stand to be near him. His victory itself is cause of this wound. The pattern of victory and wound is repeated twice more in the romance, and the symbolism is the same. In one of these cases, when Tristan kills the dragon, thereby earning the right to marry Ysolt and share the Irish kingdom, the dragon's tongue, cut out as a symbol of the victory, overcomes Tristan and makes him helpless.

Tristan's arrival in Ireland promises solutions to these conflicts, as the heroine's mother, also called Ysolt, cures his wound. Healing is an important function of women in the Tristan story and in other romances as well. On three other occasions women serve as healers—or are asked to—when men have incurred wounds in an attempt to win land or women. Tristan's mother first comes to his father when he has been wounded in a tournament by the rival duke. The father and mother make love, and after that the father is cured. This suggests that sexual intercourse is understood to be the curative agency, and the supposition gets support from the fact that the healing of Tristan by Ysolt's mother takes place when they are alone in her chamber, in a faintly erotic scene. In fact, this symbolism may provide the real meaning of Tristan's passion, for which the love potion is so clearly only an excuse: in the embraces of Ysolt he is seeking a cure for the continually reopening wounds in his self-image. On his second voyage to Ireland, when he has been rendered helpless by fumes from the dragon's tongue, he is healed by Ysolt and her mother together. After the final battle of the romance, a battle which is undertaken to win back the wife of the second Tristan and in which the second Tristan is killed, Tristan sends for the heroine, for she is, he says, the only one who can cure his wound.

The cure, however, brings new troubles, and as before they are involved with family relationships and self-image. It quickly becomes apparent that Tristan's existence in Ireland is endangered by his too-close involvement with the royal family there. To prevent recognition by Queen Ysolt, who is Morholt's sister and knows the name of her brother's slayer, Tristan takes the pseudonym Trantris, turning himself upside down, so to speak. Later he undertakes the courtly education of Ysolt the daughter, thus making himself a kind of parent figure for the woman who is soon to become his lover and the wife of his lord (and uncle). As wooer (for Mark) and then as lover of Ysolt, Tristan usurps Mark's place, just as he had earlier done in defending the realm against Morholt. Queen Ysolt refrains from killing the helpless hero only because she has previously cured him and because he is their savior (from the dragon). Since the dragon and Morholt are both father figures, we see that Tristan's symbolic family involvements have been the cause of both his predicament and his salvation. Now, however, implications of incest are being added to those of father killing, for it is really in the role of mother that the women of this story have curative powers, Ysolt's mother being the one who prepares the love potion.

Once these events are set in motion, Tristan begins to undergo a series of symbolic self-conflicts that suggest some additional facets of his personality fragmentation. The first of these is with an evil steward who claims heroine and kingdom for himself after the dragon is dead. In his desire to win Ysolt and in his claim to have slain the dragon, the steward is simply a crude version of the hero. Tristan's conflict with him is a conflict between the noble pretenses of the romance and the underlying, unattractive aims of the hero. A similar struggle underlies Tristan's rescue of the heroine from another alter ego, the Irish harpist who attempts to abduct her. The conflict here is between the man who only dreams of possessing this most beautiful and desirable woman (the harpist) and the fictional man she herself desires (Tristan). The harpist's unlawful violence is similar in nature to Tristan's "heroism," but maintenance of the romance's fantasy demands that violence, at least toward the heroine, be rejected and that she be won as a result of courtesy, intelligence (Tristan outwits the harpist), and her own choice. Neither the steward nor the Irish harpist is killed. Because they are identified with the hero, to do so would be to kill him, and that in

fact is what happens when later the death of another Tristan substi-
tute (Tristan the Dwarf) leads directly to the death of the hero
himself.

Ysolt also has a number of alter egos. One of these is Brengvein,
her maid, who becomes an important character just at the point
when Ysolt's involvement in the plot has brought about confusion
in her own self-image, when she becomes at once the lover of
Tristan and the wife of Mark. Brengvein is Ysolt's constant com-
panion and adviser. She substitutes for Ysolt on her wedding night,
and later she becomes the lover of Tristan's close companion
Kaherdin. When Tristan builds his love shrine, he includes a statue
of Brengvein along with that of Ysolt, and he kisses both. It is clear
that these two characters represent different and conflicting aspects
of a single personality and that, even though the relationship be-
tween them changes somewhat with the progress of the plot, their
symbolic value remains essentially the same throughout.

Brengvein seems to be a kind of chaste Ysolt—"chaste" being
used here to include not only virginity before marriage but also
faithfulness afterward and the appearance of virtue always. She
takes Ysolt's place in Mark's bed when the heroine has disqualified
herself for a royal marriage by her lovemaking with Tristan. The
immediate result of this substitution is a crisis of self-image similar
to those that Tristan has already experienced: Ysolt, having de-
cided that Brengvein knows too much, attempts to kill her, order-
ing two "thralls" or "workmen" to do the deed. Brengvein wins the
servants' pity with an allegorical story stressing the relationship
between chastity and marriage: when the servants ask what she has
done to be condemned, she says that she and Ysolt were both given
white silk nightgowns on their departure from Ireland; Ysolt soiled
hers on the trip over and prevailed on Brengvein to lend hers for the
wedding night.

Brengvein, of course, symbolizes the appearance of chastity
rather than true chastity, as is made clear when she teaches Ysolt
answers to allay the king's suspicions. When Tristan and Kaherdin
get an opportunity to enjoy three pleasure-filled nights with the
women of their desires, Brengvein resists for the first two by using
a magic pillow to put Kaherdin to sleep, but she grants him her
favor on the third night. In a climactic sequence, Brengvein con-
fronts Ysolt with a litany of their sacrificed honor, blaming the
heroine's lechery for their problems; then she reports Ysolt's un-

chasteness to Mark, an act that results in Tristan's banishment from the court.

Standing for the maintenance of a chaste appearance and, consequently, for the marriage to Mark, Brengvein is an expression of conscience pains over the heroine's unfaithfulness, a sort of superego to Ysolt's id. Ysolt's decision to kill Brengvein represents a giving-in to lustful desires, which is immediately repented because it entails the death of one part of the personality. Brengvein's complaints and betrayal of her lady represent a victory for feelings of obligation to social demands. Underlying these incidents is a continuing theme of self-conflict, caused in this case by the dual need for sexual gratification and for social acceptability.

The last important alter ego of the heroine, Ysolt of the White Hands, originates from a split in the hero's perceptions. Tristan's marriage to Ysolt of the White Hands represents one further step away from his original submerged desire, the combined mother-lover-wife. By means of this step the lover's goal is made socially acceptable, but the wife contains within her so little of the originally desired object that she has no real appeal. Tristan marries Ysolt of the White Hands primarily because of her name, which allows him, while courting her, to sing songs about his real beloved. Like actual marriage among the medieval nobility, this one results from practical considerations: Tristan wants to forget the first Ysolt and finds that the second, in addition to having the same name, has a good reputation and carries herself in a proper courtly manner. Her family, in turn, seeks the marriage so that the militarily indomitable Tristan will stay and protect the dukedom. But, to Tristan, Ysolt of the White Hands is inferior to the first Ysolt, both because she is less beautiful and because she is the daughter of a duke, whereas the first is a queen. As a result, Tristan refuses to have sexual intercourse with his wife and sets about building an elaborate shrine where he can secretly worship the image of the first Ysolt.

This final complication leads directly to the death of Tristan, as the wife, jealous of the lover, attempts to deny her to Tristan. His death is preceded by a process of symbolic self-alienation leading to symbolic self-sacrifice. Rejected by the heroine as a result of Brengvein's intervention, Tristan turns wild man and becomes, in disguise, the self that he had most feared becoming: a beggar and madman. Thus transformed, he is able to defeat Cariadoc, but this is a victory for the rational, not the passionate Tristan, and his reward is to return to Brittany and Ysolt of the White Hands. It is at this point that he is confronted by Tristan the Dwarf, a conventionally married version of the hero, whose wife has been stolen by Estult l'Orgulous of Castle Fer and his six brothers (a transparent representation of Pride and the six other deadly sins). The hero is so divided from his own passions that he is at first casual about taking the part of Tristan the Dwarf until admonished that "Tristan l'Amorous" could not be so unsympathetic to a lover. Rationality wins again, and the two Tristans kill the seven brothers—but at the cost of their own lives. In its conclusion, the story tells us that rational, socially acceptable behavior can be had only through self-denial and self-sacrifice, which mean loss of identity.

The conflicts of the Tristan story are rooted in competing desires and fantasies. Faced with medieval man's need to locate himself in a rigid, moralistic society and with his desire (also social in origin) for fruits forbidden by that society, the romance seeks answers by postulating a series of fantasy images in a fantasy world. One of the fantasies is sexual. Although it seems clear that none of the versions had any actual description of lovemaking, Thomas's version in particular seems (if we can trust Friar Robert's translation) to have contained many scenes in which the sexual imagery is explicit. These include the scene in which Tristan leaps from his bed to Ysolt's, the naked sword scene, Meriadoc's tracking of Tristan through the snow, the episodes involving the magical dog Petit Crû (the name is given in *Sir Tristrem*), and the description of Tristan's shrine to Ysolt. Contrasting with the sexuality is the insistence throughout on a code of absolute chastity, or at least on the appearance of absolute chastity. This is the standard against which Ysolt is constantly measured and, surprisingly enough, one that she is again and again able to come up to by one device or another. Ysolt is like a boy's image of his mother: a woman whose virtue is known to be compromised but who maintains the appearance of chastity in the face of constant curiosity concerning it. In Ysolt of the White Hands we have an opposing image: that of the virgin wife, who cannot perform her task of childbearing because of her unwilling "virtue" and who is driven by jealousy to the destruction of the hero. Both images betray the same kind of inner conflict evident in the various images of the hero and for the same reasons: the several desires embodied in the female characters compete with each other and with moral necessities.

These competing desires exist because marriage and, conse-
quently, love served several different and not necessarily related
purposes in the imaginations of medieval upper and middle class
audiences. In addition to companionship and physical comforts,
marriage promised the partners social acceptability and status, a
sense of identity, heirs, and psychological self-fulfillment; love,
which is the means to marriage in a society accustomed to choosing
mates, sometimes aided in the realization of these promises and
sometimes created troubles. In the romances, love and marriage
offer psychological comfort through a re-creation of the childhood
family, which in those days meant the "line" or extended kinship
group rather than the nuclear family of more recent times.[4] In such
families, the father-mother-children bonds are weaker because they
are shared with bonds to grandparents, uncles and aunts, and even
with bonds to functional (nurses and tutors) or symbolic (kings and
God) members of the family. Imaginative ties to a line family need
not be weaker than to a nuclear family, but the individual relation-
ships between child and parent or between husband and wife may
well be more distant and more easily confused with other relation-
ships. In medieval romances, we find that the father and mother
figures tend to greater extremes of good and evil than the other
characters, as if the parents were abstractions rather than real per-
sons. The father appears as benevolent king or malevolent giant,
the mother as healer or slut.

Medieval notions of love and marriage were also involved in the
individual's concept of himself, especially as it concerned social
status. The romances show us that upward social mobility was one
of the more important aims in twelfth-century society. In addition
to being a mother figure (or a sister figure) and the possessor of all
things good, the romance heroine is invariably seen as a means to a
higher social rank.

The question of sexual relationships is another matter entirely.
Sex occurs in medieval romances because marriage does, but it is
understood as a secondary benefit of marriage, or it is symbolic, or
it is a source of conflict. In *Tristan* it is both of the latter. The
fantasies of the romance are socially directed, and sexual urges get
in their way, partly because Christianity condemned them but
more so because they led to socially undesirable consequences.

This problem is built into the Tristan story, and all the authors
show their awareness of it in one way or another. Béroul's handling
of the problem is perhaps the most interesting since he is extreme

both in his sympathy for the hero and heroine and in his condemna-
tion of their love. He preaches against adultery, and yet he paints
those who would discover and prevent it as the blackest villains.
The result is a curious conflict in moral judgments, a conflict that
Béroul attempts to resolve by blaming the lovers' passion on the
love potion. They cannot help themselves, they are unhappy in
their love, and they repent as soon as the effects of the drug wear
off. Rationally and literarily, it is an unsatisfactory solution, and it
would be interesting to know what Béroul did with the end of the
story. Thomas dissociates himself from the adulterous affair by
commenting and moralizing upon it, and he is continually having
his characters rationalize their actions. Because he must keep the
fantasies of the romance at a distance, he is less sympathetic than
Béroul toward the lovers, but for the sympathy that must be there
his excuse is likewise their helplessness—that and the tragic ending,
which serves as expiation for their sins. The same is also true for
the Middle English author, whose "Tristrem the trewe" is the vic-
tim of circumstances.

THE FEMININE ANGLE

The lays of Marie de France offer us a rare opportunity to see
the romance from a woman's point of view—and women, we
should recall, probably made up a large part of the romance audi-
ence. It is generally thought that she composed these lays in En-
gland, perhaps for the court of Henry II, sometime during the
latter half of the twelfth century. Even if they were not composed
in England, they are closely associated with British tradition, and
two of them were later translated into Middle English versions.
Marie, who also put into French verse some fables of Aesop and a
version of the Purgatory of St. Patrick, says that she got the stories
for her lays from songs sung by Breton minstrels. Later English
authors repeated this claim often enough to establish the "Breton
lay" as a distinct class of romances. There are only twelve lays that
can be ascribed to Marie without reasonable doubt, plus a prologue
that appears in one of the manuscripts. The lays are short, the
longest of them running not much over 1,100 lines. All of them are
about love, and in fact all of them involve a love triangle or some
variation on one. But, like Thomas the author of *Tristan*, Marie,
though a poet of love, is far from a blind adherent to its cause. Her

poems portray love as a necessary ingredient of the happy life but also as a constant source of trouble and tragedy.

Marie's contradictory attitude toward love is apparent everywhere in the lays. She says that "those who have no good sense or moderation in love live a wasteful life, but in love it is moderation to lose all reason" (*Equitan*, ll. 15–20). She calls love a "sickness" but adds that "one who has found a loyal lover should serve her, cherish her, and do her will" (*Guigemar*, ll. 483–95). In the tales, love is a serious business, an irresistible power, upon which all attention centers. It is also good: all the lovers are objects of sympathy, and none of the happy endings occurs without love as a basis. Yet lovers are shown to be selfish, indulgent, excessive, and immoral. The excuse for the sympathy is the same as in the Tristan romances: the lovers cannot help themselves. In reality, Marie is divided between her devotion to love and her devotion to morality (also an ever-present theme), and each of her stories shows the conflict between the two.

Reading these poems, one's first impression is that they are not greatly different from the romances written by men, and thus Marie seems to reconfirm the surprising observation that this type of obviously male-oriented literature had substantial appeal for women. The reasons for this have already been discussed. Medieval women gained place and identity by marrying—unless they went into a nunnery, and that of course was understood as a marriage to Christ. For the average woman of whatever class, there was no social climbing, no opportunity for individual accomplishment, no gaining of power or wealth except as these came to her through her husband or father. Thus what she dreamed about was marriage to a man who got what he dreamed about. His fantasies became hers too. In addition, no one had yet bothered to develop a literature strictly for women. Women themselves seldom wrote fiction, and some time was to pass before they were even thought of as a distinct and significant segment of the reading public. Literacy among women, after all, was a kind of sociological accident, only becoming a deliberate aim of society at a much later period. Marie, not being a creator of new literary forms or even of new stories, had little opportunity to exercise her feminine instincts except in selecting which of the traditional romance themes she would include, which she would emphasize, and which she would reject.

Looking at what she selected and emphasized, we do find evidence of the woman's point of view. In several of the stories *(Le Freisne, Le Laustic, Le Chaitivel)* a woman is the central figure, and in one *(Yonec)* there is an obvious female fantasy: the young heroine, married against her will to an old husband and shut up by him without companions of her own age, complains aloud in solitude. Immediately a falcon flies in her window and transforms itself into a young, handsome lover who comes and goes whenever she wishes. But male fantasies also occur in several of the lays, most notably in *Lanval*, which was clearly the most popular of Marie's stories. *(Lanval* will be discussed in the next chapter.) Perhaps the major "woman's" feature of these stories is their total concentration on love and marriage and a corresponding deemphasis on fighting and social climbing. In all of the romances that we have so far considered, even *Tristan*, both fighting and social climbing are prominent, but Marie refers to fighting only occasionally and never describes it, while social climbing appears in her stories as a literary convention, not as a major concern. In several of the stories *(Bisclavret, Le Laustic, Le Chaitivel)* no class differences exist between the lovers; in others *(Equitan, Le Freisne, Yonec)* the man belongs to the higher class, but social advancement is not viewed as an important acquisition. The acquisition that is important in all the stories is love made socially acceptable.

Marie associates love with images of family, but in her stories the associations are clearer, less complicated, and less tortured than in the Tristan romances. The ever-present love triangle usually includes at least one parental figure, most often a motherlike lover or a threatening fatherlike husband. The lay of *Guigemar* is a classic example of a childhood family fantasy conveyed through thinly disguised Oedipal imagery. The hero comes from a happy family, from which he is sent away to become first a page and later a knight. Love comes to him through a symbolic virgin mother, a spotless white doe, that Guigemar mortally wounds with an arrow, but the arrow rebounds and wounds the hero too. The dying doe reveals that the only cure for his wound will come from a woman "who for your love will suffer greater pain and sorrow than any woman has ever suffered." A magic ship carries Guigemar to a land where he encounters another mother figure, an old king's young wife, the key to whose bedchamber is in the keeping of a priest. She cures the hero (the image of woman as healer also occurs in *Le Chaitivel)*, and they fall in love. When their innocent meetings are discovered by the king, Guigemar is banished and returns to his own land after exchanging tokens with the lady. The hero gone, she undergoes imprisonment and suffering until she wishes for escape, and the magic ship transports her away. She falls into the possession of another father figure, a knight called Meriadus who wishes to marry her, but she and Guigemar recognize one another through the tokens, Guigemar defeats Meriadus in battle, and he and the lady are married.

Much of the charm of this story derives from the simplicity and directness with which Guigemar's winning of mother-love is presented. The underlying identity of doe and lover is not left to doubt. The lady and the old king/Meriadus figures are simply twice removed from the real mother and father, and this proves just enough to make the fantasy allowable. It is an innocent fantasy (sex enters in only enough to be denied), and Marie handles it without embarrassment or excessive rationalization.

Similar in pattern and only a few degrees less innocent are the lays of *Milun* and *Yonec*. In both of these the love between knight and lady is physical, and in both it produces a son who eventually becomes the means by which the story is resolved. The presence of the son also helps to remind us that the lady is a mother figure, for the symbols of her underlying identity are not as obvious here as in *Guigemar*. In both lays attention centers on a conflict between love and marriage. In *Milun* the lady falls in love and has a son; then her father gives her in marriage to another man, a rich baron. Like Ysolt, the heroine frets over her husband's inevitable discovery that she is not a virgin, but nothing comes of this worry. Instead, the marriage goes ahead without quarrel, and the parted lovers continue to communicate with each other by means of a swan that carries messages between them. The swan symbolically combines the contradictions of physical love and chastity, the love having been made chaste once the son, who alone is necessary to the fantasy of family perpetuation, has been born. The happy ending comes about through two father-son confrontations. First, there is a battle between the lover (Milun) and the son, Milun having undertaken the battle out of jealousy of the son's prowess; later the son promises to kill his mother's husband, but on the way to doing this, he conveniently discovers that the husband has already died.

In *Yonec*, the desire for physical gratification is more explicit, and consequently the story verges on tragedy. The lady, married to an old rich man, is discovered to have a magical lover who comes to her when she wishes, and in a brutally symbolic scene the husband arranges to kill the falcon-lover with sharp steel blades placed in the window by which he enters the bedchamber. Eventually the son, Yonec (so named at the request of the lover-father), avenges this deed by killing the husband with his father's sword, as the lady expires on her long-dead lover's tomb.

In these and all of Marie's lays, the family is seen as having redemptive power, while physical love (lust) is destructive. *Bisclavret*, *Le Laustic*, *Le Chaitivel*, and *Chevrefoil* are all short allegories demonstrating the destructiveness of passion. Of these, *Bisclavret*, a werewolf story, is particularly interesting. The werewolf is a husband who runs wild in the woods three nights a week, doing terrible but unnamed deeds. His wife coaxes his secret from him and also finds out the place where he leaves his clothes, without which he cannot return to the shape of a man. Fearing her husband now, the wife has another knight steal the clothes, and subsequently, when the husband does not return, the two of them are married. Eventually these deeds are made known to the king, who finds the werewolf's clothes, restores his human shape and his place in court, and banishes the wife and her second husband. The lay associates sexual intercourse with bestiality and sin, symbolizing it first in the nocturnal ravages of the werewolf and later in the illicit marriage of the wife. Once the werewolf husband is separated from his wife and thus from the cause of his lust, a solution to his problem becomes possible; this explains why the werewolf, who at the beginning is an object of terror, can later become a loyal household pet to the king, attacking no one but the wife and second husband when they show up in court. The story contains so strong a rejection of physical passion that it also rejects marriage, something that is everywhere else seen as desirable.

The evil effects of passion are also evident in *Yonec*, where the dead falcon-lover's realm is left kingless until the son comes along to rule in his father's place, and in the lay of *Equitan*, in which a king falls in love with his seneschal's wife, to the ultimate harm of his kingdom. Equitan, the king, is portrayed as a good man and a good king, excepting only that he is an immoderate lover. His affair with the seneschal's wife is repeatedly condemned as a violation of his sworn duty to his vassal and is shown to have an evil effect on the realm itself. Equitan rejects the reasonable way of arranging marriages, speaking of the wife's stipulations as "the bargaining of a burgess." Allegorically, the seneschal represents reason and the wife passion; the lovers come to a symbolically appropriate end, being scalded to death in a boiling bath they had prepared for the seneschal.

A different kind of love problem has a pathetic outcome in *Les Dous Amanz*. Here the difficulty is not the lovers' passion in itself but rather inadequate dissociation of the fantasy from the underlying family image. A king who treats his daughter as a wife substitute sets an impossible task for any suitor who would win her: the prospective husband must carry the girl to the top of a mountain without stopping to rest—symbolically a sexual feat, like Tristan's great leap from the cliff in Béroul's romance. Thus when a young squire, beloved of the daughter, undertakes the task, he finds himself in direct competition with the father, who laughs at the boy's presumption. From the lady's aunt (a mother figure, as in other romances), the squire obtains a magic potion to confer strength on him, but he does not use it, relying instead on his own strength, and two-thirds of the way up the mountain he falls dead. The girl dies on his body, in a lover's embrace. The sexual conquest of the motherlike lover proves impossible without the aid of magic and image substitution.

A successful resolution of these problems is achieved in two lays, *Le Freisne* and *Eliduc*, which present a different kind of love triangle, involving one man and two women instead of the other way around. In both lays the women represent, respectively, wife and lover. *Eliduc* is structurally the simpler of the two stories. In it, the hero Eliduc becomes, by means of some complicated adventures, seneschal in two different countries, in one of which he has a wife, Guildelüec, and in the other a lady whom he loves, Gualadun. Gualadun is the mother figure, and Eliduc has won her love by protecting her and her father from an evil king. We are told that their love is chaste, and so apparently is the relationship between Eliduc and his wife, to whom he is attached only by his pledge, not by any passion. When Gualadun finds out that her lover is married, she swoons and is taken for dead until the pitying wife revives her with a magic flower, releases Eliduc from his marriage vows, and takes the veil so that the lovers can be married. In addition to the divided image of wife and lover, resolved by religious expedient, the most interesting thing here is the symbolism of the flower.

While the wife is gazing on the unconscious lover's body in a chapel, a weasel runs out from the altar and across the body. A servant kills the weasel, whereupon the weasel's mate brings a crimson flower in its teeth and revives the dead animal. Guildelüec then frightens off the weasels, obtains the flower, and uses it to revive Gualadun. The weasel's flower apparently symbolizes sexual passion, the lack of which makes unsatisfactory the marriage of Guildelüec and Eliduc, but it is a sexual symbol made holy by coming from the altar. At the end of the story, the former wife, now an abbess, instructs the new wife in religious rules and practices, and they pray together for the husband. Religious blessings on love marriages are also prominent in *Le Freisne* and *Guigemar* and were obviously of great importance to author Marie de France.

Le Freisne, after some twists of plot at the beginning, develops into a story of a lord who has taken one woman (the heroine) as a lover but whose subjects demand that he take another woman (who turns out to be the heroine's twin sister) in marriage for the benefit of the realm. The wife-to-be has all the practical benefits on her side: she comes respectably from a respectable family, she brings with her a dowry of land, and she can give her husband a legitimate heir. (The proposed wife is named La Codre, 'hazel,' and the mistress is Le Freisne, 'ash,' because "the hazel gives nuts and pleasure, but the ash bears no fruit"—not that the mistress is infertile, but she cannot give him an *heir*.) Le Freisne, in addition to being socially "barren," is of uncertain birth and parentage, having been adopted first by a porter, then by an abbess, who is called her "aunt." The romance makes a powerful case against romantic love, but it turns out that the lover is everything the wife-to-be is, and a happy ending is ensured. With her husband, Le Freisne also regains her childhood family since her father, now apprised of the girl's existence by the repentant mother, welcomes her with love. Perhaps more than any of the other lays, this one combines the elements that are positive for Marie de France into a completely happy (and completely contrived) ending.

CHILD LOVE

The romance of *Floris and Blauncheflur* is an unusual one, less so in its own day than it seems in ours, but remarkable even among medieval romances for its uncompromising favoritism of infantile sentiment. It is the story of a young boy and girl, born of different parents but raised by the same mother. The children's love for each other so troubles the boy's royal parents that they attempt to separate the children. But the devoted boy pursues his beloved to an emir's harem and is eventually reunited with her. The story was extremely popular all over Europe, versions of it appearing in Provence, Germany, Scandinavia, Italy, Greece, Spain, and Portugal. Two somewhat different French versions, both composed in the twelfth century, established the tradition from which a Middle English version derived. Probably composed about 1250, this is one of the earliest of the romances in English, being antedated only by *King Horn*.

Its appeal was obviously to an audience that longed for a lost childhood, and this helps to account for its seeming strangeness in an age like ours when the period of childhood dependence has been extended farther and farther past adolescence so that our popular literature offers mostly fantasies of becoming an adult rather than of returning to childhood. Among the medieval nobility and gentry, social pressure favored early marriages, especially for women (to whom romances like *Floris and Blauncheflur* may have had special appeal), and boys were sent out as squires or apprentices before they were fully pubescent; the same may have been true among the middle and lower classes as well. These practices, in addition to the frequent lack of a close-knit family group during the early years, appear to have resulted in a longing for and idealization of childhood that is the major social cause of the family directed desires apparent in all of the love romances. In *Floris and Blauncheflur*, however, the infantile fantasy is more direct than in most: the hero's attachment is not to a mother substitute but to a sisterlike lover who is most importantly a part of his own childhood. Right up to the end of the romance, the two main characters are referred to as "children" or with such epithets as "these two sweet things."

The beginning of the romance establishes the image of the idyllic childhood world and the theme of adult threats to it. The hero, Floris, is the child of a Saracen king and the heroine, Blauncheflur, a child of a Christian lady captured by the Saracens, but the Christian mother raises them both, lavishing love on them equally. The children are united in their birth (they are both born on the same day), in their apparent parentage and family affection, and in the similarity of their names (which mean "flower" and "white flower").[5] They are divided by barriers of sex, class, geography, and religion, all concerns of the adult world that threaten their happiness. Pressures toward alienation from the child world develop when Floris's father (the king, who represents the adult, political world) wants to educate him and, later, to send him away from home and get him married. In both of these cases the hero pleads, first successfully, then unsuccessfully, that Blauncheflur be his companion. Eventually, as a result of the king's and queen's efforts, Floris is sent away to his aunt's family, where his education is continued without Blauncheflur, and Blauncheflur is sold into slavery so that she will not stand in the way of the family's further plans for Floris. Both of these actions are equivalent to sending the children into the world. Blauncheflur, in particular, is cast adrift among the foreign and the non-Christian, being sold to a merchant who speaks many languages and who sells her to the emir of Babylon (associated with Babel?), eventually to become one of his wives. The sale is symbolically equivalent to a loss of virginity, and that in turn leads to death. Blauncheflur is exchanged for a cup (a symbol of female sexuality) on which are engraved the stories of Paris and Helen and Aeneas and Dido; when Floris returns to his own land, he is told that his sweetheart is dead, and he is shown her grave, on which is inscribed: "Here lyth swete Blaunchefloure, / That Florys lovyd par amoure." ("Par amoure" implies physical and illicit love.)

Death is the same as sexual intercourse, which means growing up. When Floris and Blauncheflur finally make love at the end of the story, he is conveyed to her room buried in a basket of flowers. After the lovemaking they are found together in a death-posture, asleep in bed facing each other, and they awake to find a drawn sword over their heads. They are then thrown in prison (a kind of grave) and brought forth to be executed by burning. Both plead to be killed so that the other will be spared, and Floris even wishes to die twice, once for himself and once for Blauncheflur.

As these incidents make clear, the image of the love-death undergoes a radical shift in the course of the romance, from a fearful to a desirable thing, and a similar shift is observable in the case of the flower imagery. At first an emblem of virginity, the flower eventually develops into a symbol of innocent deflowering and, by implication, fertility. The shift corresponds to a change in the hero's aims, from a desire to regain his childhood innocence to a desire for sexual union with the symbol of that innocence, Blauncheflur. We become aware of this change when the hero, traveling as a merchant but really searching for his lost love, tells those whom he encounters along the way:

> "But y thynke on al wyse
> For to fynde my marchaundise;
> And yit it is the most woo,
> When y it fynd, y shal it forgoo" (ll. 463–66 and 533–36).

The idea here is that by union with his virgin lover, Floris must destroy her virginity. The new, more complex significance of the flower symbol explains the flower basket scene, in which Floris, rising "upryght" from the basket, makes Blauncheflur blush and another maiden shriek with surprise.

Ambiguity also marks the sexual imagery associated with the emir's city and garden. The description of these (ll. 549–642) begins as a symbolic representation of the difficulties Floris must overcome to win his love. As would be expected, the images are conventional ones for the threatening adult world, with an emphasis on numbers, wealth, rank, and commerce—which has already twice appeared in association with the adult world. Then the imagery becomes sexual. In the center of the harem is an enormous, impregnable tower, into which the only males allowed to enter are eunuchs; near this emblem of the emir's power and sexuality lies a garden combining images of fertility and chastity, the latter being presented as a requirement for marriage. Each year when the emir wishes to take a new wife, he first sends the candidates to wash their hands in the garden's spring. If they are virgins, the water remains calm and clear, but if they are not, the spring shrieks aloud and becomes red as blood, a reenactment of their loss of virginity. The unclean women are put to death, and the rest are brought under a beautiful flowering tree called "the Tree of Love," which will drop a flower on the maiden who is to be the emir's queen. Thus the flower, as in other contexts in the tale, is a symbol linking together virginity with marriage and fertility.

The ambiguous symbolism makes possible a resolution of the romance's central problem, which is how to regain the innocence of childhood in the adult, sexual world. The resolution occurs in a most improbable ending to the story, when the enraged emir suddenly takes pity on the self-sacrificing hero and heroine, knights Floris (thus making him a man), and allows the two lovers to wed.

Both practically and symbolically, the appropriate ending to a story like this is death, as in the *Tristan* and Marie's lays of *Yonec* and *Le Laustic*. But, like most romance writers, the author of *Floris and Blauncheflur* was willing to sacrifice inevitability in the interest of a happy ending.

FRATERNAL LOVE

Another story that is rather unpalatable to modern tastes but was very popular all over Europe in the Middle Ages is that of Amis and Amiloun. We would not call this a love story, since the affection in question is between two men, yet that is precisely what it was for medieval audiences, and that is what its authors call it.

The story, which tells of two noblemen who swear eternal loyalty and subsequently sacrifice their own interests to aid each other in times of extreme hardship, is extant in Latin and many vernacular versions, including Italian, Spanish, Welsh, Dutch, German, and Norse in addition to French and English. There are two different traditions of the story, hagiographic and romantic, but all the French and English versions belong to the latter. Of concern to us are the Anglo-Norman *Amis et Amiles*, a short romance composed sometime in the twelfth century, and a longer Middle English narrative, *Amis and Amiloun*, composed late in the thirteenth century, which tells the same story but is not a translation of the French. It is usually asserted that both these romances are based upon a common Anglo-Norman original, but it is also possible that the English poem is merely an expanded and somewhat modified retelling of the French romance. There is also an Old French *chanson de geste* (continental, twelfth century) that tells the same story.

One may interpret the Amis-Amiloun romance in two ways: either as social propaganda favoring extended family attachments over the ties of the nuclear family, or as an allegory of self-realization, similar to *Tristan* and some of the lays of Marie de France. The propagandistic meanings are closer to the surface. Throughout the story, the pledge of Amis and Amiloun to be true to one another like brothers (they are not actually related although they are the same age and physically identical, like twins) takes precedence over their attachments to their childhood families, which are of small consequence in the story, and to their families by marriage. Amiloun, for instance, undertakes a trial by combat for Amis, leaving the latter in his own place, to rule his lands and to sleep with his wife. (Amis, however, does not touch her.) Later, both protagonists combine in warfare against Amiloun's wife, who has since proved false to her husband. For his part, Amis, in the climactic scene of the romance, cuts the throats of his own two sons because an angel has told him that only by sprinkling their lifeblood on Amiloun can he cure him of leprosy incurred as a result of aiding his friend. Even Amis's wife goes along with this deed because, she argues, they can always bear more children but they cannot replace a friend like Amiloun. In fact, the only obligations that seriously compete with the sworn fraternal attachment are those of duty to one's lord and to God, both of them also examples of extended family bonds, and these too are ultimately sacrificed with consequences that prove the sacrifices justified. Amis is torn between the deadly sin of killing his own children and violation of his oath to Amiloun, but when he finally decides in favor of the oath, God implicitly smiles on the decision by restoring the children to life: they are found happily playing in the nursery.

As in all the love romances, lovers' goals in *Amis and Amiloun* are modeled on family ties. There are obvious similarities between the heroes here and the child lovers in *Floris and Blauncheflur*, for, like those, Amis and Amiloun were born on the same day and raised together, then parted against their wills. Just as Floris and Blauncheflur are essentially brother and sister, so Amis and Amiloun are like brothers—a relationship that proves less embarrassing later in the plot and can therefore be admitted more openly by the author. Almost every new step in the plot places the heroes in some family-like arrangement. Amis and Amiloun are taken into the court of a duke, swear allegiance to him, and become, respectively, his butler and steward. When Amiloun's parents die, he returns to his own land, marries, and replaces his father as baron; he marries a woman who had lost both father and mother (Anglo-Norman version). Amis becomes more closely associated with the duke's family by making love to his daughter, later marrying her, and by taking over the dukedom on the deaths of the parents. And so forth. Amis's sweetheart is closely associated with her mother, the duke's wife: when Amis is accused of lovemaking with the daughter and leaves the court to seek help from Amiloun, mother and daughter both go surety for him and both are on the verge of being burned at the stake when Amiloun arrives to undertake the trial by combat in his friend's place (announcing, in a marvelously absurd line: "For, certes, it were michel unright / To make roste of levedis bright"— ll. 1234–35, and cf. the Anglo-Norman, ll. 567–68). The romance expresses no longing for childhood, however, and its real aim is to replace the childhood family by ties based on verbal agreements. The last and in some ways the climactic attachment of the romance is between Amiloun and a substitute son, called Amorant ('lover, friend'—and parallel to 'Amis' and 'Amiloun'). This young boy, a relative of Amiloun but not his son, follows the hero and cares for him during the time when he is a leper and beggar, refusing to leave him even when offered an advantageous position at court and eventually inheriting Amiloun's lands. At the same time the eventual fate of Amis's children by birth is neglected.

The important bond is "treuthe," the eternally lasting pledge that welds together sworn companions, man and wife, lord and vassal, Christian and God, and that creates the conflicts with which the romance deals. *Treuthe* is based on beauty—which is a way of saying that it comes from nature, and from God. The romance lays great stress on the beauty, natural virtue, and prowess of the two heroes, and these lead directly to their mutual pledge, just as the beauty of a heroine leads to the hero's love for her. The Anglo-Norman romance tells us that nature had fashioned Amis and Amiloun so well that they resembled angels and that this produced their love and their pledge (ll. 15–18). Likewise, the duke's daughter falls in love with Amis because he is the "doughtiest," "semlyest," "worthliest," and "fairest" of men while her beauty is conveyed in her name: Belisant ('beautiful') in the Middle English version and Mirabele ('very beautiful') in the Anglo-Norman, though there she is also called Florie ('flower'—with the same symbolism as in Floris and Blauncheflur). The young Amorant is also extremely handsome, especially in contrast to the ugliness of Amiloun's leprous visage, which, as we will see, is a product of his sin.

On another level, *Amis and Amiloun* presents a fantasy of self-realization, confronting the same kind of personal contradictions and conflicts seen in the *Tristan*. In fact, this romance contains two episodes that are strikingly reminiscent of the *Tristan*—one of them when Amis, sleeping with Amiloun's wife, places a naked sword between them as a symbolic barrier to sexual relations; the other when Amis and Belisant use deceit to win a judicial test proving that their love had been innocent when, in fact, it had not. Even more clearly than in *Tristan*, the various characters in *Amis and Amiloun* are alter egos of one another. Amis and Amiloun, born on the same day to parents of equal rank, look so much alike that they can be told apart only by their clothing. This, of course, makes possible the substitution of Amiloun for Amis in the trial by combat and the simultaneous substitution of Amis in Amiloun's kingdom and bed. The careers of the two parallel and complement one another. At first the two men are both vassals of the same duke. When Amiloun returns home and gets married, Amis enters into a love affair with the duke's daughter. When Amiloun proves Amis's love chaste, thereby making marriage with Belisant possible, Amis is living, chastely, in a married state with Amiloun's wife. While Amis is enjoying the rule and marriage that are the result of Amiloun's efforts on his behalf, Amiloun suffers the illness and degradation that are ultimately the result of Amis's sin.

At the end of the story, Amis remains in his love marriage with the children who have been born to it but who have not yet come into any inheritance, while Amiloun is left in a state of apparent celibacy, having passed on his inheritance to the substitute son Amorant. The underlying pattern involving Amis, the physical lover, and his alter ego Amiloun, the chaste husband, has a parallel in the dual role of Tristan as lover and husband. The parallels are there because the basic problem is the same: marriage is desirable as a means of self-identification and fulfillment and for the heirs which it brings, but Christian society condemns as sin the means by which these things are gained. The fantasy solution is to split the lover and husband identities into two separate persons. For Amis, lovemaking comes first and then, only after the deceptive proof of chastity, marriage; from this union real heirs are born. For Amiloun, there is no lovemaking (nothing in the romance suggests that either he or Amis has intercourse with his wife) and no true heir; his marriage ends in rejection of the wife and the defeat of her proposed lover, this defeat being the only joint action of the two heroes in the whole romance.

In keeping with its preference for nonphysical, male love, *Amis and Amiloun* consistently portrays sexual love as illicit, bestial, dangerous, and diseased. Amis enters into the affair with Belisant unwittingly, and she herself is unsympathetically treated until near the end. Their love endangers his place at court, his future prospects, and the very lives of both of them. The death by burning that she and her mother are to suffer is emblematic of uncontrolled passion. The virtuous Amiloun learns of Amis's passion and consequent danger from a dream in which he sees Amis attacked by bears (lions in the Anglo-Norman version) and other wild beasts. And Amiloun's affliction is a direct consequence of physical love, having been promised to him at the time of the successful trial by combat. In the Anglo-Norman version, Amiloun substitutes for his friend not only in the trial but also in the marriage to the heroine, and it is this marriage that makes the angel threaten him with leprosy. In the Middle Ages, leprosy was believed to be a venereal disease,[6] and Amiloun's other affliction, beggary, suggests a connection between physical love and the lower classes. In this light, Amis's sacrifice of his children, who are the product of love, is seen as an act of contrition for the sin of sexuality, and the restoration of the children's lives is a sign of God's approval of the sacrifice.

But the unforgiveable sin is not so much sexual love itself as public acknowledgement of love. Amiloun is chaste because we do not know of his relations with his wife. Amis can be made "chaste" through a trick and does not have to pay for his lovemaking itself except by sacrificing the obvious results of it. Accordingly, the worst villain in the romance is another alter ego of the heroes, a steward to the duke, whose sole function in the plot is to tell the duke of Amis's indiscretion. Amiloun has already warned his friend, at their parting, of this villain, telling Amis to guard against deadly sin, keep *treuthe* toward his lord and "honor" in himself, and beware of the false steward. When the steward sees Amis and Belisant making love and reports this to the duke, the romance writer's attitude is like that of Béroul toward a similar episode in his *Tristan:* it is the steward who has been traitorous and broken *treuthe* much more than Amis himself. The act is bad enough, but admission of it is worse. In contrast to the steward is the character of Amorant, who is an image of the hero contaminated neither by sexual relations, the rumor of them, nor by the marriage that implies them. He is linked to the other characters only by his pledge and a vague blood relationship, but he is the one in whom the disparate images of lover and husband are combined and by whose means the self-image is perpetuated. In him the problem of passionate love is overcome by finally separating it from its look-alike, attachments to other members of the society based on familial concepts.

LOVE AND COURTESY

The glossing over of problems inherent in the medieval concept of love is particularly obvious in *William of Palerne*. This romance, originally composed in Old French during the last half of the twelfth century and translated into English in the mid fourteenth century, seems dull and conventional today; even in its own day it did not share the popularity of the other romances discussed in this chapter if manuscript survival is a guide. But it does represent something like the end result of a tendency apparent in all the love romances except *Tristan*, and that is the evasion of the conflict between love and social morality by means of superficial twists of the plot and by sentimentalizing of the emotions involved. Basically, *William of Palerne* is not even a love story but rather a romance of social climbing and empire, similar to the child exile and some of the superman stories. It tells of a prince, son of the good king of Apulia, Calabria, and Sicily, who is taken from his land and family as a result of an envious uncle's plotting. The prince eventually wins back the kingdom through his own prowess and marries the daughter of the emperor of Rome, finally becoming emperor himself. The love affair between William and Melior, the emperor's daughter, is only one of several major themes in the romance; the special importance of the love affair lies in the internal conflict that it shows in the hero.

William of Palerne is a political romance, and family ties, which are elsewhere models for broader social relationships, here take on a decidedly political significance. According to the romance, rightful rule passes to the firstborn, and attempts by others, more distantly related to the reigning king, to secure the kingdom are the causes of disruption. William's uncle, desiring the kingdom for himself, conspires with two handmaidens who serve as the young William's tutors (parent substitutes), and the three try to poison the boy. When a helpful werewolf carries him off in order to save his life, the act also alienates the hero from his patrimony. The werewolf, as we find out later, is himself an alienated prince: he is Alphonse, son of the king of Spain by his first marriage, and was changed into a wolf by the king's second wife, a witch, who wanted to see her own child inherit the throne. Thus the source of evil is the ambition for rank and power in violation of the strict, socially sanctioned lines of birth inheritance. The violators of inheritance themselves are evil only insofar as their ambitions are necessary to the plot;

toward the end of the story they are either forgotten, like William's uncle, or they repent and reform, like the handmaidens and the stepmother. William's own social advancement proves justifiable because it is accomplished through marriage to the emperor's only child—and because William's natural virtue makes him worthy of empire. William does not come to control the kingdom of Spain, for no inheritance entitles him to it; instead an alliance is achieved between Spain and the empire through the lasting and sworn friendship between William and the werewolf prince.

Acceptable social climbing occurs in a symbolic way only. Once separated from his natural family, William is first adopted by the werewolf, then by a childless cowherd (his "father" for seven years), then by the Roman emperor. However, at the end of the romance, William, now made emperor, grants an earldom to the cowherd in another example of socially acceptable advancement. These motifs take on added interest in light of the evil social ambitions at the beginning, for through them we see that good rule is associated with the virtue of the working classes and with upward social mobility. The ideal ruler combines natural worth, contact with the poor, and royal birth. Contradictorily, the desire for social advancement is evil, but the advancement itself is good. To replace promises of anything more than nominal social advancement, the romance offers its audience the doctrine of *noblesse oblige*, according to which the nobility must act in service to the less fortunate and less powerful.

This doctrine is set forth clearly in various passages toward the end of the romance, particularly in a parting speech of advice that the old emperor of Rome gives to his daughter, now married to William. He instructs her to be gracious, good, and courteous to low and high alike, to be humble toward those who serve her, to be loyal in degree to her lord and his subjects, to guard against abuse and excessive taxation of the poor, and to serve law and church (ll. 5116–25). The guide here being promulgated—and later demonstrated by the actions of both hero and heroine—is the law of courtesy, the behavior expected of the nobility. Its most important ingredients are service to all, the keeping of pledges both sworn and implied, careful observation of rank, courteous speech and behavior, and Christian humility. The law is based firmly in a hierarchical view. Although observation of it constitutes virtue in anyone and although it is understood to be in mankind by nature, degrees of courtesy separate noblemen from the peasantry and humans from beasts. Where the appropriate degree of courtesy is lacking, the resulting behavior is unnatural and is the source of evil, not only for those directly involved but for the whole society. Inordinate ambition, which is a failure to observe rank, threatens misrule and bestiality; thus the stepmother's desire to advance her son too far makes a wolf of the rightful heir. Throughout the romance, courtesy is the critical test between the good and the bad characters. William displays it by nature, gathering a crowd of followers about him because of his courteous behavior while living in the woods as the cowherd's son; later, when he has returned to his own kingdom and has sent for the stepmother to restore Alphonse's human form, threatening her with violence if she does not, William and his mother greet her "with welthe and gret worchip," William helping her "curtesli" from her horse and the mother kissing her (ll. 4300–04). Other notable instances of courtesy are shown by the cowherd and the werewolf.

In contrast to courtesy is the fierce and rough animal behavior of several characters, usually the evil nobility but occasionally the lower classes as well. The story of *William of Palerne* takes place in two locales, the court and the forest, and the two are in close proximity: next to the tower of the old king's palace is a park filled with wild beasts. The court is a place of wealth and ease, where courtesy is proper but not always practiced; the forest is a place of hardship, where William fears that Melior cannot survive but where courtesy sometimes makes an appearance. William's adventures twice lead him into the woods. Once, when threatened by the uncle's plot, he is adopted by the werewolf and cowherd; another time, love takes him there.

Although the author never says so directly, the course of the plot makes it clear that physical love is bestiality, a violation of the law of courtesy. Having been taken into the emperor's court at Rome and having distinguished himself in the noble occupations of chess, hawking, and horsemanship, William becomes the object of Melior's affections. Her maid, Alexandrine, brings on love in him with a magically induced dream, the plain content of which is that Melior is available. Despite William's objections that he is of uncertain birth, the two lovers are brought together and the love illness from which they have been suffering is cured (see ll. 1029–34). They see each other regularly for years, "doing their will" or "loving *paramours*," as the author puts it, until a marriage is proposed between Melior and the emperor of Greece—who is, in addition, William's maternal uncle. To avoid accomplishment of the marriage, Alexandrine helps the lovers escape into the woods, sewn up in the skins of two white bears. There they attempt to live on wild foods and love but are actually supported by the efforts of their constant companion, the werewolf. When the bear disguises become too well known and dangerous, the lovers exchange them for the skins of a hart and hind and thus, constantly threatened by capture, they come to Palermo, William's own capital. Behind this much-rationalized episode lies the idea that they have become converted into beasts by their secret and illicit love. While in both the bear- and deerskins, they live in the wild, walking sometimes on four feet (by day), sometimes on two (by night), and they are considered "grisli" objects of fear by all who see them.

The wild stage of their existence ends when William is reunited with his mother, the father having died. She observes the two deer in her park and is able to see their clothing underneath the skins, so, dressing herself as a hind, she meets them and brings them to the court where they are cut from the skins, bathed, and clothed. (Bathing and clothing are also stages in the humanization of the werewolf later.) The wild stage is not only an image of uncourteous bestiality but serves as penance for the lovers' sin, and the transformation from bear to deer marks a stage in the successful completion of that penance. The final absolution, however, is social and not religious, coming about by reunion with the family from which the hero's ties were severed by intercourse with the mother-lover Melior. Once William's place in his own kingdom is restored, nothing is required to complete his marriage to Melior but an announcement of their wishes to the emperor. At this point in the romance, the love theme dwindles away to unimportance, and Melior becomes a secondary character, just as Alexandrine did when the lovers escaped to the woods.

In *William of Palerne* the plot symbolism and the secrecy that surrounds the lovers' meetings indicate that physical love is a threat to social order. On the surface, the author regards their desires and the similarly destructive desires of other characters as separable from the characters themselves so that, when the desires have had their required consequences in the plot, they can be ignored. This is the key to the romance's sentimentality, and it is the reason why

William of Palerne is a less troubled story than the other love romances. The social, familial, and personal conflicts found in *Tristan*, *Amis and Amiloun*, and the others are present here too, but they have become so completely enshrouded in symbol that they can be willed away at the proper time. One other factor is that *William of Palerne* does not take passionate love seriously: moral order is its predominant concern.

LOVE AND RELIGION

Le Morte Arthur (usually called the Stanzaic *Morte Arthur*) is a love story with a Christian message. Modern critics, interested primarily in the connections between this work and Malory, often treat it as a tragedy of Arthur's downfall, but the poet's attention is really centered on Lancelot and his relationships with Guenevere, Arthur, Gawain, and others. This is one version (and about the only one in English verse) of the "book of Launcelot de Lake" which, Chaucer's Nun's Priest tell us, "wommen holde in ful greet reverence."

Admittedly, it is not the usual sort of love story. Although the focus of attention is on Lancelot and Guenevere at the beginning and the end of the poem, many episodes involve Guenevere only indirectly or not at all, and in one major episode—the war with Modred and the death of Arthur—Lancelot is absent. There are only two scenes, both brief, in which we see the lovers together as lovers, and in one of these Lancelot enters Guenevere's chamber to do nothing more than take his leave of her. Besides this, the poet ignores an apparently excellent opportunity for a love scene after Lancelot has ridden alone into Arthur's castle and rescued Guenevere from execution for adultery. From later developments we know that Guenevere then goes back to Joyous Gard with Lancelot, but she is not even mentioned again until an arrangement to return her to Arthur is worked out. Instead of showing us the lovers' reunion, the poet concentrates on the enmity that springs up between Gawain and Lancelot because Gawain's brothers have been killed in Lancelot's attack.

All this, however, is typical of many medieval love romances, in which the love interest is but one element in a complex set of relationships and events. The *Morte Arthur* presents a sequence of episodes that are carefully linked together by cause and effect, and it deserves to be called a love story if for no other reason than because the love between Lancelot and Guenevere is the initial cause. The tournament at the beginning of the story is held because Guenevere has told Arthur (in bed) that his "honour by-gynnys to falle, / That wount was wide in world to sprede" (ll. 25–26); in actuality, she wants to get him out of the castle so that she can have a meeting with Lancelot. When Lancelot enters the tournament carrying the favor of the maid of Ascalot, Guenevere's jealousy results in Lancelot's departure from the court and then in her subsequent plight when she is wrongly accused of murder and has no champion. After Lancelot fights to clear the queen of the murder charge, Agravayne's plan to tell the king of the illicit love affair brings Guenevere's life in jeopardy again, and Lancelot's rescue of her, with the deaths of Gawain's brothers, creates the conflict between Gawain and Lancelot. This in turn makes possible Modred's plot and the final disastrous war, with the death of Arthur and all his followers. At the end, when Guenevere has joined a convent, she directly attributes the course of events to their passion (ll. 3640–41).

Love is the cause of the tragedy because it leads to violation of more serious social compacts. Arthur is Lancelot's friend and lord, "the noble kynge that made me knyght" (l. 2145), and an alliance between the king and his invincible knight is necessary for the protection of England. Neither Arthur nor Lancelot wants to violate the trust between them. Arthur misses Lancelot sorely when he is absent from the court and is greatly relieved to find that Lancelot is not dead. When Lancelot comes to the aid of the accused queen, the king kisses and embraces him. When the Round Table, at Gawain's urging, has mounted an attack on Lancelot in Benwike, the king constantly argues for raising the siege and returning home rather than continuing the conflict. Lancelot, for his part, refuses to fight against Arthur (or Gawain) until forced to do so. During the siege of Joyous Gard when the king follows him about the field hewing at his helmet, Lancelot will not respond, and when Bors finally attacks and unhorses Arthur, Lancelot helps the king back onto his mount—at which Arthur weeps, thinking of "thyngis that had bene ore." Both Arthur and Gawain are delighted when it appears that Lancelot has taken the maid of Ascalot as his "leman," but the love between Lancelot and Guenevere makes an irreconcilable rift in the fellowship of the Round Table.

The relationships thus interfered with are similar to extended family relationships. The king and queen are like father and mother, and the knights are like sons (or nephews) to the king. Feelings and actions that reinforce this pattern are good; those that disrupt it mean trouble. If Lancelot were to pursue a brother-sister type of love for the maid of Ascalot (when she falls in love with him, he is about to enter the tournament wearing the armor of her ill brother), the king and court would accept this joyfully. But his love for Guenevere, although it originates in the family (mother-son) relationships and is beyond his power to control, is not only illicit; it is, by implication, incestuous as well, as it threatens Arthur's position as "head of the family." Agravayne, plotting to make the love affair known to the king, puts his finger on the problem:

'The kynge Arthur oure eme sholde be
And Launcelot lyes by the quene;
  A-geyne the kynge traytor is he;
And that wote all the curte by-dene' (ll. 1681–84).

But, like the steward in *Amis and Amiloun*, Agravayne, by bringing the affair to light, is himself guilty of "treason."

In Modred's treason (which is parallel to that of Lancelot), we have an even clearer case of violation of the family unit. Modred's relationship to the king is more specific and at the same time more ominous than Lancelot's: "The kynges sister sone he was, / And eke his owne sonne, as I rede" (ll. 2955–56). His prime motive is to marry his uncle's wife (elsewhere, "hys faders wyfe"). This is seen as a direct challenge to Arthur's position and authority, as Modred creates false reports of the king's death and begins to win the allegiance of the people to himself. Arthur's later offer to make Modred his heir (without the marriage to Guenevere) is insufficient to reestablish the now-disrupted family.

The conflicts are further complicated by the familylike ties that various characters honor, especially ties of brotherhood. Gawain's long-sought vengeance on Lancelot is motivated by his sorrow over the deaths of his brothers, Agravayne, Gaheriet, and Gaheries. Like Modred, these are all nephews to the king, and Lancelot is responsible, directly or indirectly, for their deaths. As a result, Gawain feels that he must oppose Lancelot until one or the other of them is killed, and Arthur lacks the power to bring this quarrel to a peaceful conclusion. The knights who support Lancelot—Bors,

Lyonelle, and Ector—are called "brothers" to one another, and Ector is a "brother" to Lancelot. So, by implication at least, we have here a reenactment of the old Germanic family feud, in which the participants are powerless to stop the conflict once it is set in motion, just as Lancelot is powerless to deny his love for Guenevere. But, unlike the old feuds, this one occurs between subgroups of a larger and more important family, the Round Table, all the members of which owe allegiance and love to one another. This is sometimes lost sight of by those commentators who view Gawain as the villain of the romance. He is not a villain but a victim, just as Lancelot and Arthur are. As he is about to die, he is still the "good" Gawain, and the "love" between him and Lancelot is unbroken despite their deadly quarrel. The tragedy of the *Morte Arthur* is that one type of love should interfere with another, more vital type and that the strength of these various bonds should make the ultimate fall of the Round Table inevitable.

The *Morte Arthur* does not end with Arthur's death. Instead it follows Lancelot and Guenevere as they reject the worldly concerns that are now seen as the cause of the tragedy and enter, respectively, into the lives of a hermit and a nun. In a moving scene, Lancelot wishes to seal this arrangement with a kiss, but she refuses even this, and they part in sorrow. Subsequently, however, it is clear that they both find love and companionship within their new orders. The ending is an integral part of the story as the poet has conceived it, although the religious orientation is a new element: not only are the two lovers "united" in an acceptable way, but Lancelot has found the family he had unsuccessfully sought— within a religious order. The archbishop makes this clear when he invites Lancelot to be "hys broder . . . to serve God." This is a better fellowship not only because it is religious and everlasting but also because it excludes women, who are, as another bishop has told Lancelot, "frele of hyr entayle" ('frail of character,' l. 2300). In addition, Lancelot now enjoys the company of all his "brother" knights without the conflicts that have plagued him up until this time.

Le Morte Arthur and the other stories discussed in this chapter represent a new type of literature clearly distinct from the *chansons de geste* in ways that the child exile, superman, and historical romances were not. It is no wonder that such stories are thought of first when the medieval romance is mentioned. And of course these are not the only romances with love as one of their central themes; in fact, in the fourteenth and fifteenth centuries love came to dominate the romances more and more. One enduringly popular type of love romance, combining a central love theme of the wish-fulfillment variety with elements of magic and the supernatural, was the fairy princess story.

6 The Fairy Princess

ne special type of love romance tells of a hero who travels to fairyland and falls in love with a fairy princess. Such stories, which were imported from French literature, enjoyed a certain vogue in England during the fourteenth and fifteenth centuries. They are similar to other medieval romances in their use of a quest plot, with travel and physical combat standing as images of change and achievement. The heroes and heroines, whether human or supernatural, are conventional enough. Even the appearance of the supernatural world is a fairly frequent romance convention, figuring prominently in such works as the lays of Marie de France, *Arthour and Merlin*, *Richard Coer de Lyon*, and the English Gawain romances. What separates the fairyland stories from all the others is their presentation of dual worlds, one the imperfect world of reality, the other a fantasy world of great pleasures and accomplishments.

The plot of the fairy-princess romance typically concerns a hero who is almost, but not quite, an accepted member of the social and political establishment. Circumstances magnify his alienation and soon result in a period of isolation from society during which he sets forth on a quest, often one not of his own choice or making. Along the way he crosses the boundary between the real and fairy worlds and finds himself in a land where his earlier problems are alleviated and his desires fulfilled in the embraces of a fairy princess. Subsequently he is allowed to return to his own world but usually on some condition, typically that he not divulge the existence of his magical lover. The remainder of the romance concerns itself with the attempt to integrate the two worlds. Sometimes this is managed successfully, by rejection of the fairy world or suppression of its supernatural features; at other times the integration cannot be achieved.

These romances deal with various types of problems, but, with few exceptions, all the problems involve the relationship between

132

an individual (a nobleman, but not usually a king) and his society. The hero suffers the effects of the problems, but society, or the world, is the cause of them. Insofar as the hero is to blame for his own troubles, his faults seem slight: he is overly generous, inept at handling money, unschooled in the manners of society, or unprepared for the conflicts in which he unexpectedly finds himself. As a result, although the stories center their attention on the individual heroes, even seeming to be allegories of his psychological development, they eventually turn out to be confrontations of social dilemmas. Perhaps because society's ills are more resistant to fictional solutions than are problems of the individual, many of the romances in this group have unsatisfactory resolutions or, at times, no resolution at all. But this fact also makes the romances more interesting than most, and this group certainly includes some of the most appealing of the Middle English romances.

Another reason for their appeal is their use of the supernatural. While fairies, dragons, and monsters appear with reasonable frequency in the medieval romance, they are by no means to be found everywhere, and only in this group and in the Gawain romances are they central to the action. As we have already seen, the romance, no matter how fantastic it may seem to us, usually attempted to reflect its own world with some degree of realism, in its own way.

All of the Middle English fairy romances were composed either in the fourteenth or the fifteenth century. Among the earliest of them is *Sir Launfal* by Thomas Chestre, an independent version of a story told also by Marie de France in the twelfth century (*Lai de Lanval*). Like *Tristan* and *Guy of Warwick*, this seems to have been one of the perennially favorite stories of the late Middle Ages, for it comes down to us in a number of different versions, written at different times and in different places. It is an Arthurian piece, telling of an impoverished knight of the Round Table who encounters a fairy lover. She arranges for him to become rich and powerful in his own world (that is, in Arthur's court) on the condition that he never reveal her existence. When the knight later incurs the displeasure of Guenevere by repulsing her offer of love, she angers him into betraying his secret. Then she falsely tells Arthur that Launfal has made approaches to her, and the hero is on the point of being executed or exiled when his fairy lady relents and carries him off to her own land, never to be seen again by human eyes. In addition to

Chestre's poem, there was another Middle English version that comes down in three manuscripts of the sixteenth and seventeenth centuries, variously titled *Sir Landeval*, *Sir Lambewell*, and *Sir Lamwell* (all referred to here as *Sir Landeval*). These clearly derive from the same ultimate source as *Sir Launfal* but lack most of its elaboration and may have been influenced at some point by Marie's version. The date of composition of the prototype *Sir Landeval*, as of *Sir Launfal*, may have been in the early fourteenth century.

Another early fourteenth-century work is the unusual and skillfully written romance of *Sir Orfeo*, which like *Sir Launfal* has been placed by scholars in the category of Breton lays, a genre which has its origins in the short romances of Marie de France. As the names of its major characters and its plot show, *Sir Orfeo* ultimately derives from the classical legend of Orpheus and Eurydice, but the story has been greatly modified by additions from Celtic mythology and from romance tradition. The time, place, and manner in which this combination of classical and Celtic tradition took place cannot be ascertained since the romance has no direct antecedents that are extant. The story tells of Sir Orfeo, a king famous for his harping, whose wife is mysteriously carried off one day. Orfeo leaves his kingdom and sets out to seek her, eventually finding her in a place reminiscent of both fairyland and the classical land of the dead. He wins her back, returns with her, and, after testing the faithfulness of the regent whom he has left in charge of his kingdom, resumes his rule. The romance defies categories and, although placed here with the other fairy-princess stories to which it bears important resemblances, will be considered separately from the others.

Libeaus Desconus is another Arthurian romance, the story of an illegitmate son of Gawain who does not even know his own name and goes instead by the title of "the Fair Unknown." Having made his way to Arthur's court, he undertakes the task of aiding a distressed lady and, after a series of rather conventional romance adventures, finds her, transformed into the shape of a dragon. When he kisses her, she regains her human form, and soon afterward they are married. This early fourteenth-century poem is a retelling of roughly the first half of the French romance *Le Bel Inconnu*, written about 1190 by Renaut de Beaujeu. The English poem may have been composed by Thomas Chestre.[1] The six manuscripts of the English version and Chaucer's reference to it in *Sir Thopas* suggest that the romance was fairly well known.

A story which was certainly popular in the Middle Ages but which in more recent times has not received the attention it deserves is that of *Partonope of Blois*. This is an extended romance, similar to *Ipomedon* and *Guy of Warwick* in its plot but using the fairy-princess motif in the opening section, which closely parallels the beginning of the Launfal story. Partonope is nephew to the king of France and heir to Anjou and Blois; his lady is a princess of Byzantium who has learned magical powers and arranges for Partonope to be brought to her on a ship guided by unseen hands. After a long and erotic love scene, the hero violates the condition placed upon him by his lady, and she loses her supernatural powers. The romance then becomes a conventional story of Partonope battling Saracen invaders and his lady battling her conscience before she finally agrees to marry him. Among the interesting features of this romance are a number of personal and ironic side comments by the author, in a Chaucerian vein, interspersed throughout the poem. The original French version of this romance was twice translated into Middle English during the fifteenth century. One Middle English version follows the original closely, with only a few minor deletions and some added commentary by the author; the other now exists only in a 300-line fragment.

The earliest extant version of *Eger and Grime* was composed in Scotland in the middle of the fifteenth century. Another, longer version exists in several prints of the seventeenth and eighteenth centuries. Opinion is divided over the relationship of the two versions and the origins of the story. However, the names of the two heroes seem to come from Scandinavian mythology, and there is some reason to believe that an Old French intermediary existed between the original mythic story and the extant Scottish poem. In this romance the lady is not a fairy but rather the prisoner of a supernaturally powerful knight; her powers are simply curative, like those of the women in the Tristan story. Eger first seeks her out in the fairyland abode and is defeated by the knight; then Grime, masquerading as his sworn brother Eger, travels to her land, kills the knight, and wins the lady for himself. At the same time, through Grime's efforts, Eger is able to win his lady in his own world. The story thus combines a variant of the fairy-princess motif with the kind of identity substitution found in *Amis and Amiloun*.

Finally, just at the end of the fifteenth century, there is the very odd *Romans of Partenay*. This is an episodic account of the founding of the royal family of Parthenay and Lusignan (in Poitou). The story was originally composed in French prose about 1387 by Jean d'Arras, with the title *Mélusine*. This was converted into French verse by a man named La Couldrette about 1400, and about 1500 two English translations were made, one in prose and one in verse. The verse *Partenay* was based on La Couldrette. Because it is so late, because it represents a development from prose to verse (the reverse of the normal development), and because it does not seem to have been either popular, influential, or typical, the *Romans of Partenay* is a poor example of the popular verse romance. Nevertheless it does have some features that provide interesting comparisons to the other fairy romances. The opening episodes follow the conventions of this romance group very closely: a young knight, Raymond, accidentally kills his adoptive father, an earl, while on a boar hunt and subsequently encounters the fairy Melusine. With her help he becomes even more powerful than his father had been. She enjoins him to "be faithful" to her, but later he violates this injunction by looking on her while she is bathing in private, and he observes that she is a serpent from the waist down. When he reveals this knowledge publicly, the two are separated forever. The later events involving Raymond and Melusine are interwoven with the stories of their nine sons. While interesting in themselves, these minor stories do not directly concern us here. The romance concludes with two stories involving Melusine's fairy sisters and a genealogy of the royal house of Parthenay, supposedly descended from Melusine and Raymond.

THE HEROES' FAILINGS

Lanval, in Marie de France's telling of the best-known fairy story in medieval romance, lives amidst the signs of opulence and power, but he himself does not fully partake of these. King Arthur, who bestows rich gifts on all the other knights of the Round Table, neglects Lanval, and the hero, whose patrimony lies in a far-off land and who is too proud to seek his rightful rewards, has spent all his money. Arthur's treatment of Lanval and the hero's resulting poverty are undeserved, for he is handsome, brave, and beloved by the court; he has spent himself into penury, but such expense, to a medieval audience, is a virtue rather than a fault, an example of

Christian charity and of the generosity expected of a medieval nobleman and exemplified in Arthur's treatment of the rest of his court. It becomes a problem for Lanval only because his own rightful source of income, the generosity of Arthur, has been cut off. Yet Arthur is not held up to blame; to Marie, the fault lies in Lanval's circumstances and in the nature of things.

Thomas Chestre is more specific. His hero dwells "wythe joye and greet solas" among the comfortable and the famous: Perceval, Gawain, Gaheries, Agravayne, Lancelot, Kay, Ywain. Arthur shows favor toward Launfal, making him king's steward, until the time of the royal marriage with Guenevere. But Launfal does not like Guenevere because she has a reputation for taking "lemannys unther here lord," and the queen subsequently cuts off the flow of gifts to Launfal, without Arthur's knowledge. Launfal's dislike of Guenevere is part of his duty toward his sovereign, and the opposite of duty, as we are told later, would be treason.

Launfal is thus an example of a knight who, through strict adherence to the obligations of his rank, deprives himself of the outward symbols of rank as well as the ability to perform further his obligations. He has been alienated by the very system he sought to serve. Chestre emphasizes the injustice through the addition of an incident not found in the other versions: Launfal seeks lodging with the mayor of Carleon who had formerly been his "servant" but who now, seeing the hero's poverty, sends him out to sleep in the orchard. The end result, in all the versions, is that Launfal is sent forth in disfavor and isolation, lacking even the simplest accoutrements of a knight ("withoute knave other squyer").

Libeaus Desconus and Raymond are, like Marie's Lanval, noblemen alienated in some degree from their patrimony. Libeaus Desconus, who does not even know his real name (Gingelain), is the bastard son of Sir Gawain, raised secretly by his mother in the forest: "gentyll of body and of face bryght, / Bastard though that he were." He is so "nyse" ('innocent, foolish') that he never asks his real name, and his mother calls him Bewfys ('beautiful of face'), a name that is later supplanted by the title "the Fayre Un-knowe," given to him in Arthur's court. His deeds show him to be a descendant of Gawain: at one point an opponent declares that only one of Gawain's kin could have fought as well as the hero has, and later we find that only Gawain or a relative of his could have released the enchanted lady from the charm placed upon her, as

Libeaus Desconus did. His only faults are his youth and a lack of gentility, the latter of which obviously derives from his nurture in the wild and which turns out to be a useful, even a requisite trait in a knight.

Raymond also is a product of the wild. He is the youngest son, by birth, of the Earl of the Forest (in the great forest of Coulombiers) but adopted by the highly educated Earl Amery of Poitiers because his natural father had so many children and so little money. Raymond is fair, sweet, gentle, courteous, intelligent, and beloved of his foster father. He kills Amery in a hunting accident, but the author describes the accident so carefully (in order to absolve Raymond of full blame) that it is not until later when Raymond himself declares his responsibility, contemplates suicide, and eventually ends by covering up the death (on the advice of Melusine) that the reader concludes that Raymond's sword and not the wild boar caused the death. The killing is an act of savagery, appropriate to Raymond's background and the setting in which it occurs (the forest); furthermore, it is a means of advancement for the hero, for, according to a prophecy observed in the stars by Amery just before his death, any man who shall slay his sovereign in that hour will become a greater lord and more powerful than any of his kin. Nevertheless, the author takes pains to shift responsibility away from the hero although he has Raymond continue to feel guilty for the act. After the opening sequences of both romances, the heroes are left alone in the forest, Raymond to encounter Melusine, and Libeaus Desconus to travel to Arthur's court in the armor of a knight whom he has found slain in the woods.

All three of the heroes thus confront their major adventures in borrowed identities. This is even more clearly the case in *Eger and Grime*, where the two heroes are alter egos of one another. Eger is a poor knight, owning no property because his elder brother has inherited the father's lands. He falls in love with an earl's daughter who, somewhat like Guy of Warwick's Felice, refuses to take any husband except one who wins all his battles. Eger sets out to win "worshippe" but is overcome by the fairy knight Sir Gray-steel and has to return in shame. By his own assessment and that of others, he has "lost his manhood" (l. 84). Such a loss is also symbolically conveyed by the fact that Sir Gray-steel has cut off the defeated Eger's little finger and by the phallic imagery in the description of Eger's return:

His kniffe was forth; his sheath was gone;
His scaberd by his thigh was done (ll. 55–56).

Naturally, his lady will not have him, and in fact at the end of the
romance, after Gray-steel has been defeated and all other conflicts
resolved, he wins her only by first spurning her and thus reassert-
ing his masculinity. The character of Eger corresponds to the
alienated-knight stage of the other heroes. As in their cases, the
failure that causes his alienation is a small one and not his fault, for
Gray-steel himself confesses that Eger would have been the better
man "and he had beene weaponed as well as I" (l. 1039). But Eger
cannot make up for his failure; instead Grime, "a courteous
knight," takes his sworn-brother's place, using the sword Egeking,
which he has obtained from Eger's uncle. He defeats Sir Gray-steel
and wins the captive lady, then allows Eger to take *his* place and
ride back as if victorious. Grime remains with the lady from the
fairy world, and Eger marries his lady in his own world.

   The failings of Partonope are more difficult to pinpoint. While
out hunting, Partonope, the nephew and favorite of King Clovis of
France, loses the king and is left isolated in the forest. Then he is
brought to the land of his enchanted lady and lives with her for a
period of time before returning to France to find that Clovis and his
own father (not elsewhere mentioned) have both died. Behind these
events obviously lurks a patricide story like that in the *Romans of
Partenay*, but it has here been entirely rationalized away. Except for
the fact that he apparently stands to inherit a kingdom to which he
is not entitled by birth, Partonope has no observable failing—until
he encounters his princess. He does undergo a period of weakness
before coming to the enchanted kingdom—he is frightened, hun-
gry, thirsty, and fatigued—but this is entirely the result of being
lost in a wilderness that provides none of the amenities of civiliza-
tion. Partonope's personal failings come later when he is faced with
the task of finding a satisfactory accommodation between the fairy
world and his own. But that is true of the other heroes as well.
Partonope does nothing to bring his original troubles upon himself,
and perhaps that is his failing. Perhaps we are to see him as less a
man for setting forth with no task, on no quest. Certainly he suffers
as much as the others, and he goes through a period of isolation
much more intense.

   Although the heroes' original problems are various, certain patterns emerge from them, and all seem ultimately to relate to the question of manhood. As has already been indicated, lack of the qualities traditionally associated with a man seems to be the most important failing of Eger and Partonope. Libeaus Desconus is beautiful and "nyse," abandoned by his father and raised by his mother. Launfal's sensitivities concerning his manhood are very obvious, for his troubles begin in earnest when he repulses the advances of Guenevere: she accuses him of having no interest in women. Wounded, he blurts out the existence of his fairy love, thus violating his promise, losing his lady, and by consequence placing his own life in jeopardy. But an even clearer indication that manhood is the central problem comes from the fact that all the heroes with the exception of Eger and Grime find a solution first in concupiscence (not merely in lovers' promises or in marriage) and thereafter in military proofs of prowess (with the exception of Raymond, whose sons do the fighting). As might be expected, the solutions tend to create further problems of their own, especially when the proof of manhood takes the classic form of patricide—indirectly, when Raymond kills his foster father and Partonope loses his, or symbolically, when Eger fights with the father figure Sir Gray-steel and loses his little finger.[2]

In the romances, manhood requires more than sexual potency and physical mastery; it depends on self-sufficiency, which in turn requires both wealth and rank (birth). For this reason poverty becomes the major outward sign of Launfal's failings and an incidental sign of Eger's. So also alienation from patrimony is a problem for all the heroes. The rigid hierarchical society of the late Middle Ages created a situation in which wealth, rank, birth, power, fame, physical and sexual maturity seemed all fused into a single entity, lack of which meant continual frustration. For many members of the minor nobility or near-nobility, the only cure for this frustration must have lain in fantasy. No other group of romances provided this fantasy as effectively or as directly as the fairy romances.

THE REWARDS OF FAIRYLAND

Alone, outcast, in sorrow or fear, the hero suddenly finds himself in contact with the other world, the world of fairie. The transitions are sometimes subtle, sometimes surprising, often imaginatively handled, but there are certain conventional markers of fairyland's boundary that stand as clues to the reader. The commonest type of boundary marker is water: a river *(Lanval, Landeval, Eger and Grime)*, a sea *(Partonope, Eger and Grime)*, or a fountain *(Partenay)*; other markers may include a rock *(Orfeo)*, a gate *(Libeaus Desconus)*, or a tree under which the traveler rests *(Launfal, Orfeo)*.[3] Other, less traditional signs are often present. In *Lanval*, the hero's horse acts fearful; the weather is sometimes hot (all the versions of the Launfal story and *Sir Orfeo*), or fires are found burning brightly *(Partonope, Libeaus Desconus)*. In *Lanval, Partonope*, and *Orfeo*, a meadow or orchard is associated with the borderland, and in the Launfal stories and *Partenay*, the first contact with fairyland is through a group of two or three richly dressed ladies. Red and gold seem to be colors traditionally associated with the fairy kingdom *(Eger and Grime, Orfeo*, and *Libeaus Desconus*—where the hero dresses in red and gold to enter the enchanted city). And there may be unusual activities or circumstances associated with the magic land: Libeaus Desconus sees people gathering up and saving the wastes thrown out from the city of Synadon, and he and Partonope are both surprised to discover themselves in a castle that is "uninhabited" but in which the activities of life are still going on.

Crossing the borderland means passing from a wilderness state into one of civilization and even luxury. As a general rule, the travelers are in a huge forest filled with wild animals before entering a richly adorned and provided castle or city, which is the fairy kingdom. The fairy maidens who first greet Launfal bring him a basin and towel, trappings of the refined life of court and city, and conduct him to the lady, reclining in a rich bed in an elegant pavilion. Partonope, Libeaus Desconus, Eger, and Orfeo come upon magnificent cities or castles with many towers, and in *Partonope* and *Libeaus Desconus* the castles are scenes of elaborate service of the sort offered in the richest of real European courts. In the *Romans of Partenay* no city awaits the hero, but such cities are later constructed by Melusine, using her magic powers.

In the type of story represented by *Launfal* and *Partonope*, the hero encounters his princess, or her emissaries, as soon as he has entered the enchanted land; in another type, represented by *Libeaus Desconus* and *Eger and Grime*, he must first defeat a superhuman opponent before finding, and winning, the lady. Of these, the first pattern seems much more interesting since the hero's reward is not won in the way normal to the medieval romance. Instead, the cause of the reward seems to be the need for it: the heroes do not even have to ask.

Probably because the heroes' failings are associated with manhood and sexual potency, their rewards are openly sexual in nature, making this the only group of romances to contain any direct eroticism (although it is true that in *Eger and Grime*, where loss of manhood is Eger's clearly stated failing, the sexual aspect of the reward is played down). When Launfal encounters his fairy maiden, she is reclining half naked on a luxurious bed (*Launfal*, ll. 283–90; *Landeval*, ll. 97–106). In Marie's rather tame version, the lovers while away the day in kisses and embraces, and the fairy lady promises that Lanval may see her at his pleasure: he need only wish for her. In the other versions they undress and make love (see *Sir Lambewell*, ll. 173–83, for example), but even there the greatest excitement comes from the circumstances. The woman appears coy and resistant, but in fact she has arranged the encounter and makes the advances.[4] She places herself completely at his will, now and in the future. Her one stipulation, that he tell no one of her existence, only makes clear that the episode is a male fantasy, deriving directly from his feelings of need and failure. The scene with the enchanted lady in *Libeaus Desconus* offers a similar fantasy: once the hero has vanquished the enchanted knights Yrayn and Maboun, she appears to him in a threatening form, as a dragon ("worme") with a woman's face and a shining body. As soon as she has kissed the fearful hero, she changes into a beautiful naked lady, thanks him for killing her foe, and offers herself to him in marriage. It is his virtue that has effected the metamorphosis because she can be released from the charm only by kissing Gawain or one of his kin.

But the lady offers the hero more than sexual gratification. To recompense him for his combined impotence, weakness, and poverty, she grants him wealth, land, power, fame, ease—all the blessings of the cultivated life of the medieval nobility. Such rewards are implied in the description of the lady's pavilion in *Launfal* (ll. 265–82), which, along with other descriptions of the lady's attire and entourage, combines images of comfort (a pavilion), riches (enameled gold and a jewel), lordship (her father's power), and empire (symbolized by an eagle and implied by the comparisons to Alexander and Arthur). Later these promises are made explicit, as the lady gives Launfal a never-empty purse (described as a sex-wealth image: ll. 319–24) and a horse, a squire, and a pennon, all of which will assure him of success in battle. With these provisions,

Launfal regains his place at court and becomes famous. He also becomes attractive to Guenevere.

The other enchanted ladies bring their lovers similar rewards. Released from the charm, Libeaus Desconus's lady grants him fifty-five castles along with her hand in marriage. He also, in a sense, recovers his birthright, by being revealed as the son of Gawain. Partonope, heir by birth only to Anjou and Blois, stands to rule over the empire of Byzantium by marrying his princess, in addition to gaining the life of ease that he enjoys while with her and the military prowess that implicitly results from their union. In *Eger and Grime* the lady, named Loosepaine because "a better leeche was none certaine," possesses curative powers that are applied to both heroes. But, along with herself, the "fairest lady that was livande," she also brings to Grime an earldom (granted him by her father and confirmed with a royal feast) and gifts including two gold robes. Eger gains his lady, a fee of 100 pounds, and an "erles lande." Melusine, by means of a trick, enables Raymond to secure a large amount of land and bears him sons who greatly expand the family's power and influence.

Thus the princess provides fulfillment of all the hero's desires, physical and social, and compensation for all his shortcomings. The pattern reveals a great deal regarding the symbolism of women in the medieval romance in general and regarding the role of erotic, courtly love; it helps to explain the importance of worldly love and some of the reasons why it must be kept secret, both by the heroes and (incidentally) by the writers of romance. The desire for wealth, power, and physical love (though not necessarily the possession of these things) was sinful, and from this conflict come the feelings of guilt that occupy the attention of the middle and later sections of the fairy romances.

The best of the erotic, wish-fulfillment episodes in medieval English romance is the opening sequence in *Partonope of Blois*, and it illustrates all the features so far discussed. The whole passage is pervaded by feelings of mystery, anxiety, and outright fear. These sensations are only partly counteracted by the narrative, which progressively describes the secret granting of a series of unspoken wishes. Lost, cold, and hungry, Partonope emerges from a forest and finds an unoccupied ship, on which he falls asleep. Then the sails miraculously unfold, and the ship transports Partonope to a rich and marvelous town, surrounded by fertile land and nestled against an enormous harbor, large enough for 10,000 ships. Inside the royal palace Partonope finds great light everywhere, fine clothes laid out on every side, and a table set for a lord. Invisible hands serve him, and torches lead his way to a warm bedchamber with a richly curtained bed. When Partonope undresses and gets into the soft bed, the chamber instantly goes dark.

Partonope now hears someone coming softly across the floor: it is a young maid "of grette degre," who gets into the bed and then, discovering his presence, reluctantly allows him to stay. He is fearful, but thoughts of pleasure overcome his wits, and he attempts to touch her. She repulses him, and the two lie quietly through the night. In the morning he again reaches forth timidly and puts his arm over her. She asks him to let be but offers no resistance; he embraces her, intertwines his legs with hers, and they make love. Although, as it turns out, she has previously fallen in love with him and arranged for his arrival, she says that she would not have relented if resistance had been within her power. He promises to serve at her command, like a prisoner. In exchange for his promises never to attempt to see her and to prove himself as a knight, she entertains him for a year in the magic city, offering him all the delights he can wish or imagine, excepting only other human companionship.

This complex fantasy sequence, dreamlike in its quality, encompasses all the interrelated rewards hitherto observed to be subjects of desire in these romances. Partonope's fairy lady symbolizes self-improvement, gained first in fantasy, then in reality: this is indicated by her name (Melior), her position (she is princess of the ancient and wealthy empire of Byzantium while he is only heir to a region of France), her extensive education from which she derives her magical powers, the name of the town that she has created for him (Chief d'Oire—which seems to mean 'the main city of the road'), and the demands for accomplishment that she places upon him. The ship that carries Partonope, always sleeping, to and from Chief d'Oire symbolizes the entrance into the dream state in which all these events occur.

WILDERNESS AND CIVILIZATION

The dream world achieved by the heroes in these romances is a city or court world, fitted out with all the accoutrements of civilization. There the hero is bathed, clothed, served, and fed by fairy hands, just as the medieval nobility was cared for by its human servants. There he passes his days in hunting and his nights making love in a warm, comfortable bed. There he may be cured of his wounds or receive other benefits from science and art. There all the wealth of the world is brought together to ensure his safety and ease. By contrast, the land the hero comes from is a savage wilderness that is roamed by wild beasts constantly threatening his life and that provides no food, drink, or shelter. This is not the love forest of the Tristan story but the harsh antithesis of a world subdued by man and made fit for human habitation.

In *Libeaus Desconus*, *Partenay*, and *Partonope*, the two worlds stand in obvious contrast to one another. Libeaus Desconus is from the forest and, like the forest, is savage. His contact with the cultivated life in Arthur's court is not enough to remove the wildness from him until he comes to the magnificent palace and subdues the two "clerks" who have built it with their educated magic. In the *Romans of Partenay*, Raymond, similarly, is a forest child whose deeds are savage while he is in the wild. He lives in a kingdom whose major cities (Rochelle, Macon, *et al.*) are not yet founded and through which the great, wild forest of Coulombiers still stretches. After his marriage to Melusine, she causes the trees to be uprooted and cities to be built overnight by magical means. In the Launfal romances and in *Eger and Grime*, the contrasts are not so obvious, yet the heroes still pass through wilderness and come to a place of civilized ease. Marie's *Lai de Lanval* opens with a brief description of Arthur's (cultivated) court being driven out by the attacks of Picts and Scots to the wild land of Wales.

In light of these contrasts, the introduction of *Partonope of Blois* takes on great interest. In both the French and English versions, the poem begins with a long preface recounting the destruction of Troy and the subsequent founding of the French kingdom by Marcomiris, one of Priam's sons; then follows a brief mythical history of France, culminating in the rule of Clovis, Partonope's uncle. This might be explained as a conventional opening, following the example of such poems as the *Aeneid* and Wace's *Brut*, but it is probably more directly related to the main action of the romance than that. The whole passage seems to be an attempt to explain the difference between a successful and an unsuccessful kingdom. Priam fails as a king because he is "ferse," "felle," and hates his people; they in turn hate him and are willing to allow the Greeks to overrun the land. In addition, Priam makes Anchises, a "knave," his chief justice, and Anchises (in addition to his later betrayal of the city) ignores the nobility to take care only of his friends (ll. 113–15). This complex of political failings leads to the fall of the city, and Marcomiris, along with other sons of Priam, escapes, eventually to found his own rule in France. We are told that France was at that time wild—a situation not entirely without its attractions, for, as the author remarks, "eche man was lorde of hys owne thynge." Marcomiris builds cities and establishes good laws, but he is succeeded by his son Ludon whose rule is evil: "chorles he cheresede, and no-thynge jentyle." Ludon's son is the good king Clovis, who is converted to Christianity, fights against the Saracens, and treats all men properly according to their rank.

The political ideas inherent in this passage seem to represent the point of view of the lower nobility. Rank and its privileges are held to be an undebatable, unqualified right, yet at the same time the doctrine of the king as servant to the people is maintained. In other words, the established hierarchy is a good thing as long as it keeps the lower classes in their place, but when kings can do as they please, something has gone wrong with the system. It is good for each man to be lord of his own, unless this applies to kings and churls. Readers with such attitudes were probably the main audience for the other fairy romances as well.

The reason for the lower nobility's special interest in the court and civilization is that it was the group that was protected by these institutions and that most benefited from them. Yet it was not the one that created them and thus might well think of the cities and palaces as having come into existence by magical, superhuman means. The city and its ways were necessary to the continuation of the lower nobility's perquisites; the builders and maintainers of the city, while they were people with whom the audience desired to associate itself, were also somewhat alien—objects of suspicion and dread. They knew more and could do more, so perhaps they were supernatural. At the same time, these makers and managers could affect the audience in undesirable as well as desirable ways. The civilization, once created, was beneficial, but it could fail and thus bring hardship to those who depended upon it. Furthermore, the civilization made demands upon its members, and these demands, when inadequately fulfilled, implied failure in the individuals. To this, the fantasy solution was alliance with the makers and, ultimately, mastery of the civilization itself, but this process seemed beyond accomplishment by practical methods. It was necessary both to defeat and succumb to the makers. By a natural extension of the family-romance myth, this could be achieved by rejecting (slaying) the civilization emblemized as father and uniting oneself with it as emblemized by the mother-lover. Thus the illogical and impossible quest for a society that serves but does not master becomes simply a quest for a satisfactory image of society. All the adverse factors having been embodied in the abstract or father image, societal benefits can be concentrated and isolated in the figure of the fairy lover who brings riches and power.

FAIRIES AND CHRISTIAN BELIEF

An additional problem in these romances involves the true nature of the fairy princess from the Christian point of view. Because of their pagan origins and because they did not fit into the Christian hierarchical world view, fairies could most easily be explained as manifestations of devils.[5] Other explanations were possible, but for the medieval reader the suspicion that fairies were devils must always have been present. Partonope constantly worries over this possibility until his mind is set at rest by the lady herself. Marie's Lanval "fears" that his lady may be a fairy, and the half-woman, half-dragon form of the women in *Libeaus Desconus* and *Partenay* is more than a hint of their association with Satan.

The problem in fact has causes much deeper than the mythical origins of fairies. The delights experienced by the hero, taking place as they do in another world, are clearly suggestive of a heavenly paradise, but they are just as clearly worldly delights. By a commonplace of medieval tradition, such delights are the temptations of the devil. In the romance, worldly delight is also a distraction from the duties of a knight: Partonope, like Chrétien's Erec, eventually regrets that his pleasure is keeping him from the life to which he is committed. Melusine is of course a devil in reality. This is indicated by the fact that she bears sons all of whom carry some significant defect: Uriens has one red eye and one gray eye, Oede has a red shining face, Guy has one eye lower than the other, and so forth. Another indication is her disappearance every Saturday, during which time she is a serpent from the waist down. And when her secret is revealed, she becomes completely and at all times a serpent. Even when the romance writers try to Christianize their heroines, suspicions about them lurk in the background and tend to cloud the stories' resolutions, for the fact is that these romances do, by medieval Christian standards, seek their consolation in worldliness. The authors' assurances are just superficial attempts to disarm criticism.

The real accommodation with Christian conscience is reached either by ignoring the suspicions, as in the Launfal stories (which reject them as false) and *Partenay* (which accepts them as true), or by rationalization of the fairy lady into a helpful human woman, as in *Eger and Grime*. *Partonope* eventually has the supernatural Melior lose her magic powers and become a conventional romance heroine. *Libeaus Desconus* combines ignoring the problem with the kind of character-splitting technique that we have seen in *Tristan*, *Amis and Amiloun*, and many other romances. Before the climactic scene in Synadon when Libeaus Desconus is finally united with his lady, he wins the right to live with another lady, called La Dame Amoure, who is a beautiful but unchaste sorceress, living in the Ile d'Or. She receives him, removes his clothing and dresses him in rich cloth, entertains him with minstrelsy, and gives him her love—the usual acts of the fairy lady. But she is a betrayer and a distraction from his mission (see ll. 1491–95). He is soon admonished for his weakness and proceeds with the task of freeing the lady of Synadon, who will offer him the legitimate, nonsatanic delights of marriage.

REVELATIONS AND RESOLUTIONS

In the less rationalized form of the fairy-princess story, the lady places a condition on the continuation of her services to the hero. Launfal's mistress forbids him to tell anyone of her existence on pain of separation and withdrawal of favors. Melior tells Partonope that if he attempts to see her as she comes to him in the darkened bedchamber he will die and she will lose her good name. Melusine warns Raymond to "be faithful," a condition that is violated when he sees that she is half a serpent on Saturdays and then tells others about it. The common element in these injunctions is that they forbid public revelation and scrutiny. The paradise offered by the fairy lady is a dream world, a land of the imagination, and attempts to investigate it or to make it known to others result in its loss. *The Romans of Partenay*, in which Raymond permanently loses Melusine as a result of his betrayal, may represent the original form of the legend, except that it lacks one element found in both the Launfal story and *Partonope of Blois*. Launfal is lured into betraying his promise through the efforts of the mother figure Guenevere, who taunts him with his apparent lack of interest in women; Partonope's mother, with the help of the bishop of Paris (who also preaches to the hero a sermon against earthly love), presents her son with a magic lantern and convinces him that he should use it to see his love. He does, and "alle naked ther had he the syghte / Off the feyreste shape creature / That ever was formed thorowe nature." Melior's beauty is an indication that she is not a devil-enchantress as had been feared, but Partonope's betrayal has broken the spell. The lantern's revelation leads directly to further information about Melior—her heritage, her history, etcetera—but it dispels the magic fantasy and she becomes a mere woman, without special powers. In the light she looks like an ordinary mistress, and so her prophecy that she would lose her good name comes true (although Partonope does not die). In an earlier form of the legend, the forbidden revelation may have concealed the information that the fairy lover and the mother were the same; in the romances it merely maintains the necessary separation of the dream world from the real world.

The revelation brings with it suffering. For Raymond it means pain and decline throughout the kingdom; for Launfal it leads to disfavor in the court (again) and the threat of death or exile; for Partonope it initiates a period of insanity and savagery in the forest (the conventional "wildman" phase of medieval romances). All represent a reversion from the civilized state of the earthly paradise. Salvation comes about through the intervention of a woman, as Launfal's mistress pities him and relents or as Partonope is discovered in the forest by Urake, Melior's sister, who nurses him back to health and brings about a reunion between the hero and the heroine.

All of the fairy romances insist on the inviolability of the separation between the two worlds. Launfal's mistress comes to him in a dream, experienced only by him. As long as he keeps the dream secret, he enjoys its benefits, but Guenevere, in effect, challenges the reality of the dream. Launfal responds by asserting that his lady is not only real but better than Guenevere—that is, better than the reality that is compromised by the judgments of the world. This is partly a false assertion, for the fairy lady is not real. Launfal consequently loses his dream. The restoration of it, out of pity for the now hopeless hero, comes about in a magnificent display of beauty and wealth, as the fairy lady's train appears in Arthur's court, followed by the lady herself. This is a reassertion of the dream, and it is proved better than reality but not more real, for Launfal must now abandon his own world and stay forever in fairyland.

The Romans of Partenay keeps the worlds separate by parting Raymond and Melusine, in a scene heavy with pathos. In *Partonope of Blois*, the hero's betrayal of trust destroys the fairy world entirely, supplanting it with a more ordinary romance world in which Partonope must win his lady all over again. Neither *Eger and Grime* nor *Libeaus Desconus* has a true fairy world to begin with; in both, the conventional romance land supplants it from the start. Yet Libeaus Desconus must still reject La Dame Amoure before he can find his lady of Synadon, and the two heroes of *Eger and Grime* end up marrying their separate ladies in separate kingdoms. Even when the original story has been rationalized to these degrees, it seems, contact between the two worlds must be avoided. The dreams remain dreams.

Such solutions are unsatisfactory in a practical sense, and the romances bear evidence of this fact in their imperfect endings. The romances that reject the fairy world have the more successful resolutions, but even in these there are difficulties. Eger and Grime both have their ladies and their earldoms, but Eger still bears the mark of his damaged manhood and the secret shame of not having recouped his losses through his own efforts. Partonope's Melior is still heir to Byzantium but no longer has her magic powers. The English *Libeaus Desconus* ends with Yrayne, one of the clerks who had imprisoned the lady, still at large and the hero worried about future efforts of Yrayne's sorcery; Renaut's version ends even more inconclusively when, after a second visit to La Dame d'Amore and a reunion with his transformed princess, the hero seems likely to return to the Ile d'Or once again. In all these, as in the Launfal and Melusine stories where the main characters are removed to fairyland at the end, the open-ended resolutions signal the potential return of the problems, both personal and societal, with which the romances began.

THE ABDUCTED QUEEN

Sir Orfeo is one of the most interesting of the Middle English romances, as a moderately large body of scholarship on it attests.

Among the reasons for the interest in it are its literary associations, its origins, its departures from standard romance conventions, and the obscurity of its meaning. It is a Breton lay, one of a group that contains some of the most entertaining of the English romances (including *Sir Launfal* and Chaucer's *Franklin's Tale*). Breton lays have proved puzzling to scholars because, although these poems contain announcements that they are Breton lays, it is hard to see precisely what this indicates or why they are categorized in this way. *Sir Orfeo*, although its fairyland atmosphere suggests Celtic and hence perhaps Breton backgrounds, derives its story from classical literature. Its prologue in the Harley and Ashmole manuscripts, however, tells how these poems originated in the oral tradition of Brittany and in general terms outlines their subject matter.[6] The question of the poem's classical and medieval antecedents is just as puzzling. Even without the names of characters and places, we could see that this is a version of the Orpheus legend, but details of the plot are strangely and unaccountably altered. Orfeo is a famous harper but he is also a king. His queen is spirited away into the other world, a land ruled by a fairy king (otherwise unidentified), and Orfeo seeks and wins her back with his music. At this point, however, the romance completely parts company with the ancient legend: instead of a violated condition and the ultimate loss of the queen, we have a happy ending in which Orfeo returns to his kingdom, successfully tests the faithfulness of the steward left as regent, and has his wife and kingdom restored. Such departures from the original story seem to suggest a complicated transmission and extensive modification of the legend, but the proper names indicate that this is not the case. The reasonable conclusion seems to be that the author of *Sir Orfeo* has consciously combined the classical story with the conventional fairy romance and, in the manner of other medieval authors, attributed his creation to a fictional oral tradition.

A further cause for interest is that although it clearly belongs to the fairyland group of romances, *Sir Orfeo* departs as dramatically from its conventions as it does from its classical sources. The most important conventional element is the journey, central both to the Orpheus legend and to the Orfeo story, to and from the other world (fairyland). The perception of this central similarity was probably the seed from which the romance grew. The circumstances of the journey are also conventional enough, the encounter taking place in an orchard under a tree and the transportation to the other world happening by magical means. The fact that the encounter occurs first through a dream is unique among the English romances, and the 100 knights and 100 ladies who accompany the fairy king on snow-white horses are unusual although they are paralleled by the ladies who appear at the fairy borderland in other stories. The fact that no magic is required to return from the other world is again conventional. Other major similarities to the standard fairy romance are the nature of the other kingdom itself, the wilderness through which Orfeo must pass (this also is found in the Orpheus story), and the happy ending which results when the characters are united in one of the worlds.

The elements that seem to be original in *Sir Orfeo* when it is compared to the other fairy romances are, at the outset, that the hero is not only a nobleman but a reigning and married king and that he has no discernible failings. As a result, fairyland can be neither a compensation nor a fulfillment of wishes, and this is a highly significant departure from the usual pattern. Then too, it is the woman and not the man who is first transported to fairyland. In context, this constitutes the loss for which compensation is sought through Orfeo's journey. The final solution lies not in the stable attainment of a new life but in reestablishment of the original condition and relationship of Orfeo and Heurodis. Finally, and this is surprising when compared not only to other fairy romances but also to all medieval romances, the ending establishes an heir to the throne who is not related by blood to the hero. Romances commonly end with descriptions of the family dynasties brought into existence by the hero, but here stability and justice of rule outweigh in importance the hero's personal contribution. Thus, in this as in other respects, *Sir Orfeo* emphasizes the reestablishment of the old rather than the creation of something new.

The established order is described for us at the beginning in the usual romance superlatives: King Orfeo is "an heighe lording," "a stalworth man and hardi"; Heurodis is "the fairest levedi . . . that might gon on bodi and bones"; Traciens is "a cité of noble defens": beautiful people in a secure city. This order is disturbed with surprising suddenness and with no clear indication of the cause. It is May, when "o-way beth winter schours," and Heurodis goes with two maidens "of priis" to enjoy the flowers and birds in an orchard. They sit down under "a fair ympe-tre," and "this fair quene" falls asleep. When she awakes after a long nap, she immediately begins to scream, scratch her face until it bleeds, and tear her "riche robe," for in her dream the fairy king has appeared and commanded her to come live with him forever. The next day she returns, as ordered, to the tree, and, despite Orfeo's seeking of counsel and 1,000 armed knights whom he arranges in a defensive barrier around her, she is snatched away.

It comes apparent that the intruder into Orfeo's happy world is death. He himself places this interpretation on it when he sees Heurodis after her dream (ll. 107–08). When the queen is gone, there is mourning for her, and Orfeo is so sorrowful "that neighe his liif was y-spent." And when he decides to follow after her, he makes provisions for the guidance of his kingdom and instructs his barons to call a parliament and choose a new king when they hear that he is dead (ll. 215–17). Subsequently, when Orfeo discovers his wife again at the fairy court, he sees her surrounded with images of death in life: wounded men, drowned men, men without heads or arms (ll. 387–404).

Although the fairy kingdom represents death, it is not an unpleasant state of being. Heurodis, terrified at her dream and at the prospect of separation from her husband, says that the fairy knights appear "fair" to her. The company are all on snow-white steeds, dressed in clothing "as white as milke," and the fairy king wears a crown made of precious stones shining as brightly as the sun. Before commanding her to come with him the next day, the king shows her his kingdom and palace with its rivers, forests, and rich steeds, promising comforts that contrast with the king's threat that she will be torn limb from limb if she does not go with him. When Orfeo arrives in the fairy kingdom, he too finds it a beautiful place and thinks that it must be "the proude court of Paradis." Fairyland is indeed, in this poem, an image of death as medieval man saw it, combining the terrors of bodily harm and separation with the promised joys of the other world, which is here seen as a court and kingdom like that left behind by Orfeo, yet much more magnificent. Except for the added richness and the images of pain and death seen there by Orfeo, the correspondence between the fairy king's court and worldly courts is exact: there is a gate with its porter, a hall in which the king and queen are enthroned, and a welcome to traveling minstrels. Through their symbolic death, Orfeo and Heurodis (who is found here asleep under her ympe-tree) have only exchanged one court for another, richer one, but nonetheless both are eager to return to their own.

The problems associated with the journey to fairyland are also problems associated with death. Primary among them are isolation, loneliness, and separation from loved ones, and this is the part of the experience that most affects Orfeo and his queen. Combined with all this is the helplessness of the situation: "ther was non amendement." But the romance also takes a broader, less personal view, recognizing the political effects of death in the problem of succession. The fact that Orfeo has no children, though it is never mentioned, makes it necessary for him to provide a new ruler when he leaves. A temporary solution is provided in his appointment of the steward as regent and his command to call a parliament when he is dead; the permanent solution comes later, after Orfeo returns in disguise from fairyland, tests the sentiments of the steward (by claiming that King Orfeo is dead), finds him faithful, and there-upon designates him successor to the throne.

Finally, there is the problem of death as leveler. With the disap-pearance of Heurodis and Orfeo's decision to seek her, the hero puts aside his royal robes and takes on a sclavin, a pilgrim's garb, and goes barefoot out of the castle gate into the wilderness, where for ten years he suffers the hardships of the poor (the wild-man phase). The contrast between this life and Orfeo's former life in court is clearly etched: he lives "in gret malais" because he has exchanged his robes, bed, and castle for rivers, forests, and woods (ll. 239–56). It is to be noted that rivers, forests, and woods are considered benevolent as long as they are part of the royal estate and associated with the castle; outside of the royal domain all is hostile wilderness, within which the poor must struggle for exis-tence and from which the nobility is protected by the court and civilization. The orchard and the ympe-tree, though part of the civilized world, are enough a part of the natural world to allow entrance to the fairy king, whose advent forces Orfeo to confront all those things against which the court protects: loneliness, poverty, hardship, nature, death. From a king skilled in harping, Orfeo is reduced to a poor minstrel (a state with which the author of the romance would naturally sympathize), and it is in this role that he comes to the greater court of the other world, begs entrance at the gate, and attempts to win back his wife. Once she is won, Orfeo becomes a suppliant again to his own court, still traveling as "a minstrel of pouer liif" and taking his lodging with "a beggar, y-bilt ful narwe." As such, he tests the faithfulness of the steward, and part of the test is to see whether the steward will act kindly toward one who seems rough and impoverished. He does, and the threats of the world outside the court are overcome.

The means by which these threats are overcome is ultimately courtliness itself. Foremost among the courtly abilities that enable Orfeo to win back his wife and kingdom is his skill on the harp, which in a number of other prominent medieval romances, including the *Romance of Horn, Tristan*, and *Le Bone Florence of Rome*, serves as evidence of the hero's innate nobility and courtly accomplishment. As in the classical legend, Orfeo is able to tame the wild beasts of the forest with his harping, and he plays so well in the other-world court that the king promises to grant any request that Orfeo wishes to make. In the Middle English poem, the harp also becomes the means by which Orfeo identifies himself to the steward at the end. In fact, the harp gains entrance for Orfeo to both courts, and by contrast it is his rough and wild appearance that brings suspicion on him in both places. Curiously, this appearance is the only reason given by the fairy king for refusing Orfeo's request to have Heurodis returned. The objection is quickly overcome when Orfeo reminds the king of his own courtly obligation to honor his word. Throughout this scene, the hero's speech is painstakingly polite and formal, in contrast to the king's more blunt and direct addresses. In the concluding scene, Orfeo again exhibits carefully polite speech and appeals to the steward's courtly virtues, including pity toward the poor and faithfulness to his superiors and to his sworn word.

The appreciation that this romance shows for the benefits of the courtly, civilized world and the concern over that world's fragility ally the poem closely with the other romances of this group. But *Sir Orfeo* avoids the wish-fulfillment aspects found in most of the fairy romances and shows a greater sophistication regarding the personal and political values of courtly civilization. In addition, the author is willing to confront the problem of death. The confrontation, it is true, is incomplete. The poem's conclusion manages a kind of solution to death as a political fact but evades the more difficult personal problem by invoking the happily-ever-after formula. Still, the author does probe beyond superficial social concerns, and he does not imply that courtliness can overcome death, a form of evasion that one might expect to find in popular literature. Careful adherence to civilized behavior and courtly formalities can serve as protection against the surrounding wilderness, real and spiritual, and it can help to allay the fear of death. Orfeo and his queen do die at the end, however, leaving the steward to rule in their place, and final resolutions are left to Christian faith.

The fairyland stories, with their sympathetic heroes, their emphasis on human love, and their imaginative use of the supernatural, are among the most attractive of medieval romances for modern readers. But while these tales were entertaining readers of the late Middle Ages, other new types were coming into existence and becoming at least as popular. Perhaps the most popular among medieval audiences was a type that has little appeal today. This is a large and varied group of adventure romances, usually written in stanzas with obvious rhythms, and concentrating on social, even domestic themes.

7 *Family Affairs*

The fourteenth century saw a new type of chivalric romance appear in England, one in which sentiment and social melodrama predominated over adventure and pathos. These new romances owe obvious debts to the earlier types, especially to the superman and love romances, but are distinct in several ways. For one thing, they are usually much shorter (1,000 or 2,000 lines) than those of the previous century—in keeping with a general tendency toward shorter verse narratives during this period—and the favored verse form is the tail-rime stanza. (Appearing first in some late thirteenth-century romances, tail rime, with its jingling and often monotonous rhythms, quickly supplanted the octosyllabic couplet as the commonest verse form for popular stories in England before apparently falling out of favor in the fifteenth century.) Most of the new romances may have been originally composed in Middle English. Although the group as a whole derives its plots from a body of folk legends with representatives throughout Europe, only two of them, *Octavian* and *Chevalere Assigne*, have identifiable French sources. A large number of these romances come down to us in dialects of the Midlands, especially the east and north Midlands. This may mean that the new romances found their most receptive audience there, or it may mean that they were popular in London and the other growing cities of England where the north and east Midland dialects were gradually gaining dominance.

The nature of the new romances suggests an audience with less refined tastes and less leisure time than the audiences of the exile, superman, and love romances. One thinks immediately of the increasingly literate middle classes, but what we see may only be evidence of a broader audience for all literature in English, as the courts and their literature became gradually less isolated from the rest of society toward the end of the Middle Ages. The sentimental and domestic nature of these romances might lead to the guess that they were written predominantly for women. Women are fre-

quently the central characters, and even when a man is the center of
attention his exploits are carried on in service to a woman. The
problems dealt with are usually marital and familial, and the virtues
promoted are domestic ones, including especially a conventional
religious piety for which the fourteenth-century romances are nota-
ble. Correspondingly, politics and military virtues are downplayed
or conspicuously absent. The heroes do engage in battles, but they
are either perfunctory ones or else they are narrated in details so
gruesome as to convey an antipathy toward all warfare, even the
virtuous warfare of the hero.

The central concern in the typical fourteenth-century romance
seems to be with the family. Whereas earlier romances present
patterns of self-realization through social climbing and the winning
of kingdoms or else concentrate on lovers struggling to find hap-
piness in a hostile world, the new romances tend to center about
disrupted family or domestic situations and the trials that ensue
until the family unit can be reunited. Tendencies in this direction
may be seen in the earlier romances of *Tristan* and *Partonope of Blois*
and in the later *Romans of Partenay* (which could actually be con-
sidered a domestic romance), but in all these the ultimate aim is the
winning of kingdom or lady, and that is clearly secondary in the
typical domestic romance. Domestic romances begin with happy
marriages, not with well-ruled kingdoms; the fact that the main
characters are emperors, princesses, and earls is less important than
that they are husbands and wives, fathers and daughters. Disrup-
tion of the family comes about through violation of marital taboos,
characteristically through adultery or the suspicion of it, and the
perils that ensue involve characters who are either literally or sym-
bolically relatives and lovers. The lovers may marry and the hero
may achieve a kingdom, but the trials end only when the family is
reestablished, often in the second or third generation after warfare
and time have taken their tolls among the original group of charac-
ters. Such reunions can happen because the individual is less im-
portant than the family unit. The patterns of familial relationships
in these romances are complex, often confusing. Sex and illicit
desires are always rearing their heads.

There has been much scholarly discussion of the interrelation-
ships among these romances and of what that implies regarding
their sources.[1] The plots come ultimately from several groups of
fairy tales in which a hero or heroine passively suffers a period of

trial or misfortune. In the fairy-tale versions, the trials usually occur after a character has committed or been accused of committing a crime such as incest or infanticide. The more sophisticated medieval literary versions de-emphasize or modify this aspect of the stories and often convert them instead into allegories of Christian patience and faith, as in Chaucer's tales of Constance and Griselda. While the same kind of reshaping occurs in some of the popular romances (see chapter nine), it is not characteristic of the romances under consideration here. They are more likely to substitute jealousy or infidelity for the more primitive crimes of the fairy-tale versions and to see these marital misdemeanors as the causes of the heroes' misfortunes. Margaret Schlauch has argued that the incest, infanticide, husband killing, and animal or monster births of the fairy tales reflect actual practices or fears during an earlier period and that the original stories dealt with problems involved in the transition from a matriarchal to a patriarchal society.[2] If this is so, the romances have updated the stories by replacing the original social problems with more contemporary ones and particularly with the problem of marital infidelity, which seldom appears in the fairy tales at all.

THE FATHERLESS CHILD

Sir Degaré, seemingly the earliest of the domestic romances, also establishes one of the major patterns for the group. It could not have been composed later than about 1330 because it appears in the Auchinleck Manuscript, and it is extant in five other manuscripts as well as several early prints. This modest popularity was deserved, for it is an entertaining and well-told narrative. What makes it especially interesting, however, is its relative openness about the family connections, real and symbolic, of its characters. Although its general story pattern and many specific incidents of its plot are paralleled again and again in medieval romance, no other romance so strongly suggests comparison with the Oedipus legend and no other so clearly betrays the meanings of the involved relationships among its characters.

The story concerns a young knight, abandoned as a baby and raised first by a merchant and then by a hermit, who seeks and finds his parents and finds a wife for himself in the process. The hero's name—and he is the only character in the romance with a name—is from the French *égaré*, meaning 'strayed, abandoned, isolated,' as the author explains (ll. 253–55). The early part of the story tells of the parentage, birth, and abandonment of the child. His mother is a princess, the only child of a powerful king and a queen who died bearing her. With the queen gone, the relationship between father and daughter is suggestive of passionate love: "This maiden he loved als his lif." In fact, when Degaré is born, his mother's motive for abandoning him is fear that the king will be thought to be the father. This king has proclaimed that anyone who wants to marry his daughter must first defeat him in a tournament.

The hero's father is a fairy knight who forces his affections on the princess one day when she is lost in the forest. The circumstances of the ravishing scene are reminiscent of the fairy-princess romance, but the knight in the forest is not a wish-fulfillment object; rather, he is a substitute for the king-father, a fact which the romance underscores by having the ravishing take place on a day set aside by the king in remembrance of his queen. Under these circumstances, it is necessary for the princess to conceal her pregnancy and to send the child away when he is born. However, she leaves with him a pair of gloves and instructions that he shall love no woman unless the gloves will fit her: that woman will be his mother. She keeps with her a token for identification of the father: a sword, the tip of which has been broken off in a fight with a giant. The main purpose of this introductory section to the romance is to set up a situation in which Degaré can fight both fathers and marry his mother without seriously violating the social and religious laws of the time.

Degaré is thus placed in the conventional romance situation of seeming to know his parents (who are middle class) and his "uncle" the hermit but finding that he has an unknown "real" family. The task set before him is to seek out his true father. The search leads him through a series of battles with menacing, fatherlike opponents. The first of these is a large, filthy dragon, clearly representing the adult as seen from the child's point of view. Degaré, who despite his strength is still a child and a rustic, confronts the dragon armed only with a club, kills him, and in return is offered land, treasure, and a wife. Because the gloves fit none of the court ladies, the hero declines these offers but he does accept knighthood and abandons his club in favor of knightly arms.

In the second battle Degaré accepts the challenge of his grandfather, the king, and consequently wins the right to marry his own mother. The tournament bout against the king seems again to suggest the process of reaching manhood, for Degaré first suffers heavy (and unjust) punishment from the king before finally deciding to respond in kind and proving superior because of his greater strength. So that the marriage with the mother can be carried out, the romance writer now has Degaré forget about the glove test until after the ceremony, when he suddenly remembers it in time to prevent consummation of the marriage. The mother's response to finding her son is one of joy, tinged only with slight regret at the marriage—which of course can be easily undone.

Immediately after this episode, Degaré's search for his father resumes and carries him to a land where another threatening male, a "stern knight," guards a beautiful maiden. This is another scene out of the fairy romances. The maiden, of course, is the one whom Degaré can and will marry for good. But before that happens and after he has killed the stern knight, he sallies forth one last time and confronts a "doughty knight" who turns out to be his real father, the excuse for the battle between them being that Degaré was hunting deer in the knight's forest. The fight begins, but the father recognizes the son by means of the broken sword, and the romance hastens toward the final reconciliation.

It is perfectly apparent that family relationships are the subject of this romance, and the underlying problem seems to be fear that they may become too close to be socially and psychologically acceptable. Specifically, the attachment of child and parent seems to be feared, as in the case of the king-grandfather and princess-mother (which is really the initial problem to appear in the story) and in the case of Degaré's marriage with his mother. A corollary fear has to do with the competition between males of different generations. At the same time, the family that is whole and close (and noble) is an object of intense desire. One wants mothers who are beautiful and marriageable, fathers who are strong and worthy opponents.

Oedipal patterns occur in society and literature at all periods, but the specific idea that one must marry one's mother before finding a lover and fight with one's father before the sword (sexual potency) can become whole is extremely interesting here. The implied social background of such stories is one in which family relationships are held in esteem but are really not close. This is reflected in the actual situations and experiences of the romance characters but even more so in the combined desire for and fear of close relationships. The intricate and contrived family connections of *Sir Degaré* are a way of achieving the appearance of closeness combined with safeguards against the dangers of full emotional involvement.

As in the fairy romances, the envisioned rewards in *Sir Degaré* are more material than interpersonal. They are presented to us in a description of the maiden's castle where Degaré stays before fighting the stern knight (ll. 749–845). The picture is one of comfortable opulence: there is a fire, bare-legged damsels bringing food, a dwarf who sets the table and lights torches, harp music, and a warm bed. In addition to this service and comfort, the promise that the maiden offers to Degaré consists of lands and her body "at thi wille." True personal relationships in this and the other domestic romances consist almost entirely of sentimental exclamations, such as this from the doughty knight: "O Degarre, sone mine! / Certes ich am fader thine!"

Somewhat less neatly arranged Oedipal patterns occur in many medieval romances and are especially typical of the domestic romances. Manuscript groupings suggest some close connections among several of these romances and in particular between *Sir Degaré* and five others which are included with it in Cambridge University Library MS Ff.2.38. The five are *Sir Triamour, Sir Eglamour of Artois, The Earl of Toulous, Octavian,* and *Le Bone Florence of Rome.* For the time being we will consider only the first two of these; the others will be discussed later in this chapter. *Eglamour* and *Triamour* are both tail-rime romances written in the north Midland dialect during the mid and late fourteenth century, respectively. Of the two, *Triamour* exhibits the more obvious similarities to *Sir Degaré.*

Like Degaré, Triamour is a knight in search of his father, whom we know to be the king of Aragon. Triamour has not, however, been separated from his mother; instead, she has been exiled by a false accusation of adultery and, carrying the future hero of the romance in her womb and accompanied only by an "old knight" and his dog, she travels through a wilderness, eventually coming to Hungary, where her son is born. The mother is a less important and less problem-producing figure than the mother in *Sir Degaré.* Since she is never really separated from the hero, she is not an object of desire and he does not pursue her. As a result she does not have to be marriageable, and thus *Sir Triamour* avoids the strange father-daughter relationship found in *Sir Degaré*. In Hungary, Triamour's mother almost drops from view, waiting only to be reconciled with her husband at the end of the romance. Her main function during the intervening period is to withhold from Triamour the identity of his father, whom he is determined to find. Meanwhile, the role of heroine is taken over by the young princess of Hungary, who falls in love with Triamour because of his military success.

Triamour's first battle is in a tournament to win the princess's hand in marriage, and this also provides him an opportunity to face and defeat his own father in combat (the relationship being unknown to both of them). Subsequently, and before giving his full attention to the winning of the princess, Triamour shows up in his father's kingdom, first being threatened with loss of his right hand for poaching and then serving successfully as his father's champion in single combat against an invasion by the emperor of Almain. This completes the father-son combat phase of the romance, and all that remains is the discovery of identities and the reunion at the end of the story. In the meantime, however, Triamour again gets involved in a different kind of family warfare, as two giant brothers of the emperor of Almain's champion attempt to waylay him and as another brother seeks to wed the heroine. Triamour literally cuts this opponent down to size, slicing his legs off at the knees and then taunting him.

During Triamour's search for his father, he encounters several male characters, any one of whom is potentially a model for the hero. Among these are the emperor of Almain and the champion's two brothers, all of whom fight battles for revenge, which is an admirable trait in all medieval romance. These characters are unsatisfactory models because their revenge is unjustified. Moradas, the emperor's champion, is another potential model, but he is remarkable only for his strength, which is not great enough to overcome Triamour; nevertheless, he is treated almost as a sympathetic character during his brief appearance in the romance. His brother Burlond, Triamour's final opponent, is the worst of all of these: not only is he pressing marriage on the reluctant heroine, but he also goes back on his word in the battle with Triamour. Still he is not as bad as the deceitful steward Marrok. In contrast to all these characters, the hero's father Ardus looks good, despite his gullibility when told that his wife is unfaithful, his inability to overcome Triamour in the tournament, and his apparent impotence when faced by the emperor's invasion. His virtues—and they are the virtues that count most in this romance—are faithfulness, humility, a certain amount of intelligence, and a sense of justice.

The values of the romance show through even more clearly in another character, the old knight Sir Roger who accompanies the queen in her exile and who, by virtue of his plot function, is symbolically a father to Triamour. Roger is the meekest of all the characters in the romance. Originally, he was sent with the queen as an insult to her: as a punishment for her supposed adultery, she is sent from the palace in "simple" clothes, on a battered and blind horse, and with this old knight for company. Yet Roger is "curtes," "kynde," and devoted to his charge. When attacked by Marrok's band of more than forty men, he defends himself valiantly and, surprisingly, kills almost all of them before Marrok spears him from behind. Roger dies, but his faithfulness lives on in his dog, appropriately named True-Love. In one of the most notable effusions of sentiment to be found in medieval romance, the author narrates the story of how the dog fought alongside his master, licked his wounds in an attempt to heal him when he was down, buried him when he was dead, lay on his grave for seven years, and finally hunted Marrok down and avenged his master's death. "Grete kyndenes," the author remarks, "ys in howndys!" The sentimentality of these events anticipates that of the final reunion between Ardus and his queen. In both scenes, and throughout the romance, we observe a bias toward emotional but nonsexual attachments. At the end, for example, the reuniting of the old king and queen gets the author's attention rather than the reuniting of the young hero and heroine. The romance concentrates on male rivalries and attachments almost to the exclusion of male-female relationships. Apart from the requisite happy marriage with many children at the end, the only male-female love affairs are unpleasant or unemotional ones.

Sir Triamour is a testament to the importance of family even when sexual attachments are almost totally rejected. In fact, the romance alternates between ignoring sexual matters and treating them with suspicion. This is nowhere better illustrated than in the opening lines that present to us the childless marriage of Ardus and Margaret and describe Margaret's refusal of Marrok's sexual advances. Wanting an heir, Ardus resorts to prayer, and this results in the begetting of the hero, unknown to Ardus. Two things immediately happen: Ardus leaves on a crusade for the Holy Land, and the queen becomes involved in events that lead to an accusation of adultery. Thus the romance, once having admitted to the necessity of sexual intercourse, reacts by separating (and purging) the participants and by viewing the resulting pregnancy as probably illicit. Looking at it this way, we might well conclude that what makes Marrok evil is not so much his falseness as his aggressive sexuality. Certainly Triamour shows no such inclination: his only advances toward the princess are military ones, and when he fights for her in the tournament, she is only seven years old. *Sir Triamour* goes a step beyond *Sir Degaré* in proposing as an ideal the marriage freed not only of emotional involvement but also of physical attraction. In truth, *Sir Triamour*'s best image of "true love" is the love of a dog for its dead master.

GIANTS AND OTHER MONSTERS

The romance of *Eglamour of Artois* concentrates on father-son relations in a different and more systematic way. The story is in two parts, the first dealing with the competition between Eglamour and his lady's father, the second centering around the competition between Eglamour and his own son Degrebelle. The Degrebelle section is the one that parallels the plots of *Sir Degaré* and *Sir Triamour*. It begins with the conception of an illegitimate son and the exiling of the pregnant mother. After giving birth to Degrebelle in the wilderness, she is separated from him for fifteen years, during which time he grows up, is knighted, and distinguishes himself in arms. Eventually he wins the right to marry her by fighting in a tournament, and the marriage ceremony is completed before she discovers from his coat of arms that he is her son. There is then a battle between father and son, which Eglamour wins, before all the main characters are reunited in marriage.

The first part of the story is an interestingly elaborated version of the contest to win the lady. Instead of a contest *with* the father, it is a contest set *by* the father, a variant pattern that is seen in other romances as well. Eglamour has fallen in love with a woman of higher rank, but her father (the earl of Artois) will consent to the marriage only if Eglamour successfully survives three feats of arms.

When he completes them, however, the earl welshes on his part of the bargain, having previously sent his daughter away carrying Eglamour's "bastard" child. At this point the competition between father and would-be son-in-law becomes overt, but the earl avoids direct conflict by taking refuge in a tower. This contrasts with the competition later between Eglamour and Degrebelle, which is successfully worked out through physical combat, in a tournament with a formal declaration of the winner. Retribution comes to the earl for his faithlessness and evasion of conflict when at the end of the romance he falls from the tower and breaks his neck.

Except for its geographical setting, which will be discussed later in this chapter, the second part of the romance is similar enough to *Sir Degaré* and *Sir Triamour* to need no further consideration. The first part, however, is an unusual version of the search for parentage through marriage, for in fact Eglamour's love for the earl's daughter symbolizes the wish to become part of a noble family, and the conflict with the earl is equivalent to a search for a satisfactory parental figure—a search that fails with the earl's deceit and succeeds later only when Eglamour himself becomes the parent figure. What is most interesting of all, however, is the romance's obvious allegorization of this process. The names of the earl and the hero are parallel. The earl's name, Sir Princesamour, is probably to be interpreted as 'love for the nobility'; Eglamour probably means 'love for equals.' The names suggest the hero's aspiration for equality with those above him and the earl's determination to keep the social barriers where they are. The other major characters have names that more or less indicate their plot functions. The heroine is Cristabelle, which probably means 'the fair Christian'; Belamy, Eglamour's squire and counselor, means 'good friend,' and Degrebelle, the hero's son, is probably *d'égaré bel*, 'the fair waif.'

The three tasks set for Eglamour represent three stages in the winning of the lady. The first task is to bring a hart from a walled cypress forest guarded by the giant Arrake, who fights with an iron club. This battle, in which Cristabelle aids her lover, represents the overcoming of parental opposition. Giants commonly symbolize adults, especially fathers, and the fact that this one lives nearby suggests a connection with the earl. In both *Sir Degaré* and *Sir Triamour*, poaching on the father's land is emblematic of the son's incursions into the realm of parental authority, and it probably has the same meaning here. Harts, in medieval literature, ordinarily represent lovers, with a pun on 'heart.' The wall around the forest would symbolize either the father's castle or his protectiveness toward the daughter, and the cypresses and iron club suggest the threat that he poses to the hero.

The second task is to kill a wild boar that feeds on Christians in the distant land of "Sedoyne" and then to kill Marrasse, brother of Arrake and owner of the boar. These battles over, the king first offers Eglamour the kingship of Sedoyne and the hand of his daughter Organata ('heritage, lineage'?); when Eglamour refuses these, the king gives him a horse, and Organata gives him a gold ring that will protect him from death. She promises to wait for him, and eventually she marries Eglamour's son. The boar fight probably represents the overcoming of the hero's uncivilized background and instincts, perhaps even of his physical passion for Cristabelle. The uselessness of his spear and the repeated loss of his horses seem to indicate a challenge against which ordinary types of physical strength are impotent. The fact that Eglamour is given an all-night bath before confronting Marrasse indicates that this is a battle between the civilized and the uncivilized, between the clean and the unclean, even between the Christian and pagan (Arrake and Marrasse are similar to the names given to pagans in other romances). This is a very difficult battle for Eglamour, and he must take twelve weeks to rest up after it. It is interesting that after the battle Eglamour pledges his troth to Cristabelle and spends the night with her. This certainly means that he has won her in all but a legal sense, but if the boar is meant to symbolize physical passion, there is a kind of paradox involved: Eglamour must conquer his desire in order to realize it.

The third test, the killing of a dragon in Rome, is narrated briefly and has a fairly obvious meaning. Rome, being the headquarters of the Church and the historical seat of European government, represents the political and religious opposition that the suitor must overcome even after he has conquered the objections of the lady's family and his own failings. Actually, political power seems to be most in the author's mind here, for he does not mention the Church or the pope, and he identifies the ruler in Rome as Octavian, a name associated not only with the Roman Empire but with its period of greatest influence and power. After defeating the dragon, which, like the boar, has left many dead strewn about the landscape, Eglamour is nursed back to health, for a year, in the

chamber of the emperor's daughter Diateur ('nurse'?). Having over-
come family, self, and society, Eglamour has succeeded in his origi-
nal venture, but when Sir Princesamour goes back on his word and
thus proves an unacceptable father, the final resolution of the ro-
mance must await the achievement of a satisfactory father-son rela-
tionship brought about in the combat and reconciliation of
Eglamour and Degrebelle.

   A very close parallel to the Eglamour story exists in the some-
what later *Sir Torrent of Portyngale*, a fast-paced, confusing, repeti-
tious compendium of conventional motifs, which might well be
considered an unconscious parody of the whole romance genre.
Except for different names, a greater number of battles, and a few
other variations in detail, the plot of *Torrent* is exactly the same as
that of *Eglamour*. The villainous father is Calamond, king of Por-
tugal, whose adamant opposition to the hero and general unreliabil-
ity eventually bring him to a "foule end"; Torrent, an earl's son,
wants to marry Calamond's daughter Desonell, but the king insists
that first he must kill a giant. When he does, the father sets another
task for the hero, another giant must be slain, and so on. In all,
Torrent stabs, stones, and drowns to death some five giants with
exotic names like Be-gon-mese, Slongus, and Weraunt, in exotic
places like an island in the Aegean, the city of "Hungry," and the
forest of Brasill in Norway. Along the way he also eliminates sev-
eral dragons, rejects offers of marriage to two princesses, and ac-
cumulates various trophies of victory, including a pair of lions, a
sword named Adolake made by Velond, a magic steed once owned
by the King of Nazareth, and the sword of Prince Mownpolyard-
nus. Despite the father's constantly renewed promises of kingdom
and daughter, all this fails to bring success to the hero, so he and
Desonell sleep together one night. When her father discovers that
she is pregnant he banishes her into the wilderness, where she gives
birth to twins. Eventually she and her grown-up sons are restored
to Torrent, after he has spent the interval crusading in the Holy
Land and after the required father-son battle and recognition have
taken place. Then the whole family returns to Portugal so that
Torrent and Desonell can get married, the two sons become rulers
of Jerusalem and Greece, and Torrent is chosen emperor of Rome.
In this grandiose scheme, conquest of the father-opponent becomes
equivalent to the conquest of all evil and the conquest of the world,
secular and spiritual.

ANIMAL CHILDREN

A romance similar to these four but one in which the fairy-tale origins are plainly evident is the short English version of the Knight of the Swan legend, *Chevalere Assigne*. The modified alliterative long lines in which this poem is written as well as a few northern forms interspersed in the predominantly east Midland dialect may indicate that it was originally composed in the north of England sometime in the latter half of the fourteenth century. The story is known from other romances as well as from fairy tales and had been connected, in the late Middle Ages, with the semihistorical, semilegendary figure of Godfrey of Bouillon. The story itself is of the Constance type, the folklore backgrounds of which have been traced by Suchier, Rickert, Schlauch, and others.[3] In the common form of the legend, a mother is falsely accused of some crime in connection with the birth of her child and is either exiled or threatened with death until being vindicated and restored to favor, usually by her child. In the folklore versions, her crime is usually said to be infanticide or giving birth to animals (or monsters). The accuser is often an incestuous father or a wicked mother-in-law. Relics of this folklore ancestry may be found in all the domestic romances. For example, infanticide, cleaned up by being modified into child-abandonment, is a central feature of *Sir Degaré*, *Eglamour of Artois*, *Octavian*, and *Torrent of Portyngale* in addition to the present romance. Hints of animal or monster birth occur here and in *Eglamour of Artois*, *Emaré*, and *Torrent of Portyngale*. *Emaré* has an incestuous father, and characters in *Sir Degaré*, *Le Bone Florence of Rome*, and other romances show evidence of being influenced by this feature of the folk stories. There are wicked mothers-in-law in *Emaré*, *Octavian*, and *Generides* (a step-mother) as well as in *Chevalere Assigne*.

Although each one of these elements probably had connections with social realities during the time that the legends were first told, all such connections had become irrelevant by the late Middle Ages and were accordingly ignored or modified. A good example of this process is seen in what happened to the idea of animal birth. In folk legends mothers give birth to animals, but in the romances they are, at most, only accused of doing so. Earlier societies had apparently believed that a woman who had intercourse with an animal could give birth to an animal, but the belief did not survive in a more enlightened time. There was, however, still a notion that trafficking with the devil could result in the birth of monsters, and *Emaré*, as well as the *Man of Law's Tale*, reflects such a belief, even though such births do not actually happen in either but are only accusations leveled at the heroines. The other common modification of the animal-birth feature in the romances is to have the child (or children, since twins or multiple births are often involved) abandoned and then taken care of for a period by a lion, deer, griffin, or other wild animal. We have already seen a version of this in *William of Palerne*. In *Octavian*, the exiled mother takes her newborn twins into the wilderness, where one is carried off by an ape, then rescued by a knight, captured by thieves, and eventually sold to a Parisian villein. The other child is seized by a lion, and then both lion and child are carried off by a griffin. The lion fights and kills the griffin and nurses the child lovingly until a queen sees them and takes custody of the boy. In a similar situation in *Torrent of Portyngale*, twin sons are carried off by a griffin and a leopard, eventually ending up in the custody of a hermit and a king. The children are named Anthony Fitz Griffin and Leobertus, and both are perceived to be of noble birth. In both cases the animal nurture of the children has developed into nothing more than an emblem of their simultaneously natural and noble heritage; it is symbolic of their lineage like a coat of arms (on which these animals later appear).

At the same time several of the romances contain a sequence of action intended to disclaim such primitive notions about conception and birth. In place of animals or monsters, the mother gives birth to twins (septuplets in *Chevalere Assigne*). This raises the same kind of suspicions that the animal or monster child would raise, for there was apparently a popular belief that multiple births meant multiple fathers. The romance writers do not accept this idea; in fact, they plainly depict it as an ignorant superstition that is in itself the cause of social evil. In two of the three poems (*Chevalere Assigne, Lai le Freine, Octavian*) in which the multiple birth problem occurs, a woman declares that another woman who has had twins is an adulteress; then the accuser herself gives birth to more than one child, all three poems making it clear that no suspicion of adultery is possible. The accusation that falls upon the mothers in *Chevalere Assigne* and *Lai le Freine* is obviously divine punishment for their own false accusations against others. Although the romance authors want to show themselves among the company of the modern and enlightened, they are willing to use the folk belief about multiple fathers for the fears it arouses and its usefulness in indicating that something serious is wrong. Later, the serious problem turns out to be something other than multiple fathers.

This rationalizing of ancient myths is normal in the romances, which, despite seeking out exciting stories, still try to portray society in a believable, contemporary way. But *Chevalere Assigne* rationalizes in a way somewhat different from that of the other romances, by explaining the story as a manifestation of divine power, and that allows the romance to retain more of the fairy-tale marvels. Christian piety among the domestic romances reaches its high point here as, right from the outset, the evil in the story is blamed on Satan and his agent, the wicked mother-in-law Matabryne (see ll. 9–10), who reports the births of the king's children with the crudest possible implications (by killing a bitch that has just had seven puppies and presenting the puppies to the king as emblematic of his wife's children), attempts to have the children drowned, and puts out the eyes of a servant who has pity on them. Throughout the story Matabryne urges her son to put the queen to death, and later when one of the children, Enyas, shows up to fight for his mother, Matabryne treats him contemptuously, grabbing and pulling his hair. She is assisted in her evil deeds by a forester, Malkedras, who nearly succeeds in killing the children and who opposes Enyas in the climactic battle to prove the guilt or innocence of the queen.

Against these satanic forces, the power of God aids the good people in a variety of ways. When the children are sent into the woods, they are found and cared for by the usual hermit, who, along with the deer that gives milk for them, is an agent of Christ (see ll. 104–18). When Malkedras attempts to kill the children, he first strikes off the silver chains that were about their necks when they were born, intending to kill them afterward, but the six children (Enyas is off hunting for food with the hermit) immediately change into swans and fly off. This is a miracle, and what follows is even more clearly so. Matabryne employs a goldsmith to melt the chains down into a cup, but when the goldsmith has melted down only half of one chain, he finds that it has increased in volume so as to be enough to make the whole cup. On the advice of his wife he secretly saves the other five chains and eventually they are used to restore all but one of the children to human form. All this, the wife concludes, is "thorowe the werke of God." The final evidence of God's intervention is in the battle between Enyas and Malkedras. Enyas (who has been christened at the same time as being knighted) carries a cross on his shield, and Malkedras holds the cross in contempt. As soon as he has expressed his contempt, however, an adder springs out of the shield and strikes at the forester, and a fire leaps from the cross and puts out his eyes. In addition to rationalizing the struggle between good and evil, these evidences of God's influence also create an atmosphere in which the other marvels of the story, such as the silver chains and the metamorphoses, seem appropriate.

As in other romances, good is firmly associated with the family and evil with the forces attempting to break it up. Despite its heavy Christian pietizing, the romance really centers about the fight to retain the integrity of the family. Enyas's task is to fight for his mother, as an angel informs the hermit: "Criste hath formeth this chylde to fyghte for his moder." The hermit repeats this to Enyas, and thereupon we see evidence of the child-hero's isolation up to this time both from family and from his courtly heritage, for he has to ask what a mother is (ll. 209–15). The victory over Malkedras restores wife to husband and children to parents, all except for the one who must remain a swan and who expresses his sorrow by striking his breast with his bill until it bleeds. The romance concludes with the christening of the restored children.

FEUDS

Variation on the fight to win a mother or mother figure are found in two late fourteenth-century tail-rime romances, *Sir Degrevant* and *The Earl of Toulous*, the latter based on a historical incident. Although the heroines in both stories are the loved ones and not the mothers of the heroes, the treatment of the characters and the plot patterns serve to associate these romances with *Sir Degaré*, *Eglamour of Artois*, and others of the type. In both, a state of feud exists between the hero, a brave young nobleman with no apparent family connections, and an older man of higher rank. In the *Earl of Toulous* the heroine and the beloved of the hero is the wife of the older man; in *Sir Degrevant* she is his daughter, but she and her mother are closely associated with one another.

Degrevant and Sir Barnard, the earl of Toulous, are examples of the knight alienated from his right, as are Lanval and other romance heroes, but in the two domestic romances the cause of alienation is plainly a father figure, not societal injustice as in the story told by Marie de France and Thomas Chestre. While Degrevant, a generous but unmarried landholder, is crusading in the Holy Land, a neighboring earl breaks into his parks, robs Degrevant's rivers of their fish, and kills his foresters. Hearing of this, Degrevant demands his "ryght," but the earl responds threateningly and insultingly. A battle ensues, and the feud is on. Barnard, in the *Earl of Toulous*, is the victim of Dioclisian, emperor of Almain, who "dysheryted many a man, / And falsely ther londys wan." Responding to unjust tenancy of his land by the emperor, Barnard mounts a successful invasion against him, thus ensuring lasting enmity between the two. In both cases the aggressor's wife takes the side of the hero and argues that her husband should treat him justly, but the older man persists in his evil and in prosecution of the feud. Both romances stress the disastrous and general effects of the feud (see *Earl of Toulous*, ll. 97–108, and *Sir Degrevant*, ll. 463–64). The women are the ones most concerned about these effects, and that is why they plead for the end of the feuds. The main concern of the men, both heroes and villains, is their own rights.

The two romances touch upon some difficult problems of a personal and semipolitical nature. The personal problems concern the behavior of the heroes and heroines, who come very close to confusing self-indulgence with pursuit of justice. Just from reading the narratives, one would conclude that the outcome of battle in these romances is a foregone conclusion. Once battle is joined, neither Barnard nor Degrevant has any trouble defeating his opponents, however powerful and terrible they seem to be, and as a consequence the heroes' ultimate conquests of all the older men's lands and possessions look a good deal like opportunism. If the heroes had been made the sons of their older opponents, their excuse would be that it is normal for children to succeed to the possessions of their parents, but in order to avoid other difficulties (mainly the implications of incest), the familial bonds have been avoided here. In fact, the heroes are not even vassals of their opponents—a natural, even an expected possibility, but also one fraught with difficulties. As a result, the entire justification for the heroes' actions must rest upon the unjust aggression of the emperor and

earl at the beginning and their continued intractability. This is a
flimsy excuse, especially since the essential goodness of the father
figures must be salvaged at the end. The heroines are in an even
more questionable situation since they take the side of an interloper
against a husband in one case and a father in the other. In such
circumstances, it would be natural to ask what precisely constitutes
justice, but both romances avoid the question.

Politically, the romances raise questions of rightful succession
and of the broad effects of the feuding, which is seen as the natural
state between the younger and older men. The authors avoid the
problem of succession by arranging to have no claimants other than
the female ones to the property when the owners conveniently
expire at the end; thus the property passes to the heroes through
marriage. The problems associated with the feuding are allayed by
a glance of passing regret. Both solutions are consonant with a
feminine point of view, the one because it maintains the fiction that
women are the key to the succession, the other because it manages
to retain the effects of the feuding while regretting the feuding
itself.

Along with the feud motif, both romances tell stories of pas-
sionate love. Barnard falls in love with the empress (Dame Beuly-
bon: 'beautiful and good') when he hears a report of her beauty, and
he immediately declares that he would be willing to lose his life for
her. Degrevant sees his lady (Melidor) before loving her, but other-
wise his reactions are the same: he repeatedly risks his life to visit
her despite being warned of the "folly" of loving one's enemies.
The stories have superficial resemblances to the Romeo and Juliet
story, but the real theme here is that of the son fighting to gain the
passionately desired possessions of the father, the possessions being
represented by the women. As usual in the romances, the father
figure is more or less safely distanced from the hero. But the associ-
ation between the woman and material possessions is especially
obvious in *Sir Degrevant*, where Melidor's rich clothing and
magnificent chamber are described at length.

This chamber, called "the chaumbur of love" where "thei sleye
care," is a remarkable example of the comforts and privileges as-
sociated with the court and the woman. Unknown to her father,
Melidor entertains Degrevant with a royal feast, attended only by
the two of them and her maid. They sit on violet cushions before a
fire and eat from an ivory board supported by trestles. There is a

gilt saltcellar, basins for washing, and towels of Aylsham. The meal consists of "payndemayn" (white bread), shoulder of wild boar, "hastelettes in galantyne" (pigs' entrails in sauce), "ploverys pouderyd in paste," "fatt conyngus" (rabbits), pheasants, and cur-lews, accompanied by four kinds of wine (ll. 1409–32). The cham-ber itself is ornamented with carvings of ivory and gold, ogees and parpens, and a variety of frescoes depicting religious scenes. There is an alarm clock, glass windows, gables adorned with scenes from romance, a crystal floor, and an azure bed. The description of the bed alone occupies thirty lines (ll. 1489–1520). It has silk sheets, and on the canopy is the story of Idoine and Amadas, one of the best known of the French love romances. Here Degrevant won-ders, "When wylt thou bryng me to rest?" (When will Melidor give in to him?), but although they lie together in bed, the consumma-tion must wait until after marriage.

Because the hero's real desire is the heroine and what she repre-sents and because the romances wish to avoid the awkward per-sonal and familial implications inherent in the stories, chastity takes on special importance in *Sir Degrevant* and the *Earl of Toulous*. *Sir Degrevant* documents a conflict of sentiment as Melidor seems to vacillate between attraction and resistance toward Degrevant, her inward conflict being delightfully reflected in her dialogue, which at the beginning is cold and formal but takes on qualities of liveliness, colloquialism, and humor as her attitudes toward the hero change. The progressive crumbling of Melidor's resistance is an exciting feature of the romance, ending as it does with the two lying together every night for a year in the silk-covered bed, but it can proceed only that far without confronting the problem of "sin."

Sir Barnard's affair with Beulybon also stops at an acceptably chaste stage as, thinking him to be a hermit, she grants him alms—which he takes as a token of her love. Having thus had her virtue symbolically compromised, Beulybon redeems herself by rejecting the advances of two amorous knights. But her virtue proves to be her downfall, for the rejected knights arrange to make it appear that she has committed adultery with another young knight, and she is cast in prison, condemned to death. Little wonder that true chastity is so precious when even the appearance of illicit love has such consequences. At the end of the story Barnard, of course, marries Beulybon, but only after her first husband has died and the barons have accepted Barnard as their lord.

In the *Earl of Toulous*, the idea of the son fighting to save the mother clearly shows through the civilized rationalizations of the poem. As in the folk tales and some other romances, the hero himself is the cause of the accusation against the heroine: Barnard makes the first advance and is accepted (chastely); then a parallel but unchaste advance results in a threat to her life. Hearing of her predicament and having been assured by an abbot that she is innocent, Barnard travels to Almain, defeats the two knights in combat, and thus rescues Beulybon from burning. This leads to a compact of peace between the emperor and Barnard, the acceptance of Barnard (as steward) into the emperor's household, and then, after the emperor's death, the marriage of Barnard and Beulybon—and the birth of fifteen children. In *Sir Degrevant*, where the distance between the underlying family romance and the surface story is even greater, the heroine is never brought in jeopardy (although the threat is there), and the hero does not fight to save her. He does, of course, fight *for* her, in tournament and single combat against the other claimant to her hand, and he also fights against the father by implication when he cuts his way out of the steward's ambush. The end is the same: Degrevant is accepted into the earl's household, marries his daughter, and becomes his heir. Degrevant and Melidor have seven children.

THE PERILS OF FLORENCE

Common to most of these romances, including all those considered so far with the exception of *Sir Degrevant*, is the theme of the lady in distress. The distress usually follows one of two patterns: either the heroine is put in prison and threatened with execution (normally burning) or else she is exiled to wander in the forest or float aimlessly at sea. The second pattern is the one more frequently found in folklore; the first is a characteristic romance motif. Both the imprisonment and the exile result from false accusations having to do with the heroine's sexual behavior. The two types are often combined, and in various ways. Both are found in other romances besides those being considered here, but in the domestic romances the imperiled lady theme finds its most natural place and its most interesting development.

Whatever the meaning of this motif may have been in folk stories, in the romances peril and distress come increasingly to stand as central images of the woman's relationship to her society. There are really only two kinds of heroine in romance: the vacuous and inactive object of the hero's desire and the lady in distress. The exceptions to the rule, though interesting, are few. Both roles are passive, reflecting the actual role of most women in medieval society, but the imperiled lady at least gets a larger share of attention, sometimes the lion's share, and so we would expect to find her appearing more frequently in those romances aimed at feminine audiences. She does appear frequently in Marie de France's lays. The most significant fact about her peril or distress is that it comes about precisely because she is a woman, that is to say, as a result of her function as lover, beloved, or mother. And the threats against her are at least vaguely sexual: she is to be burned (suggestive of passion), to be sent into the wilderness (suggestive of the uncivilized, emotional life), or married to someone large and undesirable. In one variation of the theme she is raped. The nonsexual perils—imprisonment and wandering abroad—emphasize ostracism from society. The punishments perhaps represent the life to which the medieval woman saw herself condemned: emotional but inactive, accepting what happened because there was no other choice, isolated from the true centers of society.

All romance heroines suffer: that is their mode of existence. About the only act they ever perform is to resist the advances of suitors. Even heroines like Partonope's Melior, who herself arranges, magically, for Partonope to come to her castle and bed, offer resistance to the heroes. The resistance makes no sense until we see that it is just the accepted behavior of a woman. In the typical domestic romance, the woman refuses an unwanted suitor (not, of course, all suitors), and he either forces himself on her or claims that she has made love to someone else. Her refusal, her one departure from a completely passive role, then leads to her trials, which are passivity exaggerated to extremes, passivity made important and exciting. She cannot save herself from this and perhaps would not want to, since the trials are a self-aggrandizement of the heroine and therefore a kind of perverse wish-fulfillment. She can only wait for her savior, man or God, to rescue her. The pattern may have been influenced by that other form of popular literature in the Middle Ages, the saint's life; certainly the saints' lives contain the same kind of vibrant, passionate distress.

The classic romance of female distress is *Le Bone Florence of*

Rome, and it bears significant similarities to the saint's life. Yet, unlike the saints' lives, it does not end in union with God for the heroine, but with the establishment of a family. The story is by no means original in English. It was widely known both in folktale and romance versions, and, although the precise source has not been identified, it is certainly a close relative of the Old French *Florence de Rome* (early thirteenth century). Florence, the heroine, is closely associated with Rome and, through it, with all of Christendom. For this reason, the story begins with an account of the founding of Rome, and later a description of the city's marvels is combined with a description of the heroine's beauty. Politically, the conflict in this romance is between Rome and Constantinople, the center of the Eastern (and "pagan") Empire. Florence represents Christianity and its passive doctrines of meekness and humility, and so does the hero Emere, who bears on his shield a white dove and a black lion, signifying meekness and ferocity respectively.[4]

The opening section of *Le Bone Florence* presents a complex situation bearing many resemblances to the other domestic romances. Florence lives alone with her father, the emperor of Rome, her mother having died giving birth to her. Garcy, the emperor of Constantinople, hears of her beauty and determines to have her as his wife or to destroy Rome in the attempt. Garcy, however, is one hundred years old (and still a bachelor). He is a literary descendant of the incestuous father of folklore, as is the king in *Sir Degaré*, but the father figure in *Le Bone Florence* has been divided in two: into the good emperor of Rome, the real father, and the superannuated, lecherous emperor of Constantinople. Florence naturally rejects the offers of Garcy, remarking that she would rather wed a commoner than lie with this old, coughing, groaning man. When her father supports her refusal, Garcy mounts an invasion against Rome, in which the father is killed and the city seriously endangered. Florence's insistence on having some choice, on being something other than a complete pawn, has caused the destruction of her family and the threatened destruction of her land. That is the way Garcy sees it (ll. 685–87), and that is the way she sees it too: "My fadur for me hys lyfe hath lorne."

Without a family and almost without a kingdom, Florence is in a dangerous position. For the common good, the lords advise her to take a husband, but this itself promises some difficulties. The only candidates are two knights who have assisted in the defense of

Rome, Emere and Miles, sons of the king of Hungary and themselves without a family since their father has died and their mother has married a Syrian against the advice of the Hungarian barons. Emere is good and Miles is evil, as has twice been proved in the fighting. Florence prefers Emere, but at the critical moment he is in Constantinople because she has declared that he will never get into bed with her until he brings her Garcy—an indication that he must completely subdue the symbolic father before winning the right to the daughter. Despite the attempts of the Roman nobles and the pope to save her, Florence falls victim to Miles's plotting and, with an accusation of unfaithfulness hanging over her head, is drawn into the wilderness alone with the villain. Here her trials begin in earnest.

Miles is the first persecutor of Florence. Just as Emere represents what she hopes for in a husband—bravery, devotion, and, apparently, physical absence—so Miles represents what she fears. The fears are clearly sexual in nature. He beats her with his naked sword and forces her to lie with him at night. She counters this by praying (appeal to a higher but still masculine authority), and God makes Miles's desire go away. A second attempt by Miles results in the same conclusion. Meanwhile, he has given evidence of the treatment that a wife of his may expect when, after begging food from a hermit, he burns the hermit to death because he does not like the offered fare of bread and water. Miles now decides that Florence has bewitched him, and, binding her naked by her hair to a tree, he beats her with a birch rod. Although the act is suggestive of male-oriented, sadistic enjoyment, the description of the scene makes it clear that Florence's fear and distress, not Miles's pleasure, are the emotions being played up. At this moment of peril, a passing knight hears her screams and frightens Miles away.

Florence's relief is only temporary, however. In what seems an anticlimactic sequence of events, various male villains now attempt to rape, rob, and marry her. During this time she finds herself in a variety of familylike situations. The lord who rescued her from Miles takes her into his household where she serves as tutor to the lord's daughter, teaching her how "to behave hur among men," but soon afterward a knight named Machary tries to rape her. Florence hits him in the teeth with a rock, prompting feelings of revenge on his part. So one night he slits the daughter's throat, and Florence, who sleeps in the same bed with her, is accused of the murder.

Exiled and wandering once again, she drifts into the household of a
burgess. The burgess's wife treats her protectively, but the burgess
and Clarebolde, a seemingly reformed thief now serving as Flor-
ence's squire, manage to sell her into slavery on a merchant ship
and confiscate her possessions in the process. The wife's last-
minute attempt to save her fails, and now she is left at the mercy of
the mariner, who wants to marry her. She refuses, he grabs for her,
and she prays. A storm suddenly comes up, breaking the ship in
two, and Florence and the mariner are washed ashore near a nun-
nery on the Aegean.

It is an astonishing series of events, one following fast upon the
other, and all combining to suggest that Florence's life, property,
and identity itself are being threatened along with her virginity.
Her adventures are similar to those of Constance and Griselda in
the *Canterbury Tales*, but the only religious virtues that Florence
exhibits are chastity and prayer, which are social and superficial in
comparison to the constancy and patience of Chaucer's heroines.
The danger Florence is being exposed to is actually marriage. Hav-
ing rejected the old fatherly suitor, she confronts the terrors of
matrimony with a younger one. The terrors are loss of identity
(Miles threatens to set her on fire if she reveals to anyone who she
is), sexual violence, potential responsibility for the deaths of her
children (represented by the lord's daughter, whom she treats as
her own), loss of her own property, the possibility of being treated
as property herself (in servitude), and uncertainty.

The conclusion of the story expresses an impassioned vindic-
tiveness toward the heroine's persecutors. Taken into the nunnery,
Florence eventually becomes a nun herself and cures one of the
sisters who is ill; the fame of this deed travels far until it is heard of
by the hero Emere, who has been hopelessly wounded in battle and
who decides to visit the nunnery for a cure. When he comes before
Florence, all the villains are there too, each suffering from a horri-
ble disease. Miles has leprosy; Machary stands shaking, deformed,
and itching; the mariner's eyes are swollen and his limbs rotten;
Clarebolde has no feet and must be carried about in a wheelbarrow.
But the diseases are only the first part of the punishment. The
villains are told that they must confess their sins openly if they
desire relief, and they do so one after the other, so that all the
mischief against Florence is made known. During this narration,
she recognizes them (and is amused), but they do not recognize her.

Afterward, she cures all the confessed villains and Emere along with them, and then Emere executes all of them for their crimes. Through the conventional romance activity of healing, Florence establishes dominance over all the males in her life, including Emere. The execution, by burning, of the villains makes her vindication complete. With the issues of the romance thus clarified, Florence returns to Rome (apparently abdicating her vows), marries Emere, and on the first night conceives a son who will become emperor. They live happily ever after.

CAST ADRIFT

Emaré is another romance in which the action centers about an imperiled heroine. This poem of the late fourteenth century is best known for the close resemblance of its story to that of Chaucer's *Man of Law's Tale* (the Constance story), written about the same time as *Emaré* or perhaps somewhat earlier. Also about this time, John Gower included a version of the Constance story in his *Confessio Amantis*, and earlier Nicholas Trivet had told the tale in his *Anglo-Norman Chronicle* (about 1335). Chaucer and Gower both followed Trivet, but *Emaré* probably had as its source one of the folktale versions of the story, of which there were many. In many of its details, this romance shows a close kinship with folk legends. It is the only one of the domestic romances to retain the motif of the incestuous father in something approximating its original form, and other motifs such as the evil mother-in-law, the enchanted robe, and the forged letters also come directly from the folklore sources. The basic plot resembles the plots of several domestic romances, especially *Le Bone Florence*, but even more than that romance it concentrates attention on the heroine. It is the only one of these romances that contains no combats.

It is surprising that the poem should treat the incest theme as such, for although symbolic incest was a concern in late medieval society, actual incest does not seem to have been. The idea of a father asking his own daughter to marry him, as the Emperor Artyus does here, must have seemed as shocking and, what is more to the point, as odd then as it does now, and the oddity is compounded because the romance distinctly treats the emperor in a favorable light (although it condemns his incestuous desires). The story contains little to qualify, excuse, or even explain his desires.

His wife, the empress, has died shortly after giving birth to Emaré, and the young girl has been given into the care of a lady named Abro, who raises her and teaches her the standard court virtues. Besides reflecting medieval practice, this does create some distance between father and daughter, but not the same kind of distance provided in other romances. The cause of the emperor's passion is a rich cloth presented to him as a gift by the king of Sicily, a minor character who serves no other function in the story. As soon as the present has been made, Artyus conceives a longing to speak with his daughter, quickly becomes enamored of her, and proposes marriage (having previously secured the permission of the pope). When Emaré refuses, citing the obvious objections, her father has her put to sea in a boat without oars, anchor, or provisions. Immediately he regrets his actions and weeps, and the next time we see him, at the end of the story, he has come to Rome seeking penance from the pope.

Between the two appearances of the father, the romance takes a more conventional direction, developing the twin themes of the lady in distress and the search for a family. Emaré marries the king of Galicia and gives birth to a son, Segramour, but the king's jealous mother accuses the heroine of giving birth to a monster and has her put to sea once again, the son along with her. In Rome she is taken in by a merchant and his family, where she stays until first her husband and then her father arrive and tearful reunions take place. This follows the pattern of other domestic romances in which attraction to a parent is replaced by attraction to a parentlike but acceptable mate and happiness is achieved in the uniting of the whole family (here, Emaré, her father, her husband, and her son). The pseudonym that Emaré takes during the period of her wanderings, Egaré, underlines in a curious way the similarities between this and the other romances, for it is the same name as Degaré.[5] To this conventional pattern are added two other motifs that we have seen in Le Bone Florence, the suffering of the heroine while alienated from her family and the caretaker family that is an unsatisfactory final solution because it is not noble and not hers. (However, the merchant family and also the family of the steward Kadore, who takes care of Emaré in Galicia, are temporarily satisfactory, unlike the burgess family in Le Bone Florence.)

In fact, all of the families in Emaré are good, and so are all the characters except the mother-in-law. All of Emaré's difficulties stem directly from the passions of parental figures: love on the part of the father, jealousy on the part of the mother-in-law. As in the case of Emaré's father, the mother-in-law's malice seems to result from family ties that are too close, in this case the ties between her and her son. As soon as he expresses affection for Emaré, his mother instantly becomes jealous and accuses the heroine of being a "fiend." The two women are clearly rivals: the mother-in-law is called "the olde qwene." Rivalry may have been the reason for the development of the evil mother-in-law figure in the folktales, and, if so, it is one of the things that survived the transition from folktale to romance. Emaré finds her opponent in the person of her husband's mother just as naturally as the male heroes of domestic romance do battle against their fathers.[6] When the romance sets up the family as the greatest good, it usually discovers the greatest threat to happiness within the family too. The general formula for a happy marriage in romance seems to be great protestations of love and devotion, much agony at parting and joy at being reunited, but a minimum amount of interdependence and physical contact.

In *Emaré*, the apparent cause of trouble is the king of Sicily's cloth. Although this is one of the folktale elements, the romance has fully assimilated and elaborated it to serve the purposes of the current story. That it is vital to the meaning of the romance is made clear by the almost 100 lines devoted to describing it, as well as by the fact that it keeps reappearing at critical junctures and is closely associated with the heroine herself. The cloth, reworked into a robe, is the one thing put into the boat with Emaré by her father, and it is the thing that draws to her the attention of her husband-to-be and of the merchant in Rome. The description of the cloth (ll. 85–180) stresses its richness and dazzling beauty. An emir's daughter "of hethennes" wove it, depicting on three corners scenes from famous love romances *(Idoine and Amadas, Tristan and Ysolt,* and *Floris and Blauncheflur)* and, on the fourth, herself and her beloved, the son of the sultan of Babylon. The main theme apparent throughout the description is true love. The cloth represents love and beauty, especially as found in the romances, and it is this that Emaré herself also represents. This fits well with the implications of the rest of the story. Romantic love aids Emaré in finding a husband and a male protector when she needs one, but, in the established family situation that exists between her and her father, and again between her and her husband, it causes mischief. In this sense, *Emaré* would seem to be almost an antilove romance, accepting the major conventions of the genre but portraying the love advocated in romances as potentially a shocking evil.

WORLD TRAVELERS

The settings of the domestic romances are anything but domestic. Wanderings like those of Florence and Emaré are typical of the whole group of romances, and the area covered by the wanderings, if not the whole known world, is at least the whole of the world that mattered. These romances even tend to start in far-off places such as Aragon *(Sir Triamour)* or Almain, "farre yn unkowthe lede" *(Earl of Toulous)*. If they start in familiar settings, the action soon moves to more distant and romantic spots, as in *Eglamour of Artois*, which begins in Artois, just across the English Channel, and follows the major characters to Rome, Israel, and Egypt. The only exceptions to this geographical rule are *Sir Degaré* and *Sir Degrevant*. Furthermore, the places are usually real ones, the only major exception to this being in *Chevalere Assigne*, the setting of which is "Lyor." These places are never described. The romance authors simply loved the exotic names, and they would use any opportunity to introduce a new one. So in *Emaré* the gold cloth comes from Babylon by way of Sicily, and the nunnery in *Le Bone Florence* is on the river "Botayre," which runs into the Aegean Sea. *The Earl of Toulous*, when in need of a minor and suspicious character, calls him Sir Trylabas of Turkey.

Apart from its inherent appeal, the function of the geography seems to be the same as in the superman and historical romances: the conceptual threat of the great world with its alien centers of power is controlled, conquered, made familiar by the presence of these characters who think and act like one's neighbors. The symbolic conquest of the world is particularly apparent in *Sir Triamour*, where the hero defeats (in a tournament in Hungary) opponents from Lombardy, Armenia, Aragon, Navarre, Sicily, "Lythyr," "Aymere," and Almain. The romance heroes and heroines begin to travel as soon as events at home have brought them into danger and cease their travels only with the final solution of their problems. This indicates that the geography is part of the threat to them, and that home represents safety.

Although the romances show little or no acquaintance with the places that they name, the names are always given with a recognition of which are Christian, which are pagan. Places in and near the Holy Land show up with great frequency, and some romances display a marked tendency to move their characters gradually in that direction. *Eglamour of Artois* and *Torrent of Portyngale* are cases in point. The first halves of these stories, in which the heroes perform combative exploits required of them by the fathers, take place in Europe; however, the second halves, in which the heroes are united with their lovers and children, take place in the Holy Land. *Eglamour* arranges to have the hero's son Degrebelle raised in Israel while his mother has been blown across the sea to Egypt and lives there with the king, who just happens to be her uncle. In *Torrent*, Desonell and her two sons wander to Nazareth, Jerusalem, and Greece respectively. The climactic confrontation between Torrent and his sons and the reunion of the family both occur in Jerusalem, after Torrent has campaigned many years at "Quarell" and Antioch. In both poems the winning of the wife and children is transformed into a kind of crusade, whereas the proving of the hero's valor is seen as a more domestic task. The crusade image probably confirms the holiness of the matrimonial bond and at the same time suggests penance for the illicit love making earlier.

Conflicts between Christian and Saracen are in the forefront of the action of *Octavian*, a romance that exists in many versions from many lands, including an early fourteenth-century French version and two English romances derived from it. The story combines an account of a Persian invasion of Paris (ultimately suggested by the Saracen wars of the Charlemagne romances) with the motif of the accused and exiled queen, and it includes many of the stock features of the domestic romances: an evil mother-in-law, twin sons abducted by animals and raised separately, the final reunion of the family, and so forth. The story has two additional features of special interest: the character of Clement (Climent in the French version), a comic middle-class Parisian who serves as foster father to one of the sons, and a romantic love affair between this son and the daughter of the Persian sultan. The French romance is a varied, complex tale, over 5,000 lines long, with many points of interest; both English derivatives manage to cover the same ground in less than 2,000 lines, by deemphasizing one aspect or another of the story.

Although *Octavian* has a plot similar to those of many of the domestic romances, the important issues in the story have little to do with home and family. In fact, it is hard to pick a central issue out of the many themes and directions of the story, and this is the major fault of the French romance. For the most part, however, the romance's concerns are with politics and social class. Even the name of the romance indicates its concern with politics, for Octavian, to the medieval mind, was synonymous with worldly power. There are actually two Octavians in the story: the father, emperor of Rome, and his son who at the end, aided by the lion that has nurtured him for a time, brings about the final defeat of the Saracens and the rescue of the father. The elder Octavian's original problems are domestic—childlessness and the suspicion that his wife is an adulteress—but they are problems with political overtones. At first, the emperor has no heir; then, when one is anticipated, it is said to be the child of a commoner, a "garcon." After the exile of the mother, two sons are born. One, Florent (or Florentyn) is carried off by an ape and raised by the commoner (or pilgrim, or villein, or butcher, depending upon which version is read), Clement; the other, carried off and later accompanied by the lion, is raised by the mother as a nobleman in Jerusalem.

The sons represent the two sources of political power, commons and nobility, but Florent is no ordinary commoner as is his foster father. When Clement gives him money, hoping to make a money changer of him, the boy betrays his true heritage by buying a horse—an impractical act from the bourgeois point of view but the thing that Florent needs to help make him a defender of the empire against the Saracen invaders. The comic scenes involving Clement demonstrate his ineptness among the nobility, yet his services turn out to be important when he steals the sultan's unicorn, apparently a symbol of power because the sultan's military fortunes go downhill from this point. Florent, though he fights in the old and inelegant armor given him by Clement and thus betrays his links with the common people, shows nobility in all his actions and is the main champion for the Christians. He defeats the Saracen giant in single combat, and he wins the hand of the sultan's daughter and converts her to the true faith. But finally Florent and his father are both captured, and it falls to the purely noble son, the young Octavian, the lion child with his crusaderlike backgrounds in Acre and Jerusalem, to save the empire, convert the Saracens, and bring about the happy reunion.

Also similar in plot to the domestic romances but different in length and major emphasis is the late fourteenth-century romance of *Generides*. There are two English versions of the story and no known source. *Generides* is long and involved (one version contains 7,000 lines, the other 10,000), combining a tempestuous love story with a complex series of battles for the control of several Asian kingdoms. The main reason for considering it here is that it has a story that begins with domestic distrust and deceit, then parades these essentially family problems across a broad geographical scene before resolving them with the marriage of hero and heroine. The original problem is an unfaithful wife, a queen who is having an affair with an evil steward. The king compensates by having a brief affair of his own, with a princess whom he encounters in circumstances reminiscent of fairy meetings, and from this union the hero Generides is born. The rest of the story narrates Generides' battles to defend various threatened kingdoms and to win back his own from the steward who has treacherously seized power. Into this plot is interwoven the story of the hero's love for Clarionas, a sultan's daughter. There are also several subplots, including a second love affair between one of the hero's companions and his half sister, daughter of the queen and steward. At the end all the parents, evil and good alike, die before Generides finally marries Clarionas. The setting of this romance is somewhat unusual: the action takes place in India (the father's kingdom), Thrace, Persia (the heroine's kingdom), Egypt (the unfaithful queen's original home), and Syria (the mother's kingdom). The characters are all presumably pagan although the romance pays no attention to this. They speak and act just like Christians.

In this romance the geography seems to be used simply for its own sake, because the names are different and exciting and because they call up romantic associations. The same is true for many of the events in the story. *Generides* is almost an encyclopedia of conventional romance motifs. In addition to the motifs already mentioned, the story manages to include a hero's search for his father, a mother in love with her son, an incipient (but avoided) fight between father and son, a fight and recognition scene between brothers, recognition by means of tokens, a character disguised as a beggar, an abduction of the heroine, a false accusation against hero and heroine, and a heroine with curative powers. And there are obvious borrowings from earlier romances, for example, a scene in which

Generides and Clarionas are discovered sleeping side by side with a naked sword between them. The principle of *Generides* seems to be that if some of the standard fare is good, a lot of it will be even better.

The domestic romances in general are superficial and convention bound, looking forward to the popular literature of later ages, thus ensuring success by reliance on time-tested formulas. The taste of fourteenth-century audiences for domestic romances demonstrates their interest in personal and family affairs, properly mixed with the right amounts of danger, adventure, and titillation, but audiences of the same period were also beginning to enjoy another type of romance, one more social in its themes and messages, one which touched on the class conflicts that were becoming a more obvious part of the late medieval scene.

8 *Gentils and Vilains*

Class consciousness pervaded medieval society to a degree that is hard to imagine today. Social rank not only defined the manner in which men lived, setting bounds on their behavior and their prospects; it also determined the way men treated others and were treated in turn. The daily conduct of life offered constant reminders to medieval man of where he stood in the social order. The romances, even the early ones, reflect the social realities of class and hint at the existence of tensions between the classes. The typical romance hero is a social climber, sometimes regaining a high rank that he had lost, sometimes achieving a higher rank through his own prowess or virtue. Romances may have offered such fantasies as hope for the less privileged classes (the "vilains") or as a justification for the privileges of the upper classes (the "gentils"), indicating that these privileges had been earned by exercise of the same behavior that the nobility required of underlings (military service, primarily). Whatever the reason, the romances imply some lower-class dissatisfaction and some upper-class defensiveness. In the days of the early romances, there may not have been much real social climbing going on, yet the device of the nobly born but apparently common hero suggests a resistance to social advancement, actual or potential, combined with a desire to believe in the validity of the existing social order.

By the middle of the fourteenth century, in a society already becoming more open, the Black Death and the consequent lack of servants brought sudden and massive change to England. The threat to the established orders was now obvious as well as real: it could not be ignored during a century in which two kings were overthrown and thousands of peasants descended on London to protest the imposition of royal taxes.

Romances, which were written to entertain readers and not to make them understand the realities of their world, mostly overlooked the changes taking place in society or else interpreted them in conventional and comfortable ways, but there is a small group of romances which confront social change and conflict more directly than most. Some of them may have been written for professionals, tradesmen, or townspeople, groups that stood to gain rather than lose from increased social mobility, but the nature of the stories themselves indicates that they were more likely intended to allay the fears of the established classes by explaining away or somehow softening the threat. These are just about the only medieval romances that are comic, and comedy, among other things, is a means of dealing with the unpalatable and the unacceptable: we laugh at what we can neither tolerate nor change.

As would be expected, the dates of these romances are, in general, quite late. In fact, only two of the ones now extant seem to have been composed before the time of the Peasants' Revolt, and both of these are more conventional than the others and more aristocratic in their sympathies. The rest, including all of those that depict real class conflicts, date from 1400 or later. Thus the class romance is, in effect, a fifteenth-century genre and one that appears to have become more popular toward the end of the fifteenth century. The dialects of these romances indicate that the majority of them were composed in outlying districts, especially in the north and west, along the Scottish and Welsh borders. These were the areas where the old independent spirit of the inhabitants had never been successfully subdued and where rebellion against royal authority (as expressed, for example, in *Fouke Fitzwarin*) had continued to be a way of life, so it is possible that challenges to the existing class structure were felt to be much more serious there, much more a part of the ordinary course of events. However, it also seems that during the fifteenth century most metrical romances, regardless of type or subject matter, were written in the outlying areas, so the provenance of the class romances may only reflect the metrical romance's decline in popularity in and around London.

THE UNCOUTH KNIGHT

The earliest style of class romances is a variation on the conventional quest or social-climbing story, which is found in the most popular medieval romances, including *King Horn, Guy of Warwick*, and *Bevis of Hampton*. The hero is a young man of lower birth (or apparently of lower birth) who survives a series of adventures and wins for himself knighthood, a lady in marriage, and a kingdom. What distinguishes these romances is their stress on class differences and on social behavior. In addition to being from a rural or bourgeois family, the hero displays crude manners and ignorance of polite society, and he must overcome these faults in himself as well as the usual assortment of evil knights and giants.

One such romance, *Fergus*, exists in the Anglo-Norman dialect and comes down in two manuscripts containing other popular writings in French. A man who calls himself Guillaume le Clerc wrote it during the first half of the thirteenth century. It is an appealing work, filled with imaginative adventures and imagery, not unlike the romances of Chrétien de Troyes, two of which are also included in one of the *Fergus* manuscripts. Like Chrétien's romances and also like the great majority of later class romances, it is Arthurian. The hero is the oldest son of a wealthy villein (a landholder) and a wife whom we are told is noble. While plowing his father's fields one day, accompanied by a churl, Fergus sees some richly accoutered knights of the Round Table and vows to become one of them, a project that is opposed by the father but supported by the mother, who considers it a natural desire because of Fergus's heritage through her side of the family. After a fumbling and inauspicious first appearance at Arthur's court, Fergus single-handedly defeats many foes, each of whom he charges to do homage to Arthur in his name. The central theme of the romance is chivalry. From a crude, rustic blunderer, Fergus develops into a polite, well-behaved knight and thus becomes worthy to win his noble lady and her kingdom. The foes whom he faces represent stages in his social development, and at the very end of the story, after his marriage and acceptance into Arthur's court, Gawain admonishes him not to abandon chivalry, the code of the nobility, even for his wife.

The Middle English *Perceval of Galles*, written about 100 years later during the early fourteenth century, is the only Middle English romance to deal with the issue of chivalry in a manner similar to that of *Fergus*. The sources of this poem are obscure, but it bears some relationship to the important versions of the grail story by Chrétien and Wolfram von Eschenbach, written during the late twelfth and early thirteenth centuries respectively. However, if the English writer knew of the grail legend, he shows no interest in it; Perceval is important to him mainly as a hero of noble birth but rustic background who blunders his way into the fellowship of the

Round Table, gradually learning chivalric behavior in the process. His father and mother are both noble, but when his father is killed by the Red Knight, the mother retires to the woods and raises her son there. As a result, when the young Perceval sets out on his adventures, he is as ill-mannered and ignorant of society as any woodsman. The story works its way through several conventional situations as Perceval gains revenge for his father's death, wins the hand of the lady Lufamour, achieves knighthood, and finally goes on a successful quest to be reunited with his mother, in the manner of the domestic romances. The English writer does not consciously develop the theme of chivalry as does Guillaume le Clerc but instead uses Perceval's unmannered ways as a source of humor. Both romances have their sympathies on the aristocratic side. Despite the many virtues of the two heroes, both are made ridiculous, ineffectual, or unacceptable by their failure to observe the behavior of court, and social advancement is impossible for them until they learn. Even then, these romances are willing to concede advancement only to persons with some hereditary claim to nobility, and, in the early fourteenth century at least, this must have been a small concession to social realities.

In these romances, courteous behavior requires two things: inherited nobility and knowledge. Both heroes have the former and lack the latter. The knowledge they lack is not very arcane, and therein lies the humor, a condescending humor, of the stories. Fergus, having decided to join the court of Arthur and having won the grudging consent of his parents, asks his father to dub him and sets out in the father's old and battered armor; later, a chamberlain must explain to the young man that only a knight can confer knighthood on another. Once he understands this, Fergus allows himself to be dressed in finer clothes and brought to Arthur's court for a proper conferral of knighthood. However, he still does not know how one should address the king, and Gawain's intervention is required to bring about the dubbing. Perceval's understanding is even more faulty. When he is past fifteen years of age and his mother attempts to explain to him who God is, he immediately and enthusiastically sets out through the woods to find this God. When he meets Ywain, Gawain, and Kay, their rich clothes make him think that he has found the object of his brief search, and he demands to know, "Wilke of yow alle three / May the grete Godd bee / That my moder tolde mee, / That all this werlde wroghte?"

Perceval, who has never seen a horse before, is fascinated by the mounts of the three knights and goes to find one for himself. When he comes home riding a mare, his mother—with some embarrassment—tells him what it is, and thereafter, through much of the story, Perceval believes all horses to be mares. After his first successful battle, he seeks to despoil his dead foe of his armor but, not knowing how to unlace it, gives up, and decides to burn the body out of its trappings. Gawain must show him how to remove the armor properly. Perceval's skill in combat and his natural instincts show that he is noble (when he comes home on the mare, his mother recognizes that "the kynde wolde out sprynge"), but he knows nothing. The term repeatedly applied to him, as it is also to Fergus, is "fool."

The ignorant behavior of both Fergus and Perceval is embarrassingly apparent to all. For one thing, their attire gives these knights away: Fergus goes off to visit Arthur's court in his father's battered armor (which he is reluctant to exchange for better trappings), and Perceval wears goat skins. Another thing is their weapons: Fergus uses a club and an ax. But the main indication of lack of breeding is in their lapses of decorum, as when Fergus approaches Arthur and seeks lodging at the chamberlain's house with the heads of two robbers dangling from his saddle or when Perceval rides his mare bareback into Arthur's court and right up to the throne so that the horse's mouth kisses the king's forehead. The court is as astonished that Arthur tolerates such behavior as they are at Perceval's crude style of address to the king: "Sir, late be thi jangleynge! / Of this kepe I nane."

Such behavior indicates a lack of "mesure," which is the quality that Perceval's mother advises him to cultivate. His first attempt to do so is crude. He comes to an unoccupied hall in which there is a table set with food, and, remembering his mother's admonition, he eats only half the food, leaving the rest for someone else. "How myghte he more of mesure be?" asks the author ironically. "Mesure" does not mean a simple splitting of alternatives, nor does it quite mean an avoidance of extremes, for the knight's natural role constantly forces him to use extreme force in extremities of distress. The best definition of "mesure" as used in *Perceval of Galles* is the use of the appropriate response for the specific situation. The knight must know when to ask and when to demand, when to object and when to be compassionate.

The chief practitioner of this kind of "mesure" in both romances is Gawain, while Kay demonstrates a contrastingly boorish behavior. In the episode in which Perceval takes the three knights for gods, for example, Gawain and Kay show the do's and don't's of courtly behavior. To Perceval's opening question, Gawain answers "faire and curtaisely" that they are not gods. Perceval threatens to kill them unless they tell him who they are. Kay, reacting to the unreasonable threat but not considering the situation and the character of the speaker, responds sarcastically, but Gawain intervenes and answers the question, ignoring Perceval's style and his lapse of manners in not giving his own name. Then, when Perceval abruptly asks if Arthur will knight him, Gawain returns the politic answer that he does not know and Perceval should go find out. A similar incident occurs in *Fergus* when the hero first approaches Arthur's entourage with the robbers' heads on his saddle and asks to become one of Arthur's knights. Kay responds first, by ironically praising Fergus's chivalry and suggesting that he undertake a quest against the Black Knight, a task that Kay assumes will be impossible for the hero. Gawain criticizes Kay for speaking "vilainement," and intervention by Arthur prevents a quarrel between Kay and Fergus.

Both romances also contain confrontations between Gawain and the heroes. The confrontation in *Perceval of Galles* is an especially difficult one for Gawain because he is not sure whom he is facing. He recognizes the armor of the Red Knight and knows that Perceval has been wearing it, but he also knows that it might be someone else. He debates with himself briefly and decides to run a single course against his opponent in order to assess his strength and style of fighting. In the first pass, the spears of both knights break, and Perceval remarks aloud that he has never suffered a stronger blow. Gawain recognizes Perceval's "wylde" manner of speech and brings the fight to an end. There is a situational ethic involved here. Correct reaction to the situation depends on knowledge combined with good instincts. The knowledge is acquired, but the instincts are inherited. Gawain has both, while Kay has the knowledge without the instincts and the heroes have the instincts without the knowledge.

The knowledge is easily acquired. In fact, the knighthood ceremony almost seems to confer it, by a process that goes uninvestigated and uncommented upon in the romances. Perceval acts like an ignorant rustic right up until the time of his knighting and then suddenly begins to show concern and mercy toward others. Somehow he even begins to recognize the difference between mares and stallions, although no one has talked to him about this. Fergus, who does not know the proper forms of address when he seeks knighthood from Arthur, soon afterward begins to address others politely—by nature, we are told. Lack of knowledge is not only easily remedied; it can be overlooked, as the scenes mentioned earlier illustrate. The ignorant knight is a source of humor; the knight who lacks natural breeding (Kay, for example) is a cause of embarrassment and concern.

Instinct, which is inherited, is much more important than knowledge. *Perceval of Galles* makes a frequent issue of the fact that the hero's father, also named Perceval, was a knight of the Round Table and that his mother is Arthur's sister. We are told, for example, that only the son of the elder Perceval can destroy the Red Knight, the hero's first opponent and one whom the other knights seem reluctant to approach. Fergus, whose heritage is less certainly noble, displays his innate nobility at every turn of the story, using complimentary banter to turn away a young woman who has thrown herself at him, feeling ashamed of himself for hitting an opponent after he is down, and repeatedly having mercy on defeated foes who ask for it. Never does knowledge seem necessary to either hero, nor does their ignorance cost them in any vital encounter. Their bad manners make them absurd and comical but not ineffective. The message of these romances is that men with natural nobility are needed to combat evil, regardless of their outward appearances. Nobility is inherited, but sometimes it is inherited and the world does not know it.

Each romance underlines its main points symbolically. *Fergus* makes prominent use of black-white contrasts, black and white having their expected meanings. Fergus's first and chief opponent is the Black Knight, who has the ignoble trait of decapitating people (a fault shared by Fergus, but he only decapitates robbers who threaten him). Fergus carries a white shield that glows brilliantly, protects the life of the owner, turns day into night, and enables the hero to win the hand of his beloved. He has acquired the shield by doing battle with an old woman wielding a scythe. The old woman seems to be a mother figure, indicating that the protective shield is inherited and is therefore to be identified with natural abilities. She has with her a large serpent, which probably represents knowledge, as in Genesis.[1] *Perceval of Galles* contains a similar protective symbol, a ring that preserves the life of the wearer. Actually, there are two rings, one which Perceval's mother gives him and another (the protective ring) which he exchanges for the first, but both rings represent Perceval's noble heritage.

Both of these romances play to the popular notion that nobility may come from humble origins and masquerade in unlikely guises, but they both side with inherited nobility nonetheless. This is especially true of *Fergus*, where we see the conventional mark of obscured noble heritage, the great beauty of the hero, revealed as soon as he is dressed in fine clothing. Fergus's opponents, too, are typically lower class: robbers, ugly villeins, ugly porters. In fact, Guillaume le Clerc takes his opportunity to propagandize against those who would restrict the freedom of movement of the nobles when he sets up as opponents of the hero a "robber" baron who charges tolls for passing over a bridge and some evil sailors who try to charge Fergus for transportation on their ship. Both of these acts are presented as unreasonable in themselves, and later there is a contrasting example of a merchant who transports Fergus in his ship for free. The opponents of Fergus who have some claim to nobility are either cruel, informal, or insulting: they include a knight who is apparently making love to a woman in his tent and comes out to meet Fergus in his nightclothes, and Artofilas, a king's nephew who is so rude toward the heroine of the romance that she concludes he is drunk. While the sympathies of the author of *Perceval* are not quite so obviously on the aristocratic side, he shows no real favoritism for the lower classes. Both romances make only tiny concessions to the realities of a changing society, and they are clearly defensive concessions.

UPSTARTS

Two very late romances bear a certain resemblance to the Fergus and Perceval stories, except that their sympathies lie more with the commoners and they favor real social climbing. Although both of these works are assumed to have been composed sometime near the end of the fifteenth century, neither exists in a medieval manuscript, the earliest version of both being sixteenth-century printed texts. These short works (each about 1,000 lines) are lively, descriptive, humorous, and a good indication that class differences were relaxing.

The earlier of the two is probably *The Taill of Rauf Coilyear*, a Scottish poem written in the verse form and style of the alliterative revival. The story belongs to a type found in several ballads ("John the Reeve," "King Edward IV and the Tanner," and others), in which a commoner does a favor for a king and the king rewards him with lands or knighthood.[2] In the romance, Charlemagne is separated from his companions in a storm and seeks refuge at the home of a collier, a rude fellow who gives the king food, shelter, and a hard time. In return for the rough hospitality, Charlemagne (whose true identity is unknown to Rauf) invites his host to court, where Rauf has a confrontation with Roland, receives knighthood from the king, and fights a Saracen. The important issue in this story is behavior (manners) and its meaning.

The other romance is *The Squyr of Lowe Degre*, an east Midland poem in couplets, which has a standard quest plot similar to that of *Fergus* and *Perceval of Galles* but filled with improbabilities. The squire is in love with the princess of Hungary. She overhears his solitary lament and agrees to marry him if he will go abroad and distinguish himself in arms for seven years. An evil steward overhears the agreement and reports to the king, who is, however, rather favorably disposed to the squire and eventually helps him to win the daughter. But when the steward lays a trap for the hero and is killed in the ensuing fight, his men disfigure his face and put the squire's clothes on the dead body. The princess thinks the dead man is her beloved and keeps the embalmed body with her all the time that the squire is abroad winning the right to wed her. This bit of grotesquerie seems to be intended primarily to spice up the story, and it is immediately forgotten when the squire returns. The obvious theme of the romance is that anyone can climb as high as he wants to.

In fact, right from the beginning, the king of Hungary expresses such faith in social advancement that he almost seems to consider it the natural order of things:

'For I have sene that many a page
Have become men by mariage;
Than it is semely that squier
To have my doughter by this manere,
And eche man in his degree

Become a lorde of ryaltye,
By fortune and by other grace,
By heritage and by purchace' (ll. 373–80).

He stands prepared to back up his principles too, for he promises his daughter that, even if she loves one who is "poore of fame," he will make him a knight, and if she loves a rich lord he will provide a sufficient dowry. This attitude reflects the new order of Tudor England, when many titles were being granted to former members of the middle class and when the power of the "squires" in the House of Commons was recognized, and it indicates that the old court audience of the earlier romances was gone, replaced by an audience that was less rigidly class-conscious.

One indication that the romance audience had lost much of its class consciousness is that no differences in behavior or speech separate the characters in the *Squyr of Lowe Degre*, as in many earlier romances. The same thing can be said of the characters' speech in *Rauf Coilyear*: king, knight, collier, and Saracen all speak in the same style. But behavior is another matter, especially in the scenes between Rauf and the king at Rauf's home. In these, Charlemagne behaves in a conventionally polite manner, while Rauf's behavior is rough and assertive. As soon as the collier has promised lodging to the king, for example, Charlemagne thanks his host-to-be, but Rauf answers that the thanks should be given in the morning after some service has been performed to warrant them. Then as they approach the cottage, the king tries to step aside and let Rauf enter first; however, Rauf grabs the king by the neck and thrusts him in, accusing *him* of uncourteous behavior because Charlemagne's act is that of a superior, and it is inappropriate because Rauf is the host (ll. 124–28). Another example occurs when Rauf asks his guest to begin the board. Charlemagne hesitates, and Rauf knocks him down, offering the same objection: "The hous is myne, pardie" (l. 168). As in *Fergus* and *Perceval of Galles*, courtesy consists of responses that are appropriate to the situation, and this particular situation requires responses that the king has not anticipated.

The same point is made in a more conventional manner when Rauf meets Roland, whom the king has sent out with instructions to bring to court any traveler he sees. Rauf addresses Roland politely, but Roland quickly and bluntly orders Rauf to come to the court, right now. Rauf refuses and makes it clear that he will not be pushed around even though his clothes are foul: "It is na courtasie commounis to scorne." As Rauf has previously observed, he does not speak "out of ressoun," and the king, who has learned his lesson at the cottage, admits this when he makes Rauf a knight "for his courtasie." Potentially, the hero of this romance is a comic figure like Fergus and Perceval because he shares their ignorance and their rude aggressiveness, but in the later romance it is not Rauf who is comic but the situation. Rauf teaches the court a new courtesy, which is the same as the old one except seen from a different perspective, that of the middle classes. That these are middle-class romances is proved not only by the doctrines which they promote but also by the loving care with which they enumerate the paraphernalia of the upper class—the clothing, the jewels, the court trappings, the services. Both romances, *Rauf Coilyear* and the *Squyr of Lowe Degre*, spend quite a bit of time on such description.

Nothing better illustrates the changes the romance audience had undergone by the end of the fifteenth century than another episode from *Rauf Coilyear*. While Charlemagne is dining at Rauf's cottage, Rauf begins to boast of his great success in poaching. He gloats over the charges of the foresters that he always brings down the best deer in the forest, over their threats to drag him before the king for punishment, and over his continued defiance of them. Poaching was a major irritant to the nobility, just as the forest laws that made it a crime were a major irritant to the commoners. To the nobility, poaching was an act against the king, a theft of property specifically set aside, by law, for him and his court; to the forest dwellers, poaching had long been a necessary or almost necessary source of food, and many continued to practice it despite the severe penalties imposed—typically imprisonment, fines, or appropriation of land.[3] Although the earlier romances take little notice of poaching, they do glory in the royal hunts, with which poaching interfered. In the later romances, as in late medieval literature generally, poaching makes a more frequent appearance, usually being seen as a justifiable act of defiance against a harsh or remote legal administration. So it appears to be to Rauf Coilyear, although he does not seek to justify his actions. Charlemagne, however, implicitly condones the poaching by continuing to eat his supper and by remarking to Rauf that the king himself has often been glad of such fare. If there is a social doctrine here, it is perhaps that the services rendered the nobility by the commoners justify the occasional loss of a deer from the royal forests.

THE MONSTROUS CHURL AND OTHER ARTHURIAN THEMES

Another type of romance that deals in new social doctrines is the group that we can roughly designate as Gawain stories. This is a sizable and very interesting group. It is strictly an English type, although the story lines ultimately derive from French romances. In general, the Gawain romances are late, short, and rural; despite this, several of them are highly sophisticated, both in concept and in literary technique. The type seems to have come into existence during the latter half of the fourteenth century, probably in the northwestern section of the country. This is the same time and in the same place that the alliterative revival occurred, and the group includes several poems written in the alliterative long line, although the commonest prosodic form is the tail-rime stanza. The usual story line shows Arthur's court, which represents the courtly establishment, subjected to a test or series of tests in which the chivalric Gawain takes up the main challenge. The significance of the tests varies considerably, but it is usually obvious. These are stories that express specific, though various, social doctrines or ideas.

Gawain began to be a prominent figure in English romance during the first half of the fourteenth century, but he is not the central figure in the earliest romances in which he appears. In *Ywain and Gawain* his role is similar to those in *Fergus* and *Perceval of Galles:* a champion of courtesy who assists the hero and then fights a climactic battle with him because neither knows the other's identity. *Ywain and Gawain* is a free translation, somewhat condensed, of Chrétien de Troyes's *Yvain.* The English version was composed in a northern dialect between 1300 and 1350. Another early to mid fourteenth-century romance, *Libeaus Desconus* (southern dialect), makes Gawain the father of its hero, a fact that may attest to Gawain's growing popularity in England.

Gawain first appears as the main hero of English romances during the last quarter of the fourteenth century. Three works of very different character come down to us from this period. *Sir Gawain and the Green Knight*, the greatest poem of the alliterative revival, was written in a northwest Midland dialect near the end of the century. In it, Gawain successfully survives two challenges that test, respectively, the courage and manners of Arthur's court but that leave Gawain doubting his own virtue. In *The Awntyrs off Arthure at the Terne Wathelyne*, a northern alliterative poem, Gawain listens to a sermon and prophecy from the ghost of Guenevere's mother and then serves as Arthur's champion against a knight whose lands Arthur has unjustly appropriated. As in *Sir Gawain and the Green Knight*, Gawain here fights for a questionable cause because no one else will accept the challenge, and Arthur's court is presented as materially rich but morally weak. *Syre Gawene and the Carle of Carelyle*, a poem of about the year 1400 in tail-rime stanzas, has Gawain meeting a series of tests posed to him by a local land-lord from whom Gawain, Kay, and Bishop Baldwin have sought hospitality. Kay and Baldwin fail the tests, but Gawain's courtly manners and sensitivity enable him to survive them and save the lives of all three knights. Although this poem appears to be written in a Shropshire dialect, its setting is the same as that of the *Awntyrs off Arthure:* the town of Carlisle, in the northwestern corner of England. (Tarn Wadling was a small lake a few miles from Carlisle.)

The *Avowynge of King Arthur*, a northern or west Midland tail-rime romance of about 1425, is a somewhat incoherent piece in which Arthur, Gawain, Kay, and Sir Baldwin all make vows that they then must carry out. The vows of the first three are ordinary enough (Gawain's is to watch all night by Tarn Wadling); Baldwin's vows (to trust his wife and all other women, to give food to all who ask for it, and not to fear death) are the real center of interest. Arthur tests Baldwin and finds him faithful to his word; this in turn gives Baldwin a chance to moralize on the wisdom of accepting one's fate. *The Weddynge of Sir Gawen and Dame Ragnell* comes down to us in an east Midland tail-rime version written about 1450, but the story was in existence earlier than this because Chaucer used it for the *Wife of Bath's Tale*. In this romance a knight named Sir Gromer Somer Jour threatens King Arthur with a petition of griev-ance, claiming that Arthur has wrongfully given Sir Gromer's lands to Gawain. To save his life, Arthur must answer a riddle: "What do women love best?" The only way to discover the answer is for Gawain to marry an old, ugly hag, Dame Ragnell. As in the *Wife of Bath's Tale*, Gawain is subsequently faced with a choice of having his fairy wife fair by day and foul by night or vice versa, and he is rewarded by having her fair both by day and night when he lets her choose which it shall be, thereby giving her sovereignty (the answer to the riddle). In *The Jeaste of Syr Gawayne*, a late fifteenth-century tail-rime romance from the south Midlands or the south, Gawain is forced to fight a father and several of his sons in order to escape punishment for kissing the daughter. This fabliau-like story ends with the last of the sons making a bargain to get Gawain out of the way and then beating his sister.

Themes from several of these romances reappear in four short works of the period 1500 to 1550. Three of these works appear in the Percy Folio Manuscript (about 1650): *The Grene Knight*, a south Midland tail-rime romance based loosely on *Sir Gawain and the Green Knight*; *The Carle off Carlile*, a Lancashire version in couplets of *Sir Gawene and the Carle of Carelyle*; and *The Turke and Gowin*, a north or northwest Midland romance very similar in some respects to *Sir Gawain and the Green Knight* but with the Green Knight replaced by a Turk (Sir Gromer), who helps Gawain survive several unusual tests on the Isle of Man. The fourth work, *Golagrus and Gawain*, is a Scottish alliterative poem surviving in a 1508 print. The story tells how Gawain wins hospitality for Arthur's court through his courteous behavior after Kay has failed in the same attempt and how Gawain must fight against a lord (Golagrus) who has been unjustly besieged by Arthur.

The sources of these stories have been much studied, and it has been shown that the immediate sources lie in French literature of the twelfth and thirteenth centuries, particularly the First Continuation of Chrétien's *Perceval*.[4] The ultimate sources are in Celtic folktales, some of which come down in the Irish *Bricriu's Feast*, but the romances combine and interpret the original stories with complete freedom, a process which can be clearly seen in Middle English by comparing the earlier *Sir Gawain and the Green Knight* with the later *Grene Knight* or the earlier *Syre Gawene and the Carle of Carelyle* with the later *Carle off Carlile*. There are certain essential elements in all the romance versions, however, and they are significant ones. Presumably the popularity of these romances had something to do with these shared elements, despite the differences in specific details and interpretations.

In essence, the Gawain romances show a noble and powerful court that has some notable failing. Arthur is the great conqueror, the uniter of England, Scotland, and Wales, and the bringer of peace *(Grene Knight)*. His court is renowned for its wealth and its chivalry. In *Gawene and the Carle of Carelyle*, the ideals represented by Arthur's court are summed up in the portrait of Sir Ironside, who would ride out both in the heat of summer and the cold of winter. He was always an enemy of giants. His arms and apparel were rich, and he was knowledgeable in hunting and war. He had slain many dragons and wild bulls and imprisoned many strong barons. No braver knight could be found, and he always spoke reason (ll. 67–102). These, it will be observed, are mainly the virtues of service: the knight's task is to protect the people from unmanageable threats. Gawain represents the best of Arthur's court— polite, cautious, thoughtful, eager to serve; the "crabbed" Kay represents the worst—rash, haughty, insulting, self-serving.

The sins of the court are usually those of the king also although they are sometimes associated with Gawain as well. The most striking example of unjust behavior on Arthur's part occurs in *Golagrus and Gawain* when Arthur, coming upon a strongly fortified and strategically placed castle, insists on having its lord, Golagrus, do homage to him. This is in clear violation of the basic romance principle that a hero attacks no one who has not committed the first act of aggression, and in addition it ignores the repeated advice of Arthur's counselor Sir Spinagrus, who knows the situation and who warns that an attack on the castle could be costly. Golagrus is clearly the injured party, and he is a sympathetic character too, portrayed as a lord bravely trying to maintain his ancestral tradition of independence. This is a sticky situation for Gawain: he is caught between his obligations to his lord and the obligation to defend the right. Only a contrived maneuver can bring about a satisfactory ending: Gawain, having defeated Golagrus in combat, agrees to pose as the besieged lord's prisoner (much to Arthur's distress) in order to save face for Golagrus and prevent him from fighting to the death. Later, in return, Golagrus quietly abandons his objection to doing homage to Arthur.

In the *Awntyrs off Arthure* and the *Weddynge of Gawen*, Arthur is accused of taking away his challenger's lands and giving them to Gawain; in the *Carle off Carlile*, Arthur is said to have wounded the carl's knights out of enmity (ll. 196–98). A similar but less specific resentment is expressed by the Turk in the *Turke and Gowin*, who says that Arthur "behaves to try mastery" (ll. 63–65). So the commonest failing of the Round Table seems to be an overly aggressive spirit in violation of individual rights or else just an excessive haughtiness.[5] It will be recalled that a similar attitude toward established authority appears in the romance of *Rauf Coilyear*, and it also underlies the spiritual guidance given to Guenevere and Gawain by the ghost of Guenevere's mother: "Have pite one the poer whil thou art of powere" (*Awntyrs off Arthure*, ll. 170–73). Even in those romances where no complaints about Arthurian excesses of power are made, the original problems seem to arise from Gawain's insensitive exercising of his privileged status at the expense of those below him. Thus in the *Grene Knight* the testing of Gawain is motivated by the love of the knight's wife for Gawain, and in the *Jeaste of Gawayne* it is brought on when Gawain makes love to Sir Gilbert's daughter. Likewise, part of the problem in the two Carl of Carlisle romances is that the Round Table knights harbor lecherous thoughts toward the carl's wife.

In the earlier versions of the testing stories (those in Irish and French), the challenger was a member of the lower classes, a "vilain," and this is also the case in two of the English romances, *Gawene and the Carle of Carelyle* and the *Weddynge of Gawen*. But, as Larry Benson has pointed out, this identification caused certain problems for the romance writer whose sympathies were firmly committed to the nobility, and various evasions were employed to alleviate the problems.[6] The commonest evasion in the English romances was to make the challenger a member of the lesser nobility, thereby, as it were, keeping the conflict over rights and privileges in the family. But this was always done at the expense of literary effectiveness, and the best examples of these romances are those in which Gawain and his antagonist represent two conflicting classes and life-styles. Some of the original power of this conflict, however, may be retained by implication, as in *Sir Gawain and the Green Knight*, where the Green Knight, though dressed richly, has the physical characteristics associated with a villein and rides rudely into the hall to demand, "Wher is . . . the governour of this gyng?"

The most imposing villein in the English Gawain romances is the carl in *Gawene and the Carle of Carelyle*. His name identifies his social rank, for "carl" is simply the northern form of the word "churl," a pejorative term meaning a country fellow or landholder not of the nobility. That this particular carl is not a gentleman is made clear by the fact that Arthur knights him at the end of the romance and by frequent references to his lack of courtesy. When Gawain attempts to kneel to his host, the carl bids him stand, "for her no corttessy thou schalt have, / But carllus cortessy, so God me save" (ll. 277–78). Gawain and the others thus find themselves in a situation where their ordinary ideas of courtesy do them no good, and they must work out other appropriate modes of behavior.

Traditionally the carl is large, strong, ugly, and rude. The last two of these characteristics contrast with the beauty and polite behavior of the nobly born romance heroes, while the first two suggest the potential power of the lower classes in conflict with their rulers. The Carl of Carlisle (in *Gawene and the Carle of Carelyle*) is a "dredfull" man with large features, a flat nose, and a big mouth. His arms are as thick as posts and his fingers are the size of an ordinary man's legs. He drinks from a cup that holds nine gallons, and he keeps a bull, a boar, a lion, and a bear as pets. Comparisons underscore his rustic nature: his hair lies on his shoulders as broad as a "fane" (winnowing basket), and his shoulders are the width of two "tayllors yardus." When he dislikes his guests' behavior, he hits them with his fist.

Sir Gromer Somer Jour, in the *Weddynge of Gawen*, can be recognized as the traditional monstrous churl by his great strength and by his rude address to King Arthur, but the underlying class implications of the romance become obvious in the description of Dame Ragnell, the hag whom Gawain is to marry, who is made "like a baralle." Her ugliness is to a large extent the result of inadequate personal care (and age): snotted nose, yellow teeth, knotted hair— all characteristics that would separate a commoner from a noblewoman. Gawain's marriage to this creature is made all the more painful because she insists on a public wedding, thus making it impossible for him to maintain social appearances. Her behavior at the wedding feast betrays her total lack of manners. She eats as much as any six others, and she breaks her food "ungoodly" with three-inch long nails. At the end of the story, social appearances again make Gawain's choice a hard one: whether to have his wife ugly at night when he must make love to her or ugly by day when the court can see his shame.

The other romances obscure the churlish origins of the antagonist, but these origins do show through from time to time in details of the description. The antagonist in the *Turke and Gowin*, for example, is short, broad, and made "like a Turke" in his legs and thighs,

and Gawain's first challenger in *Golagrus and Gawain* is "ane woun-
der grym sire" who complains that Kay has mistreated his servant.
Apart from these slight marks of their ancestry, however, the an-
tagonists have improved both in rank and behavior over their rela-
tives in *Gawene and the Carle of Carelyle* and the *Weddynge of Gawen.*
They are, after all, the ones with the right on their side even though
Gawain is the hero and ultimate victor in combat.

Although most of these romances include fighting, victory in
combat is never a solution to the problems of the plot. More often
than not, it is an additional complication, and the real solution lies
in an accommodation or agreement between Gawain and the an-
tagonist. Even when the antagonist is a nobleman, this is not an
accommodation between equals. Gawain is of higher rank, and his
willingness to reach an agreement is a sign of his true nobility. The
solution in these romances, in short, is an enforced equality of
terms between unequal persons, brought about not by insistence on
the part of the underling but by the grace of the superior.

The various tests that Gawain undergoes in these stories also
involve the idea of equality in various ways. The most interesting
and best known of these tests is the beheading game, which appears
in *Sir Gawain and the Green Knight* and in the *Grene Knight.* (There
are variants of it in the *Turke and Gowin* and the *Carle off Carlile* and
a vaguely similar exchange of blows in *Gawene and the Carle of
Carelyle.*) The basic idea of the beheading game is a tit-for-tat agree-
ment: you cut my head off today, and I'll cut yours off later.
Nothing could be fairer than this, and apparently nothing could be
safer for Gawain, who is the one to strike the first blow. It is like
the presumed agreement between the nobility and the commoners
whereby the commoners provide food, service, and taxes to their
superiors, in return for which the nobility will render services of
their own, tomorrow. In the beheading game, tomorrow actually
comes, as the Green Knight picks up his severed head and walks
out the door, reminding Gawain of his bargain.

The other test in the Green Knight stories, the bedroom temp-
tation, stresses equality of relationships in a different way. Gawain
is given an opportunity to make love to his host's wife, but true
courtly behavior requires that he treat the host as he would treat an
equal (or a superior, since, as Rauf Coilyear has reminded us, it is
the host's house) and use restraint. *Gawene and the Carle of Carelyle*
makes the point about obedience to the host particularly clear:

Gawain gets in bed with the carl's wife when the carl commands him to do so but does not touch her, also at his host's command; later, in reward for this obedient behavior, the carl allows Gawain to make love to his daughter.

Another very similar test is found in the Carl of Carlisle stories. While being entertained at the carl's home, Kay, Baldwin, and Gawain each in turn go to the stable to see after their horses, and there they find a foal belonging to their host. Kay and Baldwin both shoo the foal from the stable to keep it away from their own more noble horses, and the host rewards each knight with a buffet. Gawain, on the other hand, leads the foal back into the stable, covers it against the cold, and feeds it because he is being fed by the carl: "'We spend her that thy master dothe gett, / Whyll that we her byne.'" This turns out to be Gawain's key test, for the carl has sworn to kill all lodgers who will not respect his authority and do his bidding, and Gawain is the first to meet the test successfully. Other tests in these romances challenge the hero's devotion to traditional chivalric principles such as the obligation to defend women in distress (*Jeaste of Gawayne, Avowynge of Arthur*) or his ability to uphold both the obligation to his lord and to the right when the two come in conflict (*Golagrus and Gawain, Awntyrs off Arthure*). In two of the stories (*Turke and Gowin, Golagrus and Gawain*) Gawain is arbitrarily made to suffer hunger like a common man when his antagonist wishes it.

The question of who has the authority and when comes to the fore in the *Weddynge of Gawen*, when Arthur is forced to answer Sir Gromer's riddle and Gawain is forced to yield "sovereinté" to his ugly wife. Dame Ragnell's answer to the riddle indicates that women, a subject class like the commoners, still desire sovereignty above all else. Then Gawain, having perhaps learned from the riddle's answer but more likely just having no choice in the matter, actually gives sovereignty to his wife, and the magical happy ending is assured. But Dame Ragnell subsequently promises complete obedience to her husband. The real bargain is not one in which either Gawain or Dame Ragnell wields all control; it is rather an exchange of sovereignty in one case for sovereignty in another, and as such it is an image of the social bargain.

The same type of social bargain underlies the laws of hospitality in the Carl of Carlisle stories. When the Round Table knights are in need of lodging, the carl must give it to them; once in his home, the guests must obey his commands unquestioningly. The lower classes have the obligation to supply the nobility, a function which the carl lavishly fulfills in the great banquet at the end of the story, but the upper classes have the reciprocal obligation to protect and respect the commoners, as Gawain and the ideal knight Ironsides do. *Golagrus and Gawain* makes the same point about hospitality. In Tuscany, Kay comes to a knight's castle and helps himself to some food he finds there in order to feed Arthur's company, which is cold and hungry. The angered knight from whom the food has been taken gives Kay a blow and sends him running back to the king. Gawain then approaches the same castle and courteously asks for food, offering to pay for it. When the knight refuses, Gawain remarks that it is the knight's right to do so, and as soon as this concession has been made, the knight immediately offers the food, remarking that everything he owns is at Arthur's disposal. The sovereignty-for-sovereignty bargain is both a moral and social doctrine, one to which the nobility as well as the commons had subscribed in principle for a long time. However, the strong emphasis on it in these late romances and the threatening power that is exercised by the "churls" are indications of the increased importance of the landholder and mercantile classes among the ranks of romance readers.

The shift in audience had profound effects upon the romance itself, so much so that fifteenth-century romances have almost nothing in common with twelfth-century romances except the continued use of a few basic plots. The late medieval verse romances were entertainments of an hour or two, for a variety of audiences ranging from the serious and sophisticated to the ill-educated. Many late romances were merely simplified versions of older stories and types. Love stories remained popular, especially love stories of a sentimental nature, but some new types emerged too, most prominent among these being the didactic romance. In addition, we begin to see the first of the antiromances or burlesques, a sure sign that the medieval verse romance was a dying form.

9 *Satire, Sermons, and Sentiment*

In the late fourteenth century the romance was still as popular and vigorous as ever, but it had undergone some discernible changes. Romances were no longer composed in French, and tastes had shifted toward shorter romances. Some themes and stories had become less popular, among them the child exile stories and the troubled love romances, and in their place we find more domestic and fairyland romances. The child exile heroes, nobly born but alienated from their heritage, were replaced by heroes of lower birth whose social advancement was real. The impossible and tragic attachments of lovers like Tristan had given way to still unrealistic but less anxious fantasies in which the lovers actually gained the hands of their ladies and lived happily ever after. More romances were being written in rural areas, especially the north and west, away from the major centers of the court, and even the verse form had changed, tail rime and alliterative verse now being preferred to the older four-stress couplet.

All of these changes show that a major though gradual shift had occurred in the identity of the romance audience. The stories that had once appealed to the nobility and the functionaries of the larger courts were now becoming the property of country families and the middle classes with their aspirations of dignity and courtliness. Several pieces of evidence indicate the nature of the new audience. From the mid fifteenth century, for example, we have a manuscript which was the property of the Ireland family living in the small town of Hale, Lancashire. This family, which had received knighthood in the previous generation, preserved three romances (*Awntyrs off Arthure*, *Sir Amadace*, and *Avowynge of Arthur*) in a coarse parchment manuscript bound between wooden covers, along with a collection of town and manor records.[1] In 1517, another manuscript, containing the Stanzaic *Morte Arthur* and a version of *Ipomedon*, belonged to John Colyns, a London mercer.[2] Indeed, in pamphlets and plays (notably *The Knight of the Burning*

209

Pestle) of the sixteenth century, chivalric romances are constantly characterized as the fare of "tradesmen, country squires, apprentices, servants, old women, the old-fashioned and the half-educated of all classes"; they were held in contempt by William Tyndale, Roger Ascham, Thomas Nashe, and Erasmus, who called the Arthur and Lancelot romances "stories for fools and old women" *(fabulae stultae et aniles).*[3]

Such contempt is natural, for as the romance audience broadened, the romances themselves became less appropriate for the more sophisticated and better-educated readers who had once made up the bulk of their audience. These readers then turned to other forms of literature and began to see the romances for what they were, purveyors of chivalrous dreams to those who had no real hope of associating with the increasingly magnificent European courts, to the same people who thronged the streets of the small towns for the royal progresses. As evidence that the broadening process was already apparent in the late fourteenth century, we have the witness of two English satires of the period 1390–1440, Chaucer's tale of *Sir Thopas* and the somewhat later *Tournament of Tottenham.*

PARODIES OF ROMANCE

Chaucer's primary audience was the royal court of England. We know this not only from the sophistication of the works themselves but from Chaucer's own association with Lionel, duke of Clarence, and John of Gaunt and from a manuscript illumination that shows him reading the *Troilus* to King Richard's court. *The Canterbury Tales,* although they make much use of popular materials, were intended for cultured readers, as the literary-philosophic machinery of such "romances" as the Knight's and Franklin's tales shows. The fictional audience, the Canterbury pilgrims, is a broader and less sophisticated group than the one that Chaucer was actually addressing, and the pilgrims continually misinterpret and underestimate the stories that they hear. Chief of the misinterpreters is the host, Harry Bailey, a middle-class innkeeper with pretensions to understanding and judgment. When the host calls upon the pilgrim Chaucer for a tale, he gets a burlesque of tail-rime romances, a subtle and complex portrayal of the status of chivalric romance in late fourteenth-century England.

The pilgrim Chaucer says that *Sir Thopas* is a rime he learned long ago and the only tale he knows, indicating that it represents an ancient literary tradition and the only one (or the only one appropriate to this audience) known to people like Chaucer.[4] The fictional Chaucer is as middle-class and unsophisticated as the host, and he delivers his romance with all due seriousness. In form and style it mimics the contemporary variety of courtly romance, with its tail rime ("ryme dogerel," according to the host), fast moving plot, self-conscious narrator's commentary, and fairyland atmosphere. The opening line invokes the traditional romance audience ("Listeth, lordes . . ."), but the beginning of the second fit ("Now holde youre mouth, par charitee") betrays the ignorance of courtly address found in much of the later and cruder English romance. Sir Thopas's lonely quest and his suddenly conceived love for an "elf-queene" recalls the plot of the fairyland romances, but, divorced from any previous troubles of the hero and occurring before he has even had a sight of the lady, the motif is reduced to meaningless convention. The giant who swears by "Termagaunt" is reminiscent of the romance Saracens, but when we find that his name is Sire Olifaunt ('elephant') and that he has three heads, we see that he has another heritage, in the "wonders" books like Mandeville's *Travels*, which were extremely popular in Chaucer's day. In each of these cases, romance conventions are used in a blundering way, as if by an author who is only superficially familiar with them.

The humor of the tale depends primarily on inappropriateness and contradictions. We are told, for example, that Sir Thopas was born in a far country (the allusion is to the exotic settings of many romances), which is then specified as Flanders "al biyonde the see." He rides through a forest that contains many wild beasts: deer and rabbits. He makes a solemn oath on ale and bread. he falls in "love-longynge" when he sees the plants growing and hears the birds sing—a conventional detail borrowed from the lyric, not from the romance.

The most important bit of inappropriateness, however, is found in the description of the hero himself, who has a face white as "payndemayn," lips as red as a rose, a scarlet complexion, and a "semely" nose (VII, ll. 724–29). To begin with, the comparisons here are wrong. Paindemain, a fine white bread, was probably a food of the upper classes but is neither a conventional nor a proper comparison for the color of a hero's face. Scarlet, an expensive dye,

also has upper-class connotations and is referred to in other ro-
mances, but as a comparison for the hero's complexion it suggests
overexertion or perhaps adolescence. Any attention at all to the
hero's nose is out of place. But the main problem with the descrip-
tion is that it suggests the romance treatment of the heroine, not the
hero, and this is especially apparent in the very conventional simile
of the "lippes rede as rose." Elsewhere we are told that Sir Thopas
was "chaast and no lechour," also a characteristic associated with
romance heroines, and thus the overall impression is of a rather
effeminate hero, the sort perhaps that women readers of romance
might appreciate. This impression is confirmed by Thopas's im-
plicitly cowardly behavior when he meets Sir Olifaunt and by the
fact that his weapon is a "launcegay," a small lance that never
appears in real romances but that Gower, in Book VIII of the
Confessio Amantis, equates with Cupid's dart. In accordance with his
appearance and accoutrements, Thopas's adventures are timid in
nature:

> And for he was a knyght auntrous,
> He nolde sleper in noon hous,
> But liggen in his hoode (VII, ll. 909–11).

Sleeping outdoors might seem adventurous to those who read ro-
mances, but it is hardly a brave act for a romance hero.

Many of the inappropriate details associate Thopas with coun-
trymen or with the middle classes. When he goes hawking, he takes
along a goshawk, a yeoman's bird, and he is praised for his archery
and wrestling, both accomplishments prized in the village but not
among the court. His cordovan shoes, brown hose from Bruges,
and "syklatoun" robe, while they are costly and noble, are not the
dress of the noble hero; they are rather the sort of thing that preten-
tious middle-class burghers would wear or long to wear. And this
middle-class orientation also explains Thopas's birthplace in Flan-
ders, the major source of fine woven cloth in the late Middle Ages.

The butt of the satire in Sir Thopas is a once-courtly literature
that had fallen into the hands of would-be courtiers and thus be-
come absurdly fantastic. Another butt is the rural and middle-class
audience itself, with its unlikely sympathies for the chivalric.
Chaucer, a former comptroller of customs and the son of a wine
merchant, tells the story seriously and respectfully; he is insulted

when the host insults the tale. The host, for his part, fails to see the humor because he lacks the sophisticated understanding to puncture pretensions so similar to his own. The courtliness of the tale (including perhaps the "dogerel" tail rime, which Robert Mannyng said was too hard for "lewed" men) passes above him, and the satire goes beyond him.

The Tournament of Tottenham is a somewhat similar but much simpler work. It was written during the second quarter of the fifteenth century, presumably in the neighborhood of Tottenham, a small town just to the north of London, although both of the extant manuscripts are in a northern dialect. The idea is the same as in *Sir Thopas*—romance conventions in the hands of the lower classes—but the classes involved are even lower (they are ignorant rustics) and the humor is cruder. The story is that most conventional of all romance motifs in which a group of "bachelors" holds a tournament to determine who is most worthy to win the hand of a young woman. But the "knights" are men of the country, "swete swynkers" and "trewe drynkers," with names like Hawkyn, Herry, Gyb, and Hud, while the "lady" is Tyb, daughter of Randolph the Reeve.⁵ The whole point of the story lies in its substitution of the rustic for the courtly. The combatants dress themselves in mats and sheepskins, put bowls on their heads for helmets, ride mares, and fight with threshing flails.

The poet obviously enjoyed these incongruities, for he passed up few opportunities to develop them. As the tournament begins, Tyb is described (like a princess by the jousting field) sitting on a gray mare, cushioned by a sack full of seeds "for scho schuld syt softe," her good brood hen in her lap, and wearing a borrowed girdle, a garland made of bones, and a brooch of sapphires. The sight of her excites Gyb so much that he spurs his mare violently and it farts. The combatants each make vows or boasts, a convention found in the *Avowynge of Arthur*, *Clariodus*, and other romances. These include Dawkyn's vow to take Tomkyn's flail from him, Hud's vow to "scomfet" them all, and Hawkyn's vow to ride through the country two or three times and not leave until he has fallen down three times—unless Tyb calls him away or he has an attack of gout. There are also descriptions of the warriors' coats of arms: Hud's bears a hedging stick and rake with fiery dragons on it and three pieces of cake in each corner; Terry's has a dough trough and baker's shovel, a saddle with no cloth, and a wool fleece. The details of the combat are handled with vigor, and at the end the winner, Perkyn the potter, goes to bed with Tyb while the village wives come to fetch their husbands home.

It is a bit surprising that romance conventions should be placed in such a humble context, among farmers and potters instead of among the country landlord and merchants who were the more likely romance readers at this time, and yet it is probable that the peasantry knew something about and tried to imitate the old chivalric customs, whether seriously or in jest. Some evidence suggests that peasant tournaments were held in Europe during the fifteenth and sixteenth centuries, although just what the spirit of these tournaments may have been is not clear.[6] Perhaps the same village tradesmen who were then producing the Corpus Christi plays were also reading and emulating the literature of the nobility. But another possibility is that the *Tournament of Tottenham* and other descriptions of peasant tournaments are sheer hyperbole, intended to draw the strongest possible contrast between a courtly literature and its uncourtly audience. In any case, the satire is not aimed at the peasants or the romance alone but at both. By drawing attention to contrasting life-styles, one fictional and the other more or less real, the poem makes us aware of the absurdity of social pretentiousness. The major audience for this sort of satire would be neither the nobility nor the peasantry but those in between, the middle classes. For them the poem would entertain by abusing the silliness of a dying literary convention and the ignorant commoners as well, and it would contain a conservative moral lesson about keeping one's place in society.

FAITH, HUMILITY, AND CHARITY

Another sign that the original romance tradition was in decline was the appearance, in the fourteenth century, of didactic and intellectualized romances. Most popular literature, the romance included, is not didactic in its main intent. It does, indeed, deal in ideas and beliefs, but usually not in an obvious way. Whereas didactic fiction narrates stories in order to draw philosophic or moral conclusions from them, most popular literature tells stories that confirm preconceived conclusions held by the author and his audience alike. In this type of work the philosophy, though rigidly maintained, seldom becomes apparent to its audience, and the ideas found in popular works are more like myth or propaganda than like lessons. When a popular genre does become didactic, it may be because the authors have lost sight of or interest in the original meanings of the form and are substituting other meanings. This apparently happened to the romance as it came to be read by a wider audience, including people to whom the old themes of just rule, the stability of Christendom, and the reality of social advancement through love or military prowess were not very important. Not all the late romances tended toward didacticism, of course. While the main stream of the tradition gradually shifted its ideas and emphasis to conform to the tastes of its new audiences, a few writers chose to use the old stories for their own contemporary purposes. Similar tendencies toward intellectualization of a popular genre can be seen in the later stages of the American western and in some recent science fiction.

The quality of the intellectualized romances varies greatly, just as the quality of the mainstream romances does. The best of them, of course, are *Sir Gawain and the Green Knight* (written about 1375–1400) and the romances of the *Canterbury Tales* (1380–1400): *The Knight's Tale, The Man of Law's Tale, The Wife of Bath's Tale, The Squire's Tale,* and *The Franklin's Tale.* Three of these—*Gawain, Man of Law,* and *Wife of Bath*—make particularly interesting studies when compared to their analogues because they are especially close to the mainstream romances in story and, to some extent, in idea. The worst of the intellectualized romances are those that show neither a feeling for the traditional themes nor any strong sense or originality. The authors of these works—Lydgate is a prominent example—seem to have felt that they needed to make the romance respectable; unfortunately their idea of respectability consisted of nothing more than the imitation of classical authors and the tacking-on of useful morals. An excellent example of this type of work is the late fifteenth-century Scottish poem *Lancelot of the Laik,* which takes one of the most exciting romance stories and treats it in a thoroughly unimaginative, pedestrian fashion, made worse by the author's apologies for his lack of skill. For this author, as for others of his time, respectability requires Chaucerian apparatus—namely heroic couplets, a division of the poem into books, and a dream-vision opening in which the author explains that he undertook the composition as penance for sins against the god of love. The lesson consists of a long, dull discourse in book II on the duties of a ruler.

Although the mainstream romances are frequently silly and monotonous, they never attain the unrelieved tediousness of works like this.

Less pretentious didactic romances, which avoid fancy rhetoric and retain more of the original romance spirit, are more entertaining, even if the obviousness of their messages makes them less interesting than the mainstream romances. At least they have the vigor of works with a real audience, for obvious lessons have their vogue too, especially during certain historical periods. The popularity of works such as the *Prick of Conscience* and the *Cursor Mundi* shows that the late Middle Ages was one of these periods, either because the audience really wanted such fare or simply because the authors thought that the audiences ought to want it. It is likely enough that the popularity was real. We recall that the host in the *Canterbury Tales*, having totally failed to appreciate the satirical wit of *Sir Thopas*, responds enthusiastically to the tedious aphorisms of the *Melibee*.

Unlike either Chaucer's romances with their complex insights or *Lancelot of the Laik* with its pretentious monotony are six fourteenth- and fifteenth-century poems that deserve to be called popular didactic romances: *The King of Tars*, *Sir Gowther*, *Sir Cleges*, *Sir Amadace*, *Sir Isumbras*, and *Roberd of Cisyle*. These works are all short, the longest being the *King of Tars* which contains fewer than 1,300 lines, and most of them are written in tail-rime stanzas. All of them concentrate their attentions on the plot and its meaning; description is relatively rare, even by comparison to other romances, and rhetoric is almost totally absent. The plots are standard ones, most of them being variations of plots found in other romances, but each plot illustrates some moral or religious lesson. The lessons are obvious and conservative ones, and all are stated clearly, even though the meaning of the romances would otherwise be clear. Most interesting of all, the philosophy of these romances is not much different from that of the standard romances of the period. There are three major themes: Christianity is the true faith; charity is good and will be rewarded; pride is evil and will be punished. Superficially, all of these are religious lessons, and certainly they are presented as such, with miracles, angels, and pious protestations appearing prominently in all six romances. Yet the true-faith message is just a more clearly stated version of the major theme of the crusading romances, that western beliefs are superior to those of the east, and the interest in charity and humility is as much social as it is religious. Both are virtues in which the middle class had an interest because charity means, in effect, that the wealthy should share their assets with those below them, and humility means that the powerful should not be too cocky.

The Kings of Tars ('Tartary') is a story about the conversion of Saracens, and it bears some similarity to the legends of Constance and Florence of Rome. The main character is not the king but his daughter, whose name is not given. In essence, the story tells how she, in order to save her father's kingdom from a Saracen invasion, agrees to marry the sultan of Damascus, then proves the truth of the Christian faith to the sultan and converts him. Like most of the Christian romances, the *King of Tars* depends upon the spectacular and the miraculous for its appeal. The central plot development consists of a miracle through which the power of Christianity is demonstrated. The lady, who has pretended to adopt the sultan's faith in order to marry him, gives birth to a child who is only a lump of flesh, without legs, arms, nose, or eyes. The sultan then realizes that his wife has not really abandoned her faith and thinks that her "fals bileve" is the cause of the child's deformity. She insists, however, that the cause is *his* religion and, as proof, instructs him to pray to his gods to make the child whole. When this proves unsuccessful, she gets a Christian priest to baptize the "flesh," and the child is instantly restored to its proper form. Another miracle occurs when the sultan is christened: his skin, previously black and "lothely," becomes white, and this demonstrates to the heroine that her husband has truly accepted Christianity.

The romance is as self-righteously one-sided and bloodthirsty as other popular religious pieces. The Saracens are ugly "hethen houndes" who love war and mercilessly slaughter the Christians, "so wilde thai were and wode." They always outnumber the Christians—ten to one at one point, 10,000 to one at another. In return, all the unrepentant Saracens are massacred at the end—30,000 of them, "both blo and blac." Nevertheless, the romance shows a rudimentary concern for all articles of faith, and this concern can look almost like an understanding of the competing religion. The Saracens have a "lawe" that must be learned, and the sultan adheres to it faithfully until it is proved inferior. The Saracens are willing to die for it, a fact which casts a bit of a shadow over the story's conclusion. But the understanding is illusory. All that the romance has done is to draw certain simple parallels between the two religions in order to create the appearance of competition—and this only to prove the superiority of Christianity. The issue is one of authority. Christianity is better because it is true, as proved by miracles. For the miracles to work, proper procedure must be followed: the heroine obtains a priest from the sultan's prison, makes sure that he knows Christian doctrine, and then has him prepare holy water for the christening. Only with these precautions will the miracle work, but, despite the talk of law and doctrine, neither behavior nor ideas are at issue here. (The Christians behave just like the Saracens.) Faith is the only thing, and the essence of this faith is made plain when the heroine instructs the newly converted sultan in Christian teachings. In the briefest possible way, she explains five necessary beliefs: the Trinity, the Virgin Birth, the Harrowing of Hell, the Resurrection, and the Last Judgment (Auchinleck Manuscript, ll. 823–70). It is a fascinating insight into popular religion, focusing as it does on the paradoxes, miracles, and personal rewards of the faith. The message of this little catechism is the same as that of the romance: believe in what you are told, however marvelous it may seem, and you will be rewarded.

Another religious-authoritarian romance is *Sir Gowther*. This odd little story combines a number of romance themes, including the fairy child, the Saracen who desires to marry a Christian princess, the Christian-Saracen war, and the superman-knight in disguise. The similarities to the *King of Tars* are many, but the theme of this work is the power of God over the devil rather than the power of Christianity over heathen religions. In addition, the romance is set apart by its unusual story of the hero's origins (the story of Robert the Devil, known from other sources) and its theme of penance. The hero, Sir Gowther, is the offspring of a devil who has appeared to the mother in the shape of her husband (compare *Richard Coer de Lyon* and *Kyng Alisaunder*). Though strong and brave, Gowther starts off as a very bad boy indeed. When sent to be wet-nursed, he sucks so hard that he kills nine nurses (thus causing their husbands to complain). As a young man he is so wicked that his supposed father, the duke of Estryke, dies of sorrow and his mother locks herself in a castle. Once he is duke, Gowther graduates to higher and higher levels of wickedness: he rapes nuns and burns down their nunnery, kills husbands and takes off their wives, makes friars jump off cliffs, burns hermits and poor widows. When finally someone suggests to him that he must be the son of a devil, Gowther and the plot set off in an entirely different direction. Having inquired of his mother and decided that he is a devil, he goes to Rome to seek absolution from the pope. His penance is to eat no food except what comes to him from the mouths of dogs and to say nothing until he receives a sign that he is forgiven. In the remainder of the story Gowther, following these instructions, defends the Holy Roman Empire against the Saracens and wins the love of the emperor's daughter. The sign of his forgiveness, expected though it is, almost rivals the marvels at the beginning of the romance. When the emperor's daughter, who is dumb like Gowther, sees him wounded in his last battle against the Saracens, she falls out of her tower and is taken for dead. But as soon as the pope and cardinals arrive for the funeral, she arises and declares that Gowther is pardoned. Then he builds the displaced nuns a new nunnery and becomes emperor.

The lesson of this amazing story is the power of God as shown through miracles. The major miracle is the conversion of the devil child into a saint: after Gowther's death, he is buried at an abbey and due to him the blind, dumb, crippled, and insane are healed "thoro tho grace of God allmyght." But the progress of the plot is marked by many other miracles, from the birth of the hero to previously childless parents, to his sudden change of heart, to the dogs who keep appearing with food in their mouths. As in the *King of Tars*, however, God's power is manifested expressly through the Church. Gowther's sins are sins against Church officials (friars, parsons), Church establishments (the nunnery), Church sacraments (marriage), and the protected of the Church (hermits and widows). The penance of Gowther and the miracle that signals his forgiveness both occur under direct supervision of the pope, whose paternal concern for his people is made clear when he says to the suppliant hero that he would have made war on him if Gowther had not come to Rome of his own accord. Gowther's stewardship of the Holy Empire, his building of the nunnery, and his sainthood also emphasize the role of the Church as the earthly instrument of God's benevolent power. The romance is really a bit of pro-Church propaganda, and it is interesting to recall that it was written at a time (about 1400) when some institutions of the Church had come under attack—by Wyclif, Langland, and others.

Along with their other messages, both of these romances assert the theme of acceptance, one of the most frequently expressed religious themes of the late Middle Ages. Take the sufferings that are sent you now, they say, and you will be rewarded later. (The rewards, incidentally, are temporal.) Two other romances built largely around this theme are *Sir Isumbras* and *Roberd of Cisyle*. These works are even more openly didactic than the *King of Tars* and *Sir Gowther*. *Sir Isumbras* is a moralized version of the popular Saint Eustace story, found also in *Sir Eglamour of Artois*, *Sir Torrent of Portyngale*, and *Octavian*. The basic plot of the Eustace legend concerns a man who loses property, wife, and children (the children being carried off by various animals) and later has them restored. In *Sir Isumbras* this loss is presented as an antidote for pride. Isumbras is a virtuous and fortunate knight, with a beautiful wife and three beautiful children, but in his pride he does not think about God's works. So an angel appears to him and gives him a choice: he can suffer sorrow either in his youth or in his old age. He chooses to take his suffering now, and promptly his trials begin. When they are over, his wealth and family are returned for the rest of his life, and after he dies he goes to heaven. To this comforting but rather ordinary theme are added several other motifs, all fairly conventional ones and not necessarily related to one another or to the main theme. The author seems to have taken every available opportunity in a short space to introduce romance clichés. There is a Saracen sultan who covets Isumbras's wife and offers one hundred pounds for her so that she can be his queen. (Isumbras makes a melodramatic refusal of this offer, but the sultan has Isumbras beaten, abducts the wife, and leaves the money.) There is an episode in which Isumbras lives as a commoner (an ironsmith) for seven years and then another in which he travels as a palmer for seven years. There is a recognition scene between Isumbras and his wife, he as palmer, she as Saracen queen, à la *King Horn*. (Actually she recognizes the 100 pounds first and then her husband.) There is a stone-putting contest and a tournament and a war to convert the Saracens in which Isumbras, his wife, and three sons, with the help of an angel, defeat 30,000 heathens.

The ironsmith episode is particularly interesting. It comes just after the hero's final misfortune (the loss of his children) and begins the process of reversal. It contains more specific detail than other such scenes in romance and indicates that the author had some interest in, if not special knowledge of, the blacksmith's trade. It also expresses a medieval version of the work ethic, certainly an unusual thing to find in a chivalric romance. Isumbras, impoverished and in grief, approaches some ironsmiths and begs for food. They respond by suggesting that he work for his living as they do, and he agrees. They put him to work as an apprentice, hauling iron ore out of a pit ("sloghe") until he has learned to build the fire and is ready to receive "mannes hyre." Even more clearly than the opening scene in which Isumbras chooses present trials for future bliss, this episode expresses a belief in the rewards-for-suffering idea. Isumbras truly works his way up the social ladder. His skills as a smith enable him to make himself a suit of armor; wearing this and riding a blacksmith's horse, he goes into battle against the heathens, where his distinguished fighting wins him a warrior's steed. The theme of the hero suffering in a humble disguise is old, but the idea of actually working for success is a new and middle-class addition.

Roberd of Cisyle ('Sicily') has the same lesson but is directed against the pride of the powerful instead of emphasizing the positive virtues of the humble, as *Sir Isumbras* does. The author of this short, moral piece begins by addressing "princes proude that beth in pres" and tells the story of an eminently successful king, the flower of chivalry, whose brothers are respectively pope and Holy Roman emperor and who "thoughte he hedde no peer in al the world" until an angel teaches him a lesson by taking his place and making him a court fool. Robert at first resists indignantly but, after suffering a series of humiliations, admits to being a fool and is restored to his throne. The lesson of this tale, stated sermon fashion in Latin with an English translation (because Robert does not understand the Latin) and frequently repeated, is that God can make the high low and the low high: "Deposuit potentes de sede, / Et exaltavit humiles." Of special interest are the confrontations of the deposed Robert with a sexton and a porter, sympathetically portrayed as innocent victims of the proud and raving king, and the fact that, like Sir Gowther, Robert is made to eat with the dogs in the palace.

The duty of the rich to share their wealth is the subject of two other moral romances, *Sir Cleges* and *Sir Amadace*. Both assert a firm belief in this duty, and both attempt to confront an obvious objection to it, namely that if the rich continue to give their wealth away, eventually they will having nothing more to give. This thinking raises the specter of total social disruption, as the virtuous nobility are systematically reduced to poverty and powerlessness. The actual threat of such disruption in medieval society was probably not very great, but the simple logic of the matter seems to have begged for a simple answer, and both romances offer the same one: God will provide.

Sir Cleges is the less complex of the two works and makes its point with greater power. The poem is actually a combination of romance and fabliau. It is set in the time of Uther Pendragon—a conventional use of Arthurian background to indicate that this is a story about the established nobility, as in the Gawain romances. Sir Cleges, a "jentyll," "fre" ('generous'), and "corteys" knight, gives all his money and food away to the poor and to minstrels until "all his good was spent awaye." Instead of complaining, however, he thanks God "of hys dysese and hys povertt, that to hym was sent," and cherries miraculously appear on a tree for him although it is Christmas time. Dressed in poor clothes, he takes these cherries as a gift to the king, and in return is eventually restored to his former state and better. It is a charming story, made even more entertaining by the addition of the fabliau element. When Sir Cleges arrives at court, he is insulted (called "chorle") and abused by the porter, usher, and steward, each of whom in turn demands one-third of whatever reward the king gives Cleges for the cherries. So when the king allows Cleges to choose his own reward, he asks for twelve strokes, to be dispensed as he sees fit, and he gives a thorough beating to the three. The episode is in keeping with the poem's lighthearted approach throughout, and no blanket condemnation of court functionaries is intended. (Cleges himself is made a steward at the end of the story.) But the treatment of porter, usher, and steward strikes a notable contrast with the treatment of similar characters in *Roberd of Cisyle*, drawing our attention to the fact that *Sir Cleges* is a more socially conservative romance than the two just discussed. In fact, the theme of liberality itself tends to justify the existing social order.

Sir Amadace takes a more somber and philosophical approach, but the main idea is the same. The lesson goes beyond praise of liberality, however, and promotes in addition the more general virtue of acceptance. Amadace, himself nearly at his last penny because of his lavish generosity, comes upon a woman grieving over the corpse of her husband, a merchant, who has died in debt because he gave away all he had to rich and poor alike. She thought he was a fool for doing so, but his answer was always that God had sent it all to him. Now his body lies unburied and stinking until the final creditor is paid. Amadace, perceiving a kinship between himself and the dead man, uses his last forty pounds to pay the debt and finance a funeral for the merchant. Then in the last half of the story a white knight on a milk-white steed assists Amadace in winning the hand of a princess in a tournament. The knight, of course, turns out to be the dead merchant who has interceded with God for the hero. But Amadace's rewards of wealth, wife, children, and kingdom are not finally confirmed until one last trial has been passed. He had promised to divide all that he won with the knight, and after the tournament, marriage with the princess, and birth of a son, the white knight reappears to insist that he be given half the wife and half the child. Amadace pleads with him, but the wife melodramatically offers her life to save her husband's word of honor. At the last moment the knight reveals who he is and spares the wife, having made the point that whoever serves God truly will be granted "alle hor will, / Till hevyn the redy waye."

Though fast-moving, the romance concentrates so exclusively on its message that attention is distracted from the story. The various episodes of the plot are obviously contrived, and everything comes much too easily to Amadace. The winning of the tournament and the princess's love are dismissed in a few lines, and then, when the king promptly offers his daughter and half the kingdom, Amadace rather absurdly answers with a simple "Gramarcy." The virtuous characters are so mindlessly virtuous in their extremities of distress that only the miraculous conclusion prevents them from seeming utter fools (a possibility that is suggested, in passing, more than once). The tale's moral philosophy is supported only by whatever apparent truth it may have and by the stage-managed happy ending. Thus, like the rest of the didactic romances but somewhat more obviously than some of them, it expresses complete faith in a benevolent order, managed by God and conferring worldly as well as heavenly benefits.

SENTIMENTALITY AND SENSATIONALISM

One of the most noticeable developments in the later years of the medieval romance is a tendency toward sentimentality. *Sir*

Amadace illustrates this tendency and so do a number of romances already discussed, including *William of Palerne*, the *Squyr of Lowe Degre*, and several of the domestic romances. The elements of the sentimental tradition in romance are very similar to those of eighteenth- and nineteenth-century sentimentalism, leading one to suspect that there were similarities in the audiences as well. Basic to both traditions is the belief in a benevolent order of things, a world in which evil is either a mistake or an exception to the general rule. The vast majority of characters in the sentimental romances are good in a very obvious and conventional sense: they are motivated by honesty, faithfulness, and a devotion to family and social ties. The evil characters are few and lack motivation entirely; in the course of the story they either repent and reform or else they are summarily eliminated when the truth of their evil deeds comes to light. A sense of childlike innocence pervades these stories. The virtuous are really as virtuous as they constantly protest that they are; the wicked, who also protest virtue, are totally wicked.

A contrasting but equally important feature of these romances is their addiction to sensationalism. This sometimes makes itself felt in horrible or grotesque situations such as the heroines' guarding of dead bodies in *Sir Amadace* and the *Squyr of Lowe Degre* or the cannibalism of the *Knight of Curtesy* (discussed below). More often it can be seen in the general extremity of situation and of passion. Hero and heroine fall in love hopelessly and forever; characters face death rather than betray their word or their virtue. The devotion to extremes carries over into the language. No sentimental author could get halfway through his story if deprived of the swoon and the word "allas." Like the sentimental literature of a later age, these romances typically have inconsistent or irrational plots that are a direct consequence of the sensationalism combined with the philosophy of benevolence. To create the extremities of distress it is necessary to ignore the intrinsic goodness of the characters, but in order to achieve a satisfactory conclusion to the story it is necessary to invoke the goodness once again. So plot complications introduced at one point are promptly and conveniently forgotten at another.

The evolving sentimental tradition in its purest form may be represented by four romances, the earliest of which is probably *The Knight of Curtesy and the Fair Lady of Faguell*, a late fourteenth-century piece that survives only in a sixteenth-century printed edition. This is an excellent example of the type. It is the story of a completely (and incredibly) chaste love with a sensational and pathetic ending. The lady, who is married, and the young knight fall in love but vow to keep their love innocent, "as chyldren that together are kynde" (l. 49). Despite the fact that this is compared to a brother-sister relationship, it actually imitates a mother-child love, for the lady's husband has in effect adopted the knight, providing him with all his wants. Like other essentially illicit relationships, this one must be kept secret because it cannot survive the suspicions of the outside world, here represented by the lord and other members of the court, who envy the favored treatment given the knight (in a kind of sibling rivalry). When word of the lovers' meetings comes to the lord, he sends the knight off crusading, after a tearful parting in which the lady vows eternal love and gives the knight a hank of her yellow hair to wear as a favor.

Since the affair, although passionate, is love in idea only, the knight must not return to the lady, and he dies while fighting in Rhodes but not until he has instructed a page to cut out his heart, wrap it in the lady's hair, and return it to her. The knight's body is to be buried in the "crosse-waie." Returning to Faguell, the page shows the heart to the lord, and he, remarking that their love "was hote in-dede," has his cook prepare the heart and serve it to the lady. Once she has eaten the heart and been informed of that fact, she again protests her chastity and prepares to die: "Sythe it is buryed in my body, / On it shall I never eate other meate" (ll. 491-92). What appeal this story had must have come from the intensely emotional symbolism and language. The surface innocence contrasts strongly with the underlying fantasy desires and creates a titillation quite unlike that found in other romances, even in those which concern illicit love-wishes.

Another story of extreme, chaste, and tragic love is *Amoryus and Cleopes*, written in 1448-49 by John Metham, a "sympl scoler of philosophye" from Cambridge, and dedicated to Sir Miles and Lady Stapleton of Ingham, in Norfolk. Metham was not a romance writer but rather a translator of miscellaneous pieces from Latin, including a palmistry, physiognomy, and some prognostications. *Amoryus and Cleopes* is not a true romance but rather a collection of varied materials, including discourses on Ptolemaic astronomy and pagan religion, dragon lore, and a pious legend about the conversion of the heathens, into which is inserted a sentimental, pathetic love story that serves as an excuse to pull all the other materials together into a single work. Metham's purpose, however, is that of a popular writer, for he says that he undertook the task of writing "to comfforte them that schuld falle in hevyness: / For tyme on-ocupyid, qwan folk have lytyl to do, / On haly-dayis to rede, me thynk yt best so" (ll. 2209-11). Metham was an unskilled but seri-ous-minded versifier in imitation of Chaucer and Lydgate, whom he claims as his "masters."[7] His love story is simply the tale of Pyramus and Thisbe, with the names and a few circumstances changed. Metham has also plundered traditional romance for a jousting contest and a dragon fight to enliven the action.

The Pyramus-Thisbe story lends itself to sentimental romance because it treats of inflamed passion in circumstances that prevent consummation. First the wall and later the lion intervene to keep the lovers from touching one another, and their desire must seek outlet through symbolic action and language. Metham does not bother to explain why the hero and heroine cannot simply seek approval of their love from their parents. Cleopes makes her love known to Amoryus by holding up and pointing to an illuminated page in a prayer book that shows a hind embracing a hart, along with some other love symbolism. He demonstrates his love for her by wearing a replica of this "conseyt" as he participates in a tourna-ment. They agonize over their feelings and their enforced separa-tion through the cranny in the wall and kiss the wall instead of each other. With a considerable amount of rhetoric, they stab them-selves to death, sacrifices to one another and to love: "O Jovys! my vyrgynyte to the I sacryfyse in this nede, / With the roseat blod off pure maydynhede" (ll. 1762-63).

Although the author appears sympathetic to this passion, he does not lose sight of the fact that it contrasts with a calmer and ultimately more satisfying "Christian" love. The love of Amoryus and Cleopes is "delectabyl woo," "lovys fevyr," "veneryan dysyre," and its ending is as stormy as its course. Another kind of love is introduced after the double suicide when a holy hermit passes by, sees the bodies, and restores the two lovers to life so that through them he can convert the whole capital city of Persia to the Christian faith. The resurrected hero and heroine are still lovers but not passionate ones. There is no more emotional language, but Amoryus says that his love for Cleopes was never greater than at the hour of their mutual baptism. They get married, have many children, die natural deaths, and are buried in a fine tomb. Cleopes is an example to all women of "trwe love, stedffastnesse and curtesy." The sudden shift in the direction of Metham's story is a reminder that, despite its increasing popularity, sentimental and passionate love continued to be seen as socially irresponsible and un-Christian. This made such love more exotic, but it also created a requirement that the love end with the death of the lovers or with the impress of conventional behavior and morality.

Roswall and Lillian is a simple, entertaining little romance in which a child hero and his homelike world come in conflict with various symbols of the adult world. It seems to have been written in the late fifteenth century, but it survives only in two printed editions, one of the seventeenth and one of the eighteenth century. It has neither the passion nor the passionate language of the other sentimental romances, but it does share their essential world view and their innocents-in-distress theme. The hero, Roswall, is a beautiful young prince exiled from home and country because of a combination of shortsighted justice and selfish treachery. His problems begin when he attempts to interfere in the adult world through motives of mercy. He releases three unhappy prisoners from his father's prison, and the father, not knowing who has done this deed, vows to kill the culprit on sight. When it becomes clear that Roswall is the guilty one, his mother and father send him from the kingdom because the father cannot betray his word, even though he now wishes he had never given it. The sympathetic parents want to send Roswall to the kingdom of Bealm where he will be received into another royal family, but this is prevented by an evil steward who deceives Roswall and takes his place during the journey to Bealm. Subsequently, the hero is taken into the home of an old, poor widow (where he is educated along with her own son) and later brought to the court of Bealm where everyone makes much of him and where the beautiful princess falls in love with him.

The steward, who replaces Roswall for his own personal advancement and who later is married (briefly) to the heroine Lillian, is the adult version of the hero. That is essentially the meaning of his treason, for the adult world is treacherous when it is not being guided by mistaken principles of conduct. While the steward masquerades as Roswall, Roswall himself goes under the name of Dissawar ('deceiver'?), a "poor" name, as we are constantly told. The story of Roswall's winning of Lillian is the standard romance plot of the disguised hero in tournament, fighting in armor of three different colors on three different days, the armor having been given to him by three knights who turn out to be the released prisoners. The conclusion sees the overcoming of the steward, the marriage of hero and heroine, and a restoration of the family situation (actually a reunion with the mother only, after the father has died). The child's fantasies of exciting private adventures occurring amid the comforts of home triumph over all else.

The late romance *Clariodus* is a sentimental version of the best-knight-in-the-world story, translated from a French prose romance by an author who was strongly influenced by Chaucer. The romance is long (over 11,000 lines) and tedious. The poet describes in detail almost anything having to do with the court and courtly behavior (fine clothing, the seating arrangements at feasts, etc.), and sentimental scenes and situations abound. The brave and handsome hero is the object of all women's affections but saves his own love for Meliades, daughter of King Philipon of England. The course of their love is marked by frequent exchanging of tokens, several tournaments, and a variety of adventures. Their feelings are passionate—her love is a "seikness" that grows about the heart—but their relationship remains honorable and chaste. The romance has one main villain, the envious Sir Thomas who is eventually executed, and a host of minor troublemakers, all of whom repent of their misdeeds. The best of these is a wonderfully cruel knight called "the Felloun but Petie," who threatens the whole countryside with revenge because his wife has been ravished. Clariodus takes up the fight, but when the Felloun finds out whom he is fighting (the worthiest knight in the world), he immediately gives up, begs mercy for his wickedness, and frees all the prisoners whom he has taken. This touches Clariodus so much that he weeps.

The plot of *Clariodus* is swelled by numerous episodes, mostly of a conventional nature. These include the rescue of ladies in distress, a fight with a lion (that turns out to be a knight transformed by magic), secret meetings between hero and heroine, crusading against the Saracens, a false accusation of treason against the hero, and a tournament with vows. In addition, both hero and heroine endure a period disguised as commoners, he as a palmer and shiphand, she as a servant dressed in sackcloth and performing such household chores as making the fire, sweeping, and going to market. Since a period of humble life was standard for the romance hero but not for the heroine, this last motif seems to imply that the role of the woman in *Clariodus* is different from that in other romances. In fact, Meliades is a more active and involved heroine than usual, and the author thinks more in terms of her point of view. Her role is still passive, but adventures affect her more directly than other heroines and we are made aware of her fear and her suffering. To a much greater extent than earlier romances, this work is directed at women, their interests, their concerns, their anxieties, and it is fitting—if somewhat overdue—that by the end of the medieval period romances should have begun to take cognizance of this long-important part of their audience.

In fact, the sentimental tradition itself was probably an offering to the women among the audience, as well as to some other new audience elements, including the laboring and merchant classes, the rural, children, and the elderly. What these people have in common that sets them apart from the original romance audience is a sense of dependency combined with a lack of excitement and significance in their daily lives. They are not concerned with the way the country is run, with the nature or reality of foreign threats, or with readjustments in social relationships; they are concerned with household, family and personal relationships, and the truth of the principles by which they live. They are not looking for the promise of personal achievement as much as for some antidote against dull routine. They want emotion, not action. The sentimental romances provided all these things. In place of politics, crusading, warfare, and social climbing, all of which are absent or played down in didactic and sentimental romance, the new romances offered simple moral lessons, absolute good opposed to absolute evil, scenes of home and family, and strong feelings. The emotion and sensationalism supplied the needed excitement, and it did so within a domestic context. The old heroes sought their challenges in Denmark, Greece, and the Holy Land; the new adventures of death and passion take place in the garden, chamber, or at the dinner table. The main characters are still noble and the main scene is still the court, but the shift in emphasis is undeniable.

The old stories, old characters, and old scenes were retained because they had set the standards for imitation and because, being unreal to the present-day audience, they offered greater possibilities for excitement and the unusual. They were also retained just because they were old and therefore implied conservatism and stability. These audiences wanted something vital and different but they did not want essential change, so they looked to ancient tales in ancient forms, to stories of King Arthur and the crusades, both of which seemed to have historical relevance but which happened in a different world. Chaucer and the author of the *Tournament of Tottenham* saw the effects of these old forms in the hands of a new audience and ridiculed the incongruity. John Metham, with his aristocratic leanings, also saw what had happened and marveled greatly that "men do noght wryte knyghtys dedys, nowdyr in prose ner ryme" as they had in older times (ll. 2105-06). He did not know, however, whether the cause of this was the "encresyng of vexacion" (that is, the civil turmoil during the Wars of the Roses) or "defaute of cunnyng" (the decline of learning—a typical scholar's complaint). It was neither. The audience for popular literature had expanded and changed and, with it, the literature itself.

What eventually happened to the popular medieval romance? In one sense we can say that it died with the Middle Ages, for romances in verse were no longer being written by the end of the sixteenth century. But it did not die without leaving descendants: two obvious ones, at least. One of these was the prose romance. Following a development that had taken place much earlier in France, English authors began almost systematically to redo the old verse romances in prose, beginning shortly after 1400. Before the end of the fifteenth century the stories of Horn (*King Ponthus*), Ipomedon, and Melusine, along with Arthurian, Charlemagne, Alexander, Troy, and Thebes legends, had appeared in prose. Other stories, never made the subject of English verse romances, were added, notably Caxton's version of the Godfrey of Bouillon legend. The prose romance flourished in the sixteenth century and left its own descendants afterward. The other popular form that developed from the verse romance was the ballad. Ballads seem to be the end result of the process of shortening and ruralization that affected the romance in the late Middle Ages. Many ballads are just brief, dramatic versions of romance stories. There are early ballads dealing with Horn, Arthur, and Gawain, and several of the later romances, including the *Knight of Curtesy* and *Roswall and Lillian*, have a distinct ballad flavor to them. A large number of ballads originated in western and northern Britain, Scotland in particular, and this conforms to a similar tendency that we have noticed among the didactic romances and that is represented by *Roswall and Lillian* and *Clariodus* as well. The two types, romance and ballad, clearly merge into one another in that famous and interesting manuscript, the Percy Folio, written about 1650. Ballads in turn have connections with still later literary forms, notably the popular song.

So the medieval verse romance was the beginning of a popular tradition that extends to the present day. In some ways it was a crude beginning, for its quality, even considered as popular work, was extremely uneven, and it often seems not to have known its audience well. In the latter respect, popular literature has certainly improved since the Middle Ages, but this is mainly the result of increased experimentation, as more readers became available for popular writings and as the costs of publication dramatically decreased. The medieval writers saw only a small segment of their potential audience (if that), worked from an inadequately small set of models, had little or no profit from their work, and faced formidable problems in the publication and distribution of their stories. Despite all this, they left a tradition that was enduring, entertaining, and important.

Chronological List of Romances

This list includes all the popular verse romances of England written between 1150 and 1500 and existing in more than fragmentary form. Brief notes on dates and editions are appended. Both French and English romances are included (French romances are indicated by asterisks), as are a few romances that are still unedited. Prose romances are excluded, with the exception of *Fouke Fitzwarin*, which is believed to be a translation of an otherwise unknown verse romance. Also excluded are the more literary romances: *Sir Gawain and the Green Knight* and the romance stories of Chaucer, Gower, and Lydgate.

Many editions of individual works are found in the following series: Anglo-Norman Text Society (Oxford); Les Classiques Française du Moyen Âge (Paris); Early English Text Society, original and extra series (London); Société des Anciens Textes Français (Paris); Scottish Text Society (Edinburgh). Several romances in English are available in two relatively recent collections: Walter Hoyt French and Charles Brockway Hale (eds.), *Middle English Metrical Romances*, 2 vols. (New York, 1930; reissued 1964); Donald B. Sands (ed.), *Middle English Verse Romances* (New York, 1966). Two basic reference works on the romances, both of which include bibliographical materials, are M. Dominica Legge, *Anglo-Norman Literature and Its Background* (Oxford, 1963), and *A Manual of the Writings in Middle English, 1050–1500*, Vol. I, ed. J. Burke Severs (New Haven, 1967).

Tristan by Thomas, after 1150. Ed. Bédier, 1902–05; Wind, 1960.
Lais by Marie de France, 1150–1200. Ed. Lods, 1959; Rychner, 1966.
Amis et Amiles, 12th century. Ed. Kölbing, 1884.
Romance of Horn by Thomas, 1170–80. Ed. Pope, 1955–64.
Roman de Toute Chevalerie by Thomas of Kent, 1170–80? Not edited.
Roman de Troie by Benoit de Sainte-Maure, ca.1184. Ed. Constans, 1904–09.
Ipomedon by Hue de Rotelande, ca.1190. Ed. Kölbing & Koschwitz, 1889.
Protheselaus by Hue de Rotelande, ca.1190. Ed. Kluckow, 1924.
Tristan by Béroul, 1190–1200. Ed. Muret, 1913; Ewert, 1963–70.
Estoire de Waldef, 1190–1200. Not edited.
Amadas et Idoine, 1190–1200. Ed. Reinhard, 1926; Hippeau, 1969.
Lai d'Haveloc, ca.1200. Ed. Bell, 1925.
Boeve de Haumtone, ca.1200. Ed. Stimming, 1899.
Fergus by Guillaume le Clerc, after 1220. Ed. Martin, 1872.
King Horn, ca.1225. Ed. Hall, 1901.
Gui de Warewic, 1232–42. Ed. Ewert, 1932–33.
Floris and Blauncheflur, ca.1250. Ed. Hausknecht, 1885.
Fouke Fitzwarin, mid 13th century. Ed. Brandin, 1930; Hathaway, 1975.
Arthour and Merlin, Earlier Version, 1250–1300. Ed. Kölbing, 1890.
Havelok the Dane, 1280–1300. Ed. Skeat, rev. Sisam, 1915.
Sir Tristrem, late 13th century. Ed. McNeill, 1886.

Amis and Amiloun, late 13th century. Ed. Leach, 1937.
Guy of Warwick, 14th century version, ca.1300. Ed. Zupitza, 1883–91.
Bevis of Hampton, ca.1300. Ed. Kölbing, 1885–94.
Richard Coer de Lyon, after 1300. Ed. Brunner, 1913.
Kyng Alisaunder, early 14th century. Ed. Smithers, 1952–57.
Lai le Freine, after 1300. Ed. Wattie, 1929.
Sir Orfeo, early 14th century. Ed. Bliss, 1954, rev. 1966.
Sir Isumbras, early 14th century. Ed. Halliwell-Phillipps, 1884; Schleich, 1901.
The King of Tars, early 14th century. Ed. Krause, 1887.
The Seege of Troy, ca.1300–25. Ed. Barnicle, 1927.
Horn Childe, ca.1320. Ed. Hall, 1901.
Sir Degaré, before 1325. Ed. Schleich, 1929.
Sir Perceval of Galles, 1300–40. Ed. Campion & Holthausen, 1913.
Ywain and Gawain, 1300–50. Ed. Friedman & Harrington, 1964.
Sir Landeval, early 14th century. Ed. Zimmermann, 1900.
Otuel a Knight, before 1330–40. Ed. Herrtage, 1882.
Otuel and Roland, before 1330–40. Ed. O'Sullivan, 1935.
Roland and Vernagu, before 1330–40. Ed. Herrtage, 1882.
Libeaus Desconus, 1325–50. Ed. Mills, 1969.
Sir Eglamour of Artois, mid 14th century. Ed. Richardson, 1965.
Octavian, Northern Version, ca.1350. Ed. Sarrazin, 1885.
Octavian, Southern Version, ca.1350. Ed. Sarrazin, 1885.
William of Palerne by William, ca.1350–61. Ed. Skeat, 1867.
Morte Arthure, Alliterative, ca.1360. Ed. Perry, 1865; Benson, 1974.
Gamelyn, ca.1350–70. Ed. Skeat, 1900.
The Gest Historiale of the Destruction of Troy, ca.1350–1400. Ed. Panton & Donaldson, 1869–74.
Athelston, ca.1355–80. Ed. Trounce, 1933.
The Awntyrs off Arthure at the Terne Wathelyne, after 1375. Ed. Robson, 1842; Gates, 1969.
Firumbras, Fillingham, 1375–1400? Ed. O'Sullivan, 1935.
Sir Firumbras, Ashmole, ca.1380. Ed. Herrtage, 1879.
The Siege of Jerusalem, 1390–1400. Ed. Kölbing & Day, 1932.
Le Bone Florence of Rome, late 14th century. Ed. Vietor & Knobbe, 1899; Heffernan, 1976.
Chevalere Assigne, late 14th century. Ed. Gibbs, 1868.
Titus and Vespasian, late 14th century. Ed. Herbert, 1905.
Sir Cleges, late 14th century, Ed. McKnight, 1913.
Ipomadon, late 14th century. Ed. Kölbing, 1889.
Sir Degrevant, late 14th century. Ed. Casson, 1949.
Sir Triamour, late 14th century. Ed. Schmidt, 1937.
Sir Amadace, late 14th century. Ed. Robson, 1842.
Generides, Couplet Version, late 14th century. Ed. Furnivall, 1865.
Generides, Stanzaic Version, late 14th century. Ed. Wright, 1873–78.
The Knight of Curtesy and the Fair Lady of Faguell, late 14th century. Ed. McCausland, 1922.
Roberd of Cisyle, late 14th century. Ed. Nuck, 1887.
Sir Launfal by Thomas Chestre, late 14th century. Ed. Bliss, 1960.
The Sege of Melayne, before 1400. Ed. Herrtage, 1880.
Duke Roland and Sir Otuel of Spain, before 1400. Ed. Herrtage, 1880.
Emaré, ca.1400. Ed. Rickert, 1908.
Sir Gowther, ca.1400, Ed. Bruel, 1886.

The Earl of Toulous, ca.1400, Ed. Lüdtke, 1881.
Le Morte Arthur, Stanzaic, ca.1400. Ed. Bruce, 1903; Benson, 1974.
The Sowdon of Babylon, ca.1400. Ed. Hausknecht, 1881.
The Song of Roland, ca.1400. Ed. Herrtage, 1880.
The Laud Troy Book, ca.1400. Ed. Wulfing, 1902–03.
Sir Torrent of Portyngale, ca.1400. Ed. Adam, 1887.
Syre Gawene and the Carle of Carelyle, ca.1400. Ed. Madden, 1839; Kurvinen, 1951.
Arthour and Merlin, Later Version, before 1425. Ed. Kölbing, 1890.
The Lyfe of Ipomydon, before 1425. Ed. Kölbing, 1889.
Merlin by Henry Lovelich, ca.1425. Ed. Kock, 1904–32.
The Avowynge of King Arthur, ca.1425. Ed. Robson, 1842.
The Tournament of Tottenham, 1400–40. Ed. Hazlitt, 1866.
The Alexander Buik, 1438. Ed. Ritchie, 1921–29.
Amoryus and Cleopes by John Metham, 1448–49. Ed. Craig, 1916.
Guy of Warwick, 15th century, 1425–75. Ed. Zupitza, 1875–76.
Eger and Grime, mid 15th century. Ed. Hales & Furnivall, 1867.
The Weddynge of Sir Gawen and Dame Ragnell, ca.1450. Ed. Madden, 1839; Sumner, 1924.
The Jeaste of Syr Gawayne, late 15th century. Ed. Madden, 1839.
The Taill of Rauf Coilyear, 1465–1500. Ed. Herrtage, 1882.
Partonope of Blois, 15th century. Ed. Bödtker, 1912.
Lancelot of the Laik, 1482–1500. Ed. Skeat, 1865; Gray, 1912.
Roswall and Lillian, late 15th century. Ed. Hazlitt, 1895; Lengert, 1892.
Golagrus and Gawain, before 1500. Ed. Madden, 1839; Stevenson, 1918.
The Grene Knight, ca.1500. Ed. Madden, 1839; Child, 1857.
The Turke and Gowin, ca.1500. Ed. Madden, 1839.
The Squyr of Lowe Degre, ca.1500. Ed. Mead, 1904.
The Romauns of Partenay, ca.1500. Ed. Skeat, 1866.
Clariodus, late 15th or early 16th century. Ed. Irving, 1830.
The Carle off Carlile, 1500–50. Ed. Madden, 1839; Kurvinen, 1951.

Notes

1. THE FRENCH BOOK

1. Quoted from MS Harley 7322 by G. R. Owst, *Literature and Pulpit in Medieval England*, rev. ed. (Oxford, 1961), p. 14n.

2. See, for example, W. P. Ker, *Epic and Romance* (rpt., London, 1922), pp. 3–4.

3. The standard work is Charles Homer Haskins, *The Renaissance of the Twelfth Century* (Cambridge, Mass., 1927). Recently, Robert W. Hanning has argued that the Twelfth-Century Renaissance brought with it "a new desire on the part of literate men and women to understand themselves as . . . what we would call *individuals*" and that chivalric romance "offered a literary form in which to work out the implications of individuality": *The Individual in Twelfth-Century Romance* (New Haven, 1977), pp. 1–3.

4. The characteristics of popular literature have been discussed in a number of recent works. One of the best of these is John G. Cawelti, *Adventure, Mystery, and Romance* (Chicago, 1976), which also contains an extensive annotated bibliography. Another excellent discussion of the romance (using that term in a very broad sense) as popular literature is found in Northrop Frye, *The Secular Scripture: A Study of the Structure of Romance* (Cambridge, Mass., 1976), especially pp. 23–26 and 56–57.

5. *Les Jongleurs en France au Moyen Âge* (Paris, 1910), pp. 116–17.

6. *The Story of England by Robert Mannyng of Brunne*, ed. Frederick J. Furnivall (London, 1887), Rolls Series, 87, ll. 71–80. Albert C. Baugh ("The Middle English Romance: Some Questions of Creation, Presentation, and Preservation" [hereafter "ME Romance"], *Speculum*, 42 [1967], 29n.) says that this passage refers to the difficulties faced by minstrels in remembering stanzaic forms, but it is clear that Mannyng means the auditors.

7. Ed. Karl Vollmöller (Heilbronn, 1883), ll. 3058–3109. In other romances it is considered a sign of virtue in a prince that he give generously to minstrels and reciters of tales: see, e.g., *Sir Isumbras* (ed. Halliwell), ll. 19–21; *Richard Coer de Lyon* (ed. Brunner), C, ll. 3775–81; *Ipomydon* (ed. Kölbing), ll. 2265–72.

8. See Dieter Mehl, *The Middle English Romances of the Thirteenth and Fourteenth Centuries* (London, 1969), p. 13.

9. "ME Romance," pp. 14–15.

10. "ME Romance," p. 2.

11. "Havelok the Dane and Society," *Chaucer Review*, 6 (1971), 142–51.

12. See the quotations and discussions in E. K. Chambers, *The Medieval Stage* (Oxford, 1903), I, 230 and 262–63; Baugh, "The Authorship of the Middle English Romances," *Annual Bulletin of the Modern Humanities Research Association* (hereafter *MHRA*), 22 (1950), 28; Baugh, "ME Romance," p. 10.

13. Ed. Andresen, ll. 8035–51. Quoted from Faral, pp. 56–57.

14. See Faral, pp. 184–89, and also Jean Rychner, *La Chanson de Geste* (Geneva and Lille, 1955), pp. 20–21.

235

15. *Le roi* is a commonly occurring title, meaning 'king of minstrels' and apparently given to the most accomplished practitioners of the art. See Faral, pp. 268–69; Chambers, I, 238–39; and Clair C. Olson, "The Minstrels at the Court of Edward III," *PMLA*, 56 (1941), 602.

16. See M. Mills's edition, *Sir Launfal* (London, 1969), pp. 60–66, and Dorothy Everett, "The Relationship of Chestre's *Launfal* and *Lybeaus Desconus*," *Medium Aevum*, 7 (1938), 29–49, for a discussion of the authorship of these poems.

17. In three articles: "The Authorship of the Middle English Romances," *MHRA* (1950); "Improvisation in the Middle English Romance," *Proceedings of the American Philosophical Society*, 103 (1959), 418–54; "The Middle English Romance," *Speculum* (1967). The 1967 article is of particular importance to the study of authorship, audience, and transmission.

18. Ruth Crosby, "Oral Delivery in the Middle Ages," *Speculum*, 11 (1936), 88–98, and George P. Wilson, "Chaucer and Oral Reading," *South Atlantic Quarterly*, 25 (1926), 285–87.

19. *La Chanson de Geste*, pp. 10–12.

20. "Die Überlieferung der Mittelenglischen Versromanzen," *Anglia*, 76 (1958), 64–73. *The Catalogue of Romances in the Department of Manuscripts in the British Museum*, Vol. 1 (London, 1883), by H. L. D. Ward is an invaluable source of information for the British Museum MSS, and E. Kölbing has given a detailed description of four English romance MSS in "Vier Romanzen-Handschriften," *Englische Studien*, 7 (1884), 177–201.

21. Laura Hibbard Loomis, "The Auchinleck Manuscript and a Possible London Bookshop of 1330–1340," *PMLA*, 57 (1942), 595–627. Loomis thought that Chaucer had access to the manuscript: see her articles, "Chaucer and the Auchinleck MS: *Thopas* and *Guy of Warwick*," *Essays and Studies in Honor of Carleton Brown* (New York, 1940), pp. 111–28, and "Chaucer and the Breton Lays of the Auchinleck MS," *Studies in Philology*, 38 (1941), 14–23. On the MS itself, see also Kölbing, pp. 178–91, and Mehl, pp. 257–58.

2. THE CHILD EXILE

1. Discussed in Walter H. French, *Essays on King Horn* (Ithaca, N.Y., 1940), p. 7.

2. John Halverson, "Havelok the Dane and Society," *Chaucer Review*, 6 (1971), 142–51.

3. On the importance of law in medieval political thought, see Walter Ullmann, *The Individual and Society in the Middle Ages* (Baltimore, 1966), pp. 46–50, and A. L. Poole, *From Domesday Book to Magna Carta* (Oxford, 1955), pp. 5–6.

4. Hanging was the usual punishment for homicide in the Middle Ages. On the tendency to make the punishment fit the crime, see Poole, pp. 403–04. Godrich is not punished; instead, he repents and is pardoned. This may have something to do with the fact that Godrich is an earl whereas Godard is only a "riche man."

5. The "Clark Kent" principle: the hero has, in effect, two different natures, one of them exciting and indomitable (almost), the other ordinary and weak. The comic book Superman, of course, is a much more exaggerated figure than either Horn or Havelok.

6. Conversely, ugliness is associated with low social status. When Horn disguises himself as a beggar, he does so primarily by disfiguring himself so that he is "unbicomelich" (*King Horn*, 1057–66).

7. The reasons given for Havelok's service betray a difference in social attitudes between the two romances, the Anglo-Norman writer viewing this service as a royal apprenticeship, the English author seeing it as a necessity of life.

3. THE BEST KNIGHT IN THE WORLD

1. Wade is mentioned several times in medieval literature as one of the well-known romance heroes, but no romance concerning him comes down to us.

2. The earliest English MS, Auchinleck (ca. 1330), divides the story into three separate poems, one ending with the marriage of Guy and Felice, the second ending with Guy's death, and the third telling the story of his son Reinbrun. The later 14th-century MS contains only the first two parts, told as a consecutive story.

3. See Ronald S. Crane, "The Vogue of *Guy of Warwick* from the Close of the Middle Ages to the Romantic Revival," *PMLA*, 30 (1915), 125–94.

4. Romances that are aristocratic in their sympathies view hunting, along with chess-playing, singing to the harp, and courtesy (especially to women), as a mark of courtliness and civilized behavior. Thus in the Old Norse translation of Thomas's *Tristan*, the hero demonstrates his courtly skills by playing chess with the Norwegian merchants, by teaching the huntsmen how to flay and dress a stag, and by singing lays before King Mark. We can compare the similar activities of Horn in the *Romance of Horn*. Later and less aristocratic romances view hunting in a different manner entirely.

5. The combat in armor of various colors became a romance convention. The idea comes from folklore, and its significance there has been commented on by Julius E. Heuscher (*A Psychiatric Study of Myths and Fairy Tales* [Springfield, Ill., 1974], p. 225), who sees the colors as symbolizing stages in the development of the consciousness—from intuition, to feeling, to willing. In the romances, however, the actual colors do not seem to be as important as the fact that the hero using them draws attention to himself while concealing his identity.

4. HISTORY AND POLITICS

1. On the usefulness of history in general, see *William of Malmesbury's Chronicle of the Kings of England*, trans. J. A. Giles (London, 1911), pp. 1 and 94, and Matthew of Westminster, *The Flowers of History*, trans. C. D. Yonge (London, 1853), I, 1. On the image of the mirror, see Ernst Curtius, *European Literature and the Latin Middle Ages*, trans. William R. Trask (New York, 1953), p. 336; James I. Wimsatt, *Allegory and Mirror* (New York, 1970), pp. 28–30 and 137–40; and *The Romance of the Rose*, trans. Charles Dahlberg (Princeton, 1971), pp. 300–03 (ll. 18013-273).

2. Preface to the *Modern History:* Giles, p. 480.

3. See T. Atkinson Jenkins (ed.), *La Chanson de Roland* (Boston, 1965), pp. xliv-xlv.

4. Kölbing and Smithers believe that both these works were written by the same person, and that he was probably also the author of *Richard Coer de Lyon:* see their editions of the two works.

5. See, for example, Maurice Powicke's discussion of the medieval veneration for law, in *The Thirteenth Century* (Oxford, 1962), pp. 84–87.

6. See Bernard J. Siegel, "Defensive Cultural Adaptation," in *The History of Violence in America* (New York, 1970), pp. 764–87.

7. See William C. Calin, *The Old French Epic of Revolt* (Paris, 1962), pp. 116 and 119.

5. Love Stories

1. See Herbert Moller, "The Social Causation of the Courtly Love Complex," *Comparative Studies in Society and History*, 1 (1959), 137–63; Moller, "The Meaning of Courtly Love," *Journal of American Folklore*, 73 (1960), 41; and C. S. Lewis, *The Allegory of Love* (rev. ed., New York, 1958), p. 12.

2. In the Anglo-Norman MSS, the name is Tristran, which Friar Robert says is from *trist homme*, 'man of sorrow,' but I use the more familiar Modern French form. The English and Norse form of the name is Tristrem or Tristram.

3. Psychological, sociological, and mythical interpretations of the Tristan story include: Denis de Rougemont, *Love in the Western World*, trans. Montgomery Belgion (rev. ed., New York, 1966), pp. 39ff.; Michel Cazenave, *Le Philtre et l'Amour: la Légende de Tristan et Iseut* (Paris, 1969); and Françoise Barteau, *Les Romans de Tristan et Iseut: Introduction à une Lecture Plurielle* (Paris, 1972).

4. See Phillipe Ariès, *Centuries of Childhood*, trans. Robert Baldick (New York, 1962), pp. 353–56.

5. The names suggest their identity with each other, their beauty, and their innocence, the flower being used here as an emblem of virginity. It is also possible to view the story as individual-centered rather than couple-centered, in which case Blauncheflur represents Floris's chastity.

6. See Walter Clyde Curry, *Chaucer and the Mediaeval Sciences* (rev. ed., London, 1960), pp. 37ff.

6. The Fairy Princess

1. The pros and cons of this supposition are discussed by Dorothy Everett, "The Relationship of Chestre's *Launfal* and *Lybeaus Desconus*," *Medium Aevum*, 7 (1938), 29–49.

2. In Chestre's version of *Sir Launfal*, the hero claims to be going to his father's funeral when he leaves Arthur's court. Subsequently he defeats several authority figures in a tournament, and immediately afterward the mother-substitute Guenevere makes her approaches to him.

3. On the mythical origins of the fairyland boundary, see T. P. Cross, "The Celtic Elements in the Lays of *Lanval* and *Graelent*," *Modern Philology*, 12 (1915), 599–609; Lewis Spence, *The Fairy Tradition in Britain* (New York, 1948), pp. 276–78; and Helaine Newstead, "The Traditional Background of *Partonopeus de Blois*," *PMLA*, 61 (1946), 925–30.

4. On the mythic backgrounds of this detail, see Spence, p. 201, and Cross, pp. 610–18. Cross believes that the stories result from a combination of two different cultural idealizations, the Celtic fée, who is "bold and imperious," and the Germanic swan-maiden, who is "timorous and shrinking." However, the pattern of the woman who first resists but ends by actively making love to the man is a common erotic fantasy.

5. This conclusion also follows from their propensity to bring bad luck: see Spence, pp. 201 and 211.

6. In the Auchinleck MS, the same prologue is found attached to the Middle English translation of Marie's *Le Freisne*.

7. Family Affairs

1. See Lillian Hornstein's discussion ("Eustace-Constance-Florence-Griselda Legends") in *A Manual of the Writings in Middle English, 1050–1500*, I, 120–32, and her bibliographies: I, 278–91.

2. *Chaucer's Constance and Accused Queens* (New York, 1927), pp. 34–47.

3. Hermann Suchier, *Oeuvres Poétiques de Beaumanoir* (Paris, 1884), SATF 31; Edith Rickert, *Emaré* (London, 1908), EETSES 99; Schlauch, *Chaucer's Constance*, esp. pp. 12–39.

4. Rome suffers just as the heroine does. Near the beginning of the romance, terrible omens, including a rain of blood and birds tearing each other in flight, foreshadow tribulations for the city, and these predictions are later fulfilled. However, the political and religious symbolism is largely forgotten by the end of the poem.

5. It also seems to appear as an element in the names Degrevant and Egraveyne (a good character in *Le Bone Florence*) as well as in Degrebelle (*Eglamour of Artois*). Further interesting correspondences are Emaré-Emere (the hero in *Le Bone Florence*) and Artyus-Ardus (the father in *Sir Triamour*).

6. See Schlauch, *Chaucer's Constance*, pp. 32–34. The other common type of villain, the evil steward, is nearly a family member too: he generally acts like one of the family, though he is not of it.

8. Gentils and Vilains

1. The equation of white with natural nobility and black with the opposite is supported by the fact that, in the great tournament at the end of the romance, Fergus rides a "cheval blondet" and Kay rides a black one.

2. There is also a tale in verse, "King Edward and the Shepherd," of the late 14th century. In this, a shepherd named Adam entertains King Edward IV, and the king later returns the favor by feasting the shepherd at court, while the court enjoys the jest of the shepherd (who will not take off his hat) addressing the king without knowing it.

3. A. L. Poole, *From Domesday Book to Magna Carta* (Oxford, 1955), pp. 33–34.

4. For example, by Jessie L. Weston, *The Legend of Sir Gawain* (London, 1897); George Lyman Kittredge, *A Study of Sir Gawain and the Grene Knight* (Cambridge, Mass., 1916); R. S. Loomis, *Celtic Myth and Arthurian Romance* (New York, 1927).

5. By way of comparison, it is interesting to note that Modred, in the Stanzaic *Morte Arthur*, easily convinces the English people that "in Arthurs tyme [was] but sorow and woo" because "Arthur lovyd noght but warynge" (ed. Bruce, ll. 2964–77).

6. *Art and Tradition in Sir Gawain and the Green Knight* (New Brunswick, N.J., 1965), pp. 21–22.

9. Satire, Sermons, and Sentiment

1. See the discussion of the MS by John Robson (ed.), *Three Early English Metrical Romances* (London, 1842), Camden Society, pp. xxxvii–xlv.

2. J. Douglas Bruce (ed.), *Le Morte Arthur* (London, 1903), EETSES, 88, vii.

3. Ronald S. Crane, *The Vogue of Medieval Chivalric Romance During the English Renaissance* (Menasha, Wis., 1919), pp. 22 and 11–20.

4. The tradition includes, as a list of "romances of prys" in the second fit

informs us, the stories of Horn, Bevis of Hampton, Guy of Warwick, and Libeaus Desconus.

5. In a sense, the incongruity hinges on a single word, "bachelery," which is used to refer to the combatants. It originally meant a group of young knights but had come to mean simply 'young, unmarried men.'

6. George F. Jones, "The Tournaments of Tottenham and Lappenhausen," *PMLA*, 66 (1951), 1124–28.

7. The poem is in rime royal and contains a temple scene (in which Amoryus first sees Cleopes) drawn straight from Chaucer's *Troilus*.

Index

241